Windows® 95 Registry For Dummies®

Y0-AGK-438

The REGEDIT window

Menu bar   Key   Active key   Value name   Value data

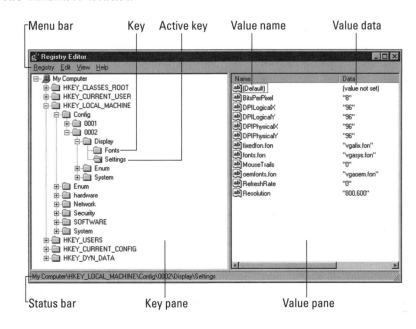

Status bar   Key pane   Value pane

A sample Registry backup batch file

Note: This **sample** batch file assumes that Windows is saved on the C: drive and the E: drive is a writable drive with a capacity larger than a 1.44MB floppy, such as a tape drive or removable storage drive. Your setup may be different; see Chapter 2.

```
@ECHO OFF
ECHO Please close all Windows programs before proceeding.
PAUSE
XCOPY C:\WINDOWS\USER.DAT E:\REG\ /H /Y /R
XCOPY C:\WINDOWS\SYSTEM.DAT E:\REG\ /H /Y /R
```

Add the following line if you want to back up profiles for multiple users

```
XCOPY C:\WINDOWS\PROFILES E:\REG\PROFILES\ /H /Y /R /S
ECHO Backup Complete!
```

...For Dummies: #1 Computer Book Series for Beginners

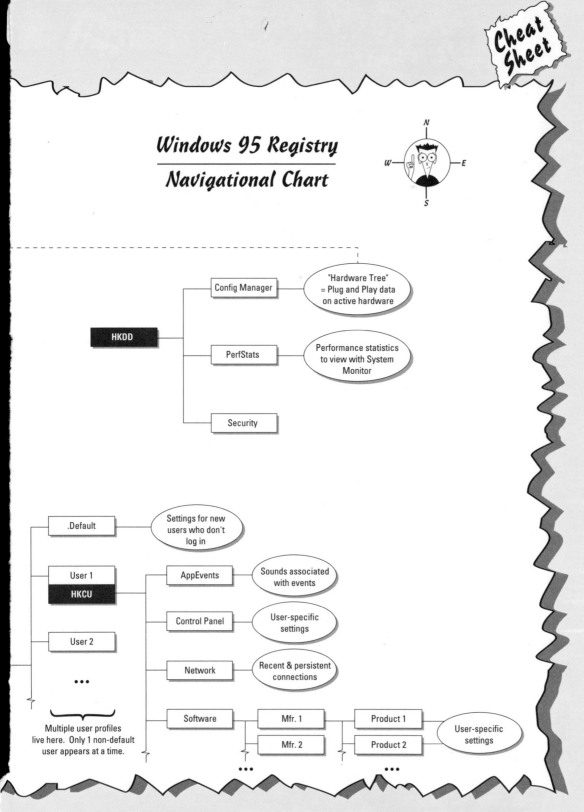

Windows 95 Registry
Navigational Chart

HKDD
- Config Manager → "Hardware Tree" = Plug and Play data on active hardware
- PerfStats → Performance statistics to view with System Monitor
- Security

HKCU
- .Default → Settings for new users who don't log in
- User 1
- User 2
- ...

Multiple user profiles live here. Only 1 non-default user appears at a time.

- AppEvents → Sounds associated with events
- Control Panel → User-specific settings
- Network → Recent & persistent connections
- Software
  - Mfr. 1 → Product 1 → User-specific settings
  - Mfr. 2 → Product 2

Windows® 95 Registry For Dummies®

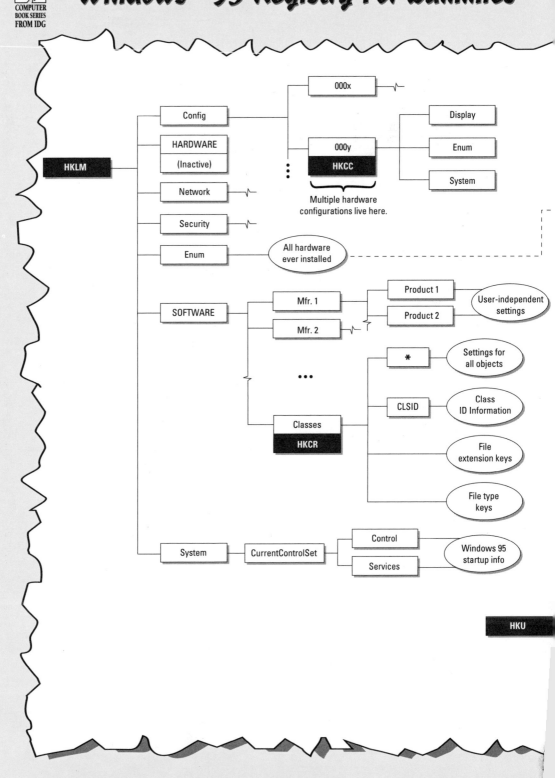

Effects of Control Panels on the Registry

Control Panel	Filename	Registry Keys Affected
Add New Hardware	SYSDM.CPL	*HKLM\Enum, HKLM\hardware, HKLM\System\CurrentControlSet\Services\Class*
Add/Remove Programs	APPWIZ.CPL	*HKLM\SOFTWARE, HKCU\Software, HKLM\SOFTWARE\Microsoft\Windows\CurrentVersion\Uninstall*
Date/Time	TIMEDATE.CPL	*HKLM\System\CurrentControlSet\Control\TimeZoneInformation*
Display	DESK.CPL	*HKCC\Display\Settings, HKCU\Control Panel\Desktop, HKCU\Control Panel\Colors, HKU* for each user. Can also modify SYSTEM.INI and WIN.INI
Fonts	*n/a*	*HKLM\SOFTWARE\Microsoft\Windows\CurrentVersion\Fonts*
Joystick	JOY.CPL	*HKLM\System\CurrentControlSet\control\MediaResources*
Keyboard	MAIN.CPL	*HKCU\Control Panel\Keyboard*
Modems	MODEM.CPL	*HKLM\System\CurrentControlSet\Services\Class\Modem, HKLM\Enum*
Mouse	MAIN.CPL	*HKCU\Control Panel\Cursors, HKCC\Display\Settings,* and (typically) *HCKU\Control Panel\Microsoft Input Devices\Mouse, HKU* for each user
Multimedia	MMSYS.CPL	*HKCU\Software\Microsoft\Multimedia, HKCU\Software\Microsoft\Windows\CurrentVersion\Multimedia, HKU* for each user
Network	NETCPL.CPL	*HKLM\Enum\Network, HKLM\Network, HKLM\System\CurrentControlSet\Services\Class\Net* (and *...~\NetClient, ...~\NetService,* and *...~\NetTrans*).
Password	PASSWORD.CPL	*HKLM\System\CurrentControlSet\Control\PwdProvider, HKU* for each user
Printers	*n/a*	*HKLM\System\CurrentControlSet\control\Print\Printers, HKCC\System\CurrentControlSet\Control\Print\Printers*
Regional Settings	INTL.CPL	*HKCU\Control Panel\International*
Sounds	MMSYS.CPL	*HKCU\AppEvents, HKU* for each user
System	SYSDM.CPL	*HKLM\System\CurrentControlSet\Control\FileSystem, HKCC\Config\Display, HKLM\Enum,* and *HKLM\Config.* Can also modify SYSTEM.INI

References for the Rest of Us! ®

COMPUTER BOOK SERIES FROM IDG

Are you intimidated and confused by computers? Do you find that traditional manuals are overloaded with technical details you'll never use? Do your friends and family always call you to fix simple problems on their PCs? Then the *...For Dummies*® computer book series from IDG Books Worldwide is for you.

...For Dummies books are written for those frustrated computer users who know they aren't really dumb but find that PC hardware, software, and indeed the unique vocabulary of computing make them feel helpless. *...For Dummies* books use a lighthearted approach, a down-to-earth style, and even cartoons and humorous icons to diffuse computer novices' fears and build their confidence. Lighthearted but not lightweight, these books are a perfect survival guide for anyone forced to use a computer.

> *"I like my copy so much I told friends; now they bought copies."*
>
> **Irene C., Orwell, Ohio**

> *"Quick, concise, nontechnical, and humorous."*
>
> **Jay A., Elburn, Illinois**

> *"Thanks, I needed this book. Now I can sleep at night."*
>
> **Robin F., British Columbia, Canada**

Already, millions of satisfied readers agree. They have made *...For Dummies* books the #1 introductory level computer book series and have written asking for more. So, if you're looking for the most fun and easy way to learn about computers, look to *...For Dummies* books to give you a helping hand.

WINDOWS® 95 REGISTRY FOR DUMMIES®

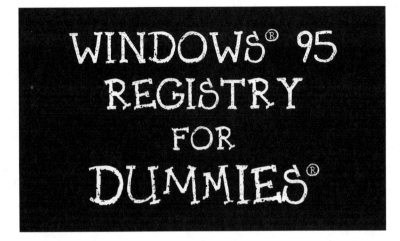

WINDOWS® 95 REGISTRY FOR DUMMIES®

**by Glenn E. Weadock
and Mark B. Wilkins**

Illustrated by Emily Sherrill Weadock

IDG Books Worldwide, Inc.
An International Data Group Company

Foster City, CA ♦ Chicago, IL ♦ Indianapolis, IN ♦ Southlake, TX

Windows® 95 Registry For Dummies®

Published by
IDG Books Worldwide, Inc.
An International Data Group Company
919 E. Hillsdale Blvd.
Suite 400
Foster City, CA 94404
www.idgbooks.com (IDG Books Worldwide Web site)
www.dummies.com (Dummies Press Web site)

Library of Congress Catalog Card No.: 98-70134

ISBN: 0-7645-0359-6

Printed in the United States of America

10 9 8 7 6 5 4 3 2 1

1E/QU/QT/ZY/IN

Distributed in the United States by IDG Books Worldwide, Inc.

Distributed by Macmillan Canada for Canada; by Transworld Publishers Limited in the United Kingdom; by IDG Norge Books for Norway; by IDG Sweden Books for Sweden; by Woodslane Pty. Ltd. for Australia; by Woodslane Enterprises Ltd. for New Zealand; by Longman Singapore Publishers Ltd. for Singapore, Malaysia, Thailand, and Indonesia; by Simron Pty. Ltd. for South Africa; by Toppan Company Ltd. for Japan; by Distribuidora Cuspide for Argentina; by Livraria Cultura for Brazil; by Ediciencia S.A. for Ecuador; by Addison-Wesley Publishing Company for Korea; by Ediciones ZETA S.C.R. Ltda. for Peru; by WS Computer Publishing Corporation, Inc., for the Philippines; by Unalis Corporation for Taiwan; by Contemporanea de Ediciones for Venezuela; by Computer Book & Magazine Store for Puerto Rico; by Express Computer Distributors for the Caribbean and West Indies. Authorized Sales Agent: Anthony Rudkin Associates for the Middle East and North Africa.

For general information on IDG Books Worldwide's books in the U.S., please call our Consumer Customer Service department at 800-762-2974. For reseller information, including discounts and premium sales, please call our Reseller Customer Service department at 800-434-3422.

For information on where to purchase IDG Books Worldwide's books outside the U.S., please contact our International Sales department at 650-655-3200 or fax 650-655-3295.

For information on foreign language translations, please contact our Foreign & Subsidiary Rights department at 650-655-3021 or fax 650-655-3281.

For sales inquiries and special prices for bulk quantities, please contact our Sales department at 650-655-3200 or write to the address above.

For information on using IDG Books Worldwide's books in the classroom or for ordering examination copies, please contact our Educational Sales department at 800-434-2086 or fax 817-251-8174.

For press review copies, author interviews, or other publicity information, please contact our Public Relations department at 650-655-3000 or fax 650-655-3299.

For authorization to photocopy items for corporate, personal, or educational use, please contact Copyright Clearance Center, 222 Rosewood Drive, Danvers, MA 01923, or fax 978-750-4470.

is a trademark under exclusive license to IDG Books Worldwide, Inc., from International Data Group, Inc.

About the Authors

Glenn E. Weadock is president of Independent Software, Inc., a Colorado-based consulting firm he founded in 1982 after graduating from Stanford University's engineering school. One of the country's most popular technical trainers, Glenn has taught networking topics to thousands of students in the United States, United Kingdom, and Canada in more than 170 seminars since 1988. He has written six intensive two-day seminars for Data-Tech Institute, including *Supporting and Troubleshooting Windows 95,* and has written and presented four Data-Tech computer videos.

Glenn is the author of *Intranet Publishing For Dummies, Small Business Networking For Dummies,* and coauthor of *Creating Cool PowerPoint 97 Presentations* (all by IDG Books, Worldwide, Inc). He has also written *Bulletproofing NetWare, Bulletproofing Windows 95, Bulletproofing Client/ Server Systems,* and *Bulletproof Your PC Network* (all by McGraw Hill, Inc.). His first book, *Exploding the Computer Myth,* deals with computers and business productivity and is used as a textbook at Rutgers University. Glenn is a Microsoft Certified Professional and member of the Association for Computing Machinery, Independent Computer Consultants Association, and American Society for Training and Development.

Mark B. Wilkins is a professor at St. Lawrence College in Kingston, Ontario, where he teaches courses in computer networks and electronics. Mark is also a popular lecturer and presenter on Windows 95 and the Registry for the Data-Tech Institute. Mark is the coauthor of *Bulletproofing Netware* with Glenn Weadock.

Glenn and Mark don't claim to know everything there is to know about the Windows 95 Registry, but between the two of them, they've learned far more than any human being should have to. They want to share with you the most important knowledge about this subject so that you don't have to spend the thousands of hours they have in studying it, reading about it, experimenting with it, and (occasionally) kicking their computers and spouting decidedly unprofessional language while trying to understand its vagaries.

About the Illustrator

Emily Sherrill Weadock is the Director of Independent Software's Digital Art Studio. An award-winning computer artist whose work has been featured in international magazines, Emily's talent ranges from technical illustration to broadcast-quality 3D animation and multimedia development. She has illustrated nine books to date, and is the co-author of *Creating Cool PowerPoint 97 Presentations.* Before trading brushes for mice, Emily enjoyed success as a mixed-media construction artist, and studied art at SMU and Baylor University.

ABOUT IDG BOOKS WORLDWIDE

Welcome to the world of IDG Books Worldwide.

IDG Books Worldwide, Inc., is a subsidiary of International Data Group, the world's largest publisher of computer-related information and the leading global provider of information services on information technology. IDG was founded more than 25 years ago and now employs more than 8,500 people worldwide. IDG publishes more than 275 computer publications in over 75 countries (see listing below). More than 60 million people read one or more IDG publications each month.

Launched in 1990, IDG Books Worldwide is today the #1 publisher of best-selling computer books in the United States. We are proud to have received eight awards from the Computer Press Association in recognition of editorial excellence and three from *Computer Currents'* First Annual Readers' Choice Awards. Our best-selling *...For Dummies®* series has more than 30 million copies in print with translations in 30 languages. IDG Books Worldwide, through a joint venture with IDG's Hi-Tech Beijing, became the first U.S. publisher to publish a computer book in the People's Republic of China. In record time, IDG Books Worldwide has become the first choice for millions of readers around the world who want to learn how to better manage their businesses.

Our mission is simple: Every one of our books is designed to bring extra value and skill-building instructions to the reader. Our books are written by experts who understand and care about our readers. The knowledge base of our editorial staff comes from years of experience in publishing, education, and journalism — experience we use to produce books for the '90s. In short, we care about books, so we attract the best people. We devote special attention to details such as audience, interior design, use of icons, and illustrations. And because we use an efficient process of authoring, editing, and desktop publishing our books electronically, we can spend more time ensuring superior content and spend less time on the technicalities of making books.

You can count on our commitment to deliver high-quality books at competitive prices on topics you want to read about. At IDG Books Worldwide, we continue in the IDG tradition of delivering quality for more than 25 years. You'll find no better book on a subject than one from IDG Books Worldwide.

John Kilcullen
CEO
IDG Books Worldwide, Inc.

Steven Berkowitz
President and Publisher
IDG Books Worldwide, Inc.

*Eighth Annual
Computer Press
Awards ➤1992*

*Ninth Annual
Computer Press
Awards ➤1993*

*Tenth Annual
Computer Press
Awards ➤1994*

*Eleventh Annual
Computer Press
Awards ➤1995*

Dedication

To Gerry Routledge, for help above and beyond the call of duty.

Author's Acknowledgments

We would like to "register" our thanks to many people at IDG Books Worldwide, including (in alphabetical order) Mary Bednarek, Heather Dismore, Angie Hunckler, Brian Kramer, Carmen Krikorian, Kyle Looper, Joyce Pepple, Jill Pisoni, and Joell Smith, as well as to the other IDG employees whom we don't know but who helped with the project. Special thanks go to Gerry Routledge for the technical review and to Jim Egan for help with nautical terminology. To the software vendors who helped us learn more about their latest products, our thanks (again alphabetically) to Jim Barrett of ISES, Giselle Bisson of CyberMedia, Tiffany Brown of Network Associates, Diane Carlini of Symantec, Bryce Cogswell, Pam Crain of Network Associates, Kristin Gabriel of Symantec, Steven Hoek, Patrick Karle of Computer Associates, Christina Karpowitz of PowerQuest, Jan Olsen of Imagine LAN, Mark Russinovich, Mike Sutherland, and Anna Thorn of Quarterdeck. Finally, to all the other writers and researchers who have added to the public store of knowledge about the Registry and therefore made our job easier, our sincere thanks as well.

Publisher's Acknowledgments

We're proud of this book; please register your comments through our IDG Books Worldwide Online Registration Form located at http://my2cents.dummies.com.

Some of the people who helped bring this book to market include the following:

Acquisitions, Development, and Editorial

Project Editor: Kyle Looper

Acquisitions Editor: Jill Pisoni

Media Development Manager: Joyce Pepple

Permissions Editor: Heather H. Dismore

Associate Permissions Editor: Carmen Krikorian

Copy Editor: Brian Kramer

Technical Editor: Gerald Routledge

Editorial Manager: Leah Cameron

Editorial Assistant: Donna Love

Production

Project Coordinators: Sherry Gomoll, Cindy L. Phipps

Layout and Graphics: Lou Boudreau, Cameron Booker, Linda M. Boyer, J. Tyler Connor, Angela F. Hunckler, Todd Klemme, Drew R. Moore, Brent Savage, M. Anne Sipahimalani, Deirdre Smith

Proofreaders: Christine Berman, Kelli Botta, Rebecca Senninger, Christine Sabooni, Janet M. Withers

Indexer: Rebecca R. Plunkett

Special Help

Seta Frantz, New Product R & D Manager

General and Administrative

IDG Books Worldwide, Inc.: John Kilcullen, CEO; Steven Berkowitz, President and Publisher

IDG Books Technology Publishing: Brenda McLaughlin, Senior Vice President and Group Publisher

Dummies Technology Press and Dummies Editorial: Diane Graves Steele, Vice President and Associate Publisher; Mary Bednarek, Director of Acquisitions and Product Development; Kristin A. Cocks, Editorial Director

Dummies Trade Press: Kathleen A. Welton, Vice President and Publisher; Kevin Thornton, Acquisitions Manager

IDG Books Production for Dummies Press: Beth Jenkins Roberts, Production Director; Cindy L. Phipps, Manager of Project Coordination, Production Proofreading, and Indexing; Kathie S. Schutte, Supervisor of Page Layout; Shelley Lea, Supervisor of Graphics and Design; Debbie J. Gates, Production Systems Specialist; Robert Springer, Supervisor of Proofreading; Debbie Stailey, Special Projects Coordinator; Tony Augsburger, Supervisor of Reprints and Bluelines; Leslie Popplewell, Media Archive Coordinator

Dummies Packaging and Book Design: Patti Crane, Packaging Specialist; Kavish + Kavish, Cover Design

◆

The publisher would like to give special thanks to Patrick J. McGovern, without whom this book would not have been possible.

◆

Contents at a Glance

Cartoons at a Glance

By Rich Tennant

page 95

page 11

page 141

page 191

page 219

page 245

page 269

Fax: 978-546-7747 • E-mail: the5wave@tiac.net

Table of Contents

Introduction

The Windows 95 Registry is a vitally important part of Windows 95. Every document that we've seen that discusses the Registry invariably refers to it as "the heart of Windows 95." That's true; the Registry contains just about every bit of information that matters about the hardware and software in a Windows 95 PC. You probably aren't aware of it, but Windows 95 and the programs you run with it use the Registry *tens of thousands of times* in a typical work session. Windows 95 can't blow its virtual nose without accessing the Registry a few hundred times.

For something so important, getting information about the Registry sure hasn't been easy. The documentation that you receive with Windows 95 doesn't tell you anything about it. (Okay, that documentation doesn't tell you much of anything about anything.) The Windows 95 software package contains practically no online help about the Registry. Even the seemingly encyclopedic, 1,500-page *Windows 95 Resource Kit* covers the Registry very lightly.

So, we thought it was about time for a book like *Windows 95 Registry For Dummies,* which provides the information you need to use the Registry safely and protect the Registry from problems that can range from inconvenient to disastrous. We give you many down-and-dirty details on how to change the Registry so that it bends to your will, rather than bending you to its. We explain cool Registry features that many Windows 95 users don't know exist, such as user profiles, hardware profiles, and system policies. We even tell you about a few Windows 95 bugs that you can fix by editing the Registry.

Windows 95 Registry For Dummies is very likely the only book you need to read or own on the subject, unless you're a professional programmer, in which case you may need to buy five or six books (but read ours first!). Certainly, our goal as authors is to include everything that the vast majority of our readers would need to know about the Registry.

About This Book

In this book, we present the essentials of the Windows 95 Registry concisely, conversationally, and (we hope!) clearly. We quickly bring you up to speed on the absolute minimum you must know about the Registry in order to use Windows 95 safely. We then take you further and show how you can use the Registry to do cool and useful things with your computer.

Windows 95 Registry For Dummies is not a tutorial. You don't have to do everything in Chapter 1 before going on to Chapter 2. You can jump here and there, finding out cool Registry tips and tricks along the way. The one caveat to this general theme is that before getting into the more heady aspects of the Registry Editor, you should read Chapter 2 on backing up your Registry and make a good backup for safekeeping. Then you can relax and explore.

Windows 95 Registry For Dummies is a reference. You don't have to commit all the various facts about the Registry, Plug and Play, and user profiles to memory (lucky for you!). Use the Table of Contents to find the topic you're interested in. Or, use the index to zero in on the specific term you're looking for. If you come across a word that's unfamiliar, you can look it up in the Glossary (Appendix A). Find the information you need, put it into action, and then set this book back on the shelf (preferably where you can get to it easily!) and get on with your life.

If you're thinking about upgrading to Windows 98, this book doesn't leave you out in the cold. We take you up into the crow's nest and give you a look through our spy glass at the Windows 98 Registry. The special preview section is based on beta software that may change.

You should know right up front that this book deals with a potentially risky subject. Viewing the Registry and modifying it through the various Windows 95 control panels isn't especially dangerous, but modifying the Registry directly, using the Registry Editor or other similar utility, can be. *You can accidentally render a Windows 95 PC unbootable, trash software settings, and lose data files as a result of using the Registry Editor.* Don't get us wrong, we encourage you to experiment with the Registry, we just want you to know that you should **always** create a fallback position for yourself in case something goes wrong. For example, back up your hard disk regularly and back up the Registry files before you make any changes to them. Chapter 2 goes into detail on how to perform these backup tasks. We'll remind you of this caution periodically throughout the book where appropriate. If you don't heed our advice and you get yourself into trouble, Chapter 15 may help you avert total disaster, but we can't guarantee it.

Finally, this book is as scrupulously accurate as we could make it. Everything you read here is something we've tested personally, usually on more than one computer. Also, every word has been scrutinized and authorized by our eagle-eyed technical editor, Gerry Routledge. Nevertheless, if you find what looks like a mistake, please let the publisher know via the online registration site described in the back of this book so we can research it and correct it if necessary. We'll thank you in the acknowledgments section of this book's next edition.

Conventions Used in This Book

Let's see: the Sacred Order of the Scarlet Elk convention, the Democratic National Convention, the Iowa Caucuses. . . .

Actually, we've made every effort to standardize how we tell you to do things and how we refer to things, because we know that you don't want to guess at what to do. Check out the following conventions:

- ✔ When we show you a keyboard shortcut, we put a + sign between the two keys that you press simultaneously. For example: Ctrl+C

- ✔ When we show you a series of commands that you use your mouse and menus to accomplish, we put an arrow between the commands. For example: File➪Save As

- ✔ When we show you a message that you get from the computer, we print that message in a monospace font, similar to what you would see on a manual typewriter. For example: `It is now safe to turn off your computer`

- ✔ When we show you something that you type into Windows 95 or another Windows 95 application, the information to enter is presented in a bold font. For example: **REGEDIT**

- ✔ When we show you stuff to enter at the DOS prompt or code to enter, it appears in monospaced font and capitalized. For example: `XCOPY C:\WINDOWS\USER.DAT E:\REG\ /H /K /Y /R`

- ✔ When we refer to a Registry key, we put that key in an italic font. (In cases where we must break a key because it's too long for a line, we do so on a syllable.) For example: *Hkey_Local_Machine\Software\Classes*

This is a hands-on book, so we give you lots of steps to follow to accomplish your Registry magic. The bolded portion of these steps are things for you to do; unbolded stuff is explanatory, as in the following example:

1. **Save any data files in open programs and close the programs.**

   This step isn't strictly necessary, but we like to walk on the safe side of the street.

2. **Give your PC the three-finger salute (Ctrl+Alt+Del) to display the Close Program dialog box.**

3. **Click Explorer and End Task.**

What You're Not to Read

Here and there, you'll see information marked with the Technical Stuff icon. This is information that isn't necessary for you to get the job done. Don't feel bad about skipping right over this stuff. If you're interested, however, go ahead and read it. Nothing ventured, nothing gained.

Foolish Assumptions

We've written this book for the broad audience of people who work with Windows 95, whether for business or pleasure. You may be a home PC user who wants to protect that machine from common problems and tune it up in useful ways. You may use Windows 95 at work, where you can't afford the downtime that Registry problems can create. You may be a part-time or full-time network administrator who's responsible for managing several Windows 95 PCs and wants to know how to set them up for minimum ongoing maintenance and maximum reliability. You may also be a consultant of one stripe or another who needs to advise others about using Windows 95. You may even be a programmer who wants a quick and friendly introduction to the Registry.

The few assumptions we do make about you as a reader are as follows:

✔ **You use Windows 95 and know enough about it to get around the desktop.** If we refer to the taskbar, the My Computer icon, or the Windows Explorer, you know what we're talking about. If not, read *Windows 95 For Dummies,* 2nd Edition, by Andy Rathbone (IDG Books Worldwide, Inc.) or take an introductory class, and then come back to this book.

✔ **You don't necessarily want to become a computer expert, but you want to understand Windows 95 more thoroughly so you can take maximum advantage of its capabilities.** If this book alone doesn't slake your thirst for Registry knowledge, we include references to a variety of additional resources on the Registry in Appendix B at the back of this book.

✔ **You're conscientious enough to actually make Registry backups before trying the various changes we suggest in this book.** (If you're not, and you prefer to live dangerously, please return this book for a refund, with which you can buy a ticket for a high-altitude bungee jump.)

✔ **You have a bona fide copy of Windows 95 and all the files that it comes with, either on hard disk, CD-ROM, or network drive.** (Some of the utilities this book discusses aren't installed as part of a typical Windows 95 installation, so you need to install them as a separate step — a procedure that requires access to the original Windows 95 files.)

✔ **You don't expect to write Windows 95 programs as a result of reading this book.** If you're a programmer, you can get a lot of great information from this book, and you certainly need to know about the Registry in order to write good Windows 95 software. But writing programs isn't our main focus here.

✔ **You don't expect to configure a network as a result of reading this book.** Some of the topics in this book pertain to a network environment, but we don't tell you how to build a network of Windows 95 computers here. For this sort of information, check out *The LAN Times Guide to Networking Windows 95* by Shimmin and Harper (Osborne/McGraw Hill) or, if you work in a company with under 100 employees, *Small Business Networking For Dummies* by Weadock (IDG Books, Worldwide).

✔ **You're no "dummy"; you just need the basics on the subject in a hurry.**

If this sounds like you, read on!

How This Book Is Organized

As with most *...For Dummies* books, you can dip in and out of specific chapters according to what your interests are and what level of knowledge you already have about particular subjects. You can certainly read this book cover to cover, and we do our best to keep it interesting if you do. However, each chapter is designed to give you all the information you need on a specific topic and not leave you hanging if you haven't read the entire book up to that point.

We've settled on a nautical metaphor to help explain the purpose of the book's six main parts. Think of this book as a voyage of discovery about the Windows 95 Registry. So put on your Wayfarers and cutoffs, stock the Igloo with wine and cheese (or beer and bratwurst), and take a look at the following navigational chart before you set sail.

Part I: All Aboard: Introducing the Registry

This part starts out by answering the question "Why do I need to know about the Registry, anyway?" We tell you what the Registry is, what it does, and how it makes Windows 95 different from Windows 3.x. The first chapter also gives you a taste of the sorts of things you can do with the Registry once you gain some familiarity with it. Chapter 2, hands down the single-most important chapter in the book, lays out the detailed procedures for backing up the Registry. Follow these guidelines and you can experiment with the Registry in the secure knowledge that if you damage something, you can always get back to where you were before you started experimenting. Chapter 3 presents the various ways you can change Registry settings without actually directly editing Registry contents, for example with Windows 95 control panels. (Whenever you have a choice between using the Registry Editor and a control panel, use the control panel; it's safer.) Finally, Chapter 4 introduces the Windows 95 Registry Editor, as well as a nifty enhanced version that comes with the Symantec Norton Utilities for Windows 95.

Part II: Hull, Keel, and Sail: The Registry Structure

Part II takes a closer look at how the Registry is put together. Chapter 5 explains what actual files constitute the Registry (yes, there's more than one), where you can find them on your PC, how to see them (they're normally hidden from view, and for good reason), and what they contain. Understanding where these files are and what they do is essential to being able to back up the Registry so you don't get into trouble that you can't get out of easily. Chapter 6 takes a look at the Registry structure from a different angle, namely, the "logical" structure. The Registry may consist of several separate files, but it appears as a single multilevel database when you view it with the Registry Editor, and you'll need to understand how Microsoft has organized that database in order to use the Registry Editor effectively. Chapter 7 zeroes in on how the Registry stores information about your PC's hardware in order to work with the *Plug and Play* standard, which Windows 95 supports so that adding and removing devices from your system is as automatic and painless as possible.

Part III: Rigging for Sea: Registry Customizing

The sailors we know get almost as much enjoyment out of tweaking and tuning their boats as they do actually sailing them. In Part III, you'll discover how to use the Registry to customize Windows 95 to your liking. Chapter 8 explains how you can customize the Windows 95 setup program so that after you install Windows 95, the Registry looks the way you want it to look. (If you only use one PC and it already has Windows 95 on it, you can skip this chapter, but if you get involved with installing multiple PCs — for example, if you're a network administrator — this stuff is great.)

Chapter 9 goes into detail on how you can customize the Registry to control what a user can do on any given Windows 95 machine. The System Policy Editor is the Registry-modifying tool that this chapter explores, and it's useful whether you're implementing a company network or just trying to figure out how to prevent little Johnny from inadvertently trashing your home Windows 95 PC. Chapter 10 investigates user profiles, a cool technique for making the Registry look and act differently depending on who logs on to the PC (also very handy for both company networks and home computers). The last chapter in this part, Chapter 11, explains ways you can tune the Registry to squeeze more speed out of Windows 95, change how the operating system looks to the user, and do things you didn't know Windows 95 could do — such as provide a multiple-choice list for choosing the program you want to use when right-clicking a data file.

Part IV: The America's Cup: Registry Mastery

Part IV is for more advanced users. Chapter 12 explains how you can know exactly what happens to the Registry when you install or remove software or hardware. The knowledge you gain in this chapter lets you troubleshoot Registry problems faster later on. It also explains how you can easily share the Registry tricks that you discover with others. Chapter 13 offers tips on clearing out Registry flotsam and jetsam — the junk that accumulates like empty sandwich bags in the ship's hold — so your Registry stays lean, mean, fast, and efficient.

Part V: Computer Overboard! Registry Troubleshooting

Windows 95 is a good operating system, but not a perfect one. It can break in a thousand different ways, most of which relate in one fashion or another to the Registry. Part V helps you deal with the occasional problems that may crop up. Chapter 14 presents the top 12 Registry-related Windows 95 problems, plus suggestions for correcting them (or at least, recovering from them). Chapter 15 gives you step-by-step instructions for recovering from Registry disasters when troubleshooting doesn't work and you must restore the Registry using an earlier version.

Part VI: Docking at the Pier: The Part of Tens

The "Part of Tens" is a standard feature of ...*For Dummies* books. Ours has one useful chapter and two frivolous ones. Chapter 16 presents ten Internet sites on the World Wide Web that contain useful information or software pertaining to the Registry. If you have an Internet connection, you'll definitely want to check out these Web sites. Chapter 17 presents ten Registry tricks that we think you'll enjoy discovering. Chapter 18 lists ten Registries that have nothing to do with Windows 95. You know, all work and no play. . . .

Part VII: Appendixes

This book has four appendixes:

- Appendix A is a glossary with concise definitions of terms used in the book.

- Appendix B is a reference and resource section that provides details on companies and products mentioned in the book, as well as a list of books and magazines that can help you get more information and stay up to date on networking trends and technology.

- Appendix C is a description of the software goodies on the enclosed CD-ROM.

- Appendix D outlines the differences between the Windows 95 and Windows NT Registries.

Icons Used in This Book

Several graphical icons highlight certain kinds of material throughout this book:

Use this icon to avoid a *gotcha* — a common trap or pitfall. Most of these little warnings come from our own experience fiddling around with the Registry. Benefit from our mistakes!

You get a CD-ROM with this book, and this icon alerts you that the accompanying text refers to software on that disc.

When you see this icon, you know we've succumbed to the temptation to editorialize a little bit. Other knowledgeable people may disagree with these opinionated comments, but they *are* based on experience.

This icon points out a bit of knowledge or comment that's worth committing to your long-term memory.

This icon clues you in to a precautionary step that, taken now, may save you a world of hurt later.

Here's material you can skip if you don't care about the nitty-gritty details, but may want to read if you like to know a bit more than the average bear.

Short suggestions, hints, and bits of useful information appear next to this icon.

This icon guides you to other sections of the book where you can find more information relative to the topic at hand.

And there you have it! We hope that this book provides a bounty of useful information that makes your Windows 95 experience more rewarding, fun, and trouble-free. If you can think of ways we could make it even better, please visit the Web site at the back of the book and let us know.

Where to Go from Here

If you don't know much about the Registry, you can find out the background stuff in Chapter 1; otherwise, proceed directly to Chapter 2 to find out how to safeguard your Registry. After that, the Registry is your oyster.

Part I

All Aboard: Introducing the Registry

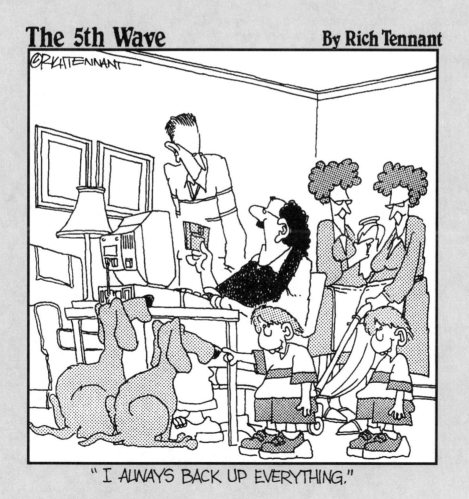

The 5th Wave   By Rich Tennant

"I ALWAYS BACK UP EVERYTHING."

In this part . . .

Sing in me, muse, of that wise man
Who wandered the Registry of Windows 95
And found that with aid from his backup plan
His hard disk could crash, his PC stay alive. . . .

Why do you need to know about the Registry? Well, we believe that everybody who uses Windows 95 or Windows 98 should know at least a little bit about it, because it's at the center of everything that Windows does.

This is the place where you get your sea legs under you for your odyssey across the Windows 95 Registry, learning the background you need and the tools you'll use to fine-tune your Registry in the safest possible way. You also find out how to batten down the hatches with an all-important backup of your Registry.

Chapter 1

Why Do I Need to Know about the Registry?

In This Chapter

▶ Defining the Windows 95 Registry

▶ Exploring the Registry's role in running Windows 95

▶ Comparing the Registry to Windows 3.x "INI" files

▶ Discovering examples of what you can do with the Registry

*I*n spite of the fact that the Microsoft-supplied product documentation all but ignores the Registry, every user needs to know about the heart of Windows 95. In this chapter, we provide you with a bird's-eye view of the Registry from which you can see what the Registry does and why it's fundamental to just about everything you can do in Windows 95. More importantly, we give you some ideas of how you can use the Registry to improve and customize your Windows 95 system.

For those of you who got your feet wet doing stuff with your INI files in Windows 3.x (by which we mean Windows 3.1, Windows for Workgroups 3.1, and Windows for Workgroups 3.11), we ground you in the differences between the old INI files you're used to and the new Registry paradigm.

So sit back, relax, and get ready to set sail.

View from the Masthead: What Does the Registry Do?

It's good to start any voyage by surveying the landscape from the masthead — looking at the "big picture." In this section, we look at what the Registry is and what it actually does for a Windows 95 PC.

Defining the Registry

If Windows 95 were an office building that you owned, then the Registry would be the wiring. You may never give the wiring much thought until the day you buy a new copier for your office, plug it into a miswired power outlet, and receive an involuntary Don King hairdo. Or, maybe, until the day you decide to improve or customize the building — for example by installing "smart" thermostats, faster elevators, or a security system.

The Registry is much the same. You need to understand it in order to fix certain problems that can crop up, and in order to customize Windows 95 to your liking. Here's our attempt at a one-sentence definition of what the Registry is and all it does:

> *The Registry is the central store of information that Windows 95 and Windows 95 programs use to track all the software and hardware on the machine, including details about how that software and hardware are configured.*

The following sections expand on key aspects of this definition in more detail.

Central storage location

One of the key features of the Registry is that it brings information that was formerly scattered around the computer's hard drive into a single place. But understanding this depends, of course, on understanding what we mean by the word *place*. The Registry contains more than one file (there may be several, depending on whether the Windows 95 PC is set up for multiple users), but the Registry's actual files don't necessarily all exist in a single directory.

The Registry still *seems* like a single place, however, because you can view all the Registry information from a single window if you use the Registry Editor tool (REGEDIT.EXE) that comes with Windows 95, as shown in Figure 1-1. The Registry Editor is covered in Chapter 4.

Figure 1-1:
The Registry
Editor lets
you see the
complete
Registry
database
within a
single
window.

Software tracking information

One of the Registry's main functions is to keep track of your PC's software (including Windows 95 itself). The Registry handles this job well with so-called *32-bit programs,* which are written expressly for Windows 95 or Windows NT, but not so well with *16-bit programs,* such as those written for Windows 3.*x.*

If every program in the world was completely compatible with Windows 95, then the Registry would know all the setup and configuration details for every program on your PC. However, Computerdom is an imperfect king-dom. The Registry's ability to track your software is subject to the following limitations:

- ✔ **Windows 95 programs.** Even 32-bit programs don't always store every setting in the Registry. Instead, they may use *private INI files* that the Registry doesn't understand. Some settings for Adobe Acrobat Reader 3.0, a 32-bit application, are stored in ACROREAD.INI. WinZip 6.1, also a 32-bit program, stores some of its own settings in WINZIP32.INI. We could provide dozens more examples, but you get the picture. For more on INI files, check out the sidebar, "History 310: INI files in Windows 3.*x.*"

- ✔ **Windows 3.x programs.** Because Windows 3.*x* has a Registry of sorts (only one section), Windows 3.*x* programs do update the Windows 95 Registry with some information at install time — such as the *file association* information that tells the program to run whenever you double-click a file with a specific suffix. Windows 3.*x* programs don't make all the entries that Windows 95 programs typically make, how-ever, such as the information that programs use to "sign in" with Windows 95 and effectively say, "This computer has program ABC installed on it, and here's how to uninstall it later." The Windows 95 Registry also can't capture information that Windows 3.*x* programs typically put into the WIN.INI file or a "private" INI file.

- ✔ **DOS programs.** DOS programs don't make any entries into the Registry, because DOS programs neither know about Windows nor care about it. If you want to know how a DOS program is set up, you must look at the program's own configuration files, and possibly also the DOS startup files, CONFIG.SYS and AUTOEXEC.BAT.

The Windows 95 Registry stores *most* of the details about Windows 95 and 32-bit Windows 95 programs; *some* of the details about Windows 3.*x* pro-grams; and *none* of the details about DOS programs.

Hardware tracking information

The Registry tracks *almost* all the hardware on your PC. The Registry contains every bit of information about any hardware that uses a *32-bit device driver,* a program designed especially to enable the Windows 95 operating system and the hardware device to communicate with each other.

(Windows 95 comes with hundreds of different 32-bit device drivers, and the Windows 95 setup program installs most of the necessary ones automatically.) Heck, the Registry even keeps details about hardware that you used to use with the PC, but later removed — presumably on the off chance that you may reinstall that stuff later on.

System configuration information

Windows 95 is a highly configurable operating system, meaning that there are zillions of settings that users and administrators can make after installing the base operating system. Similarly, most Windows 95 programs offer a dizzying array of optional settings, so (for example) if you prefer white text on a blue background in your word processor, you can set the program up that way. Finally, the hardware devices in a Windows 95 PC may have a variety of configurable settings, too: for example, whether your network interface card uses the coax cable connector or the twisted-pair cable connector. The Registry tracks all these configuration settings so that users don't need to remake them every time they boot the PC.

Real-mode device drivers

Sometimes, Windows 95 PCs communicate with some hardware devices by using software left over from earlier versions of DOS and Windows. These 16-bit programs are called *real-mode device drivers*, and they get activated by the old DOS startup files CONFIG.SYS and AUTOEXEC.BAT, instead of through the Registry.

A typical example is the real-mode device driver for a CD-ROM drive. Most new Windows 95 PCs load 16-bit CD-ROM support software in CONFIG.SYS and AUTOEXEC.BAT. For example, a line in CONFIG.SYS may look like this:

```
device=c:\d011v109.sys
   /D:toscd001
```

and a line in AUTOEXEC.BAT may look like this:

```
c:\windows\command\mscdex
   /d:toscd001 /m:15 /l:e
```

Windows 95 and Windows 95 programs typically don't need these lines in CONFIG.SYS and AUTOEXEC.BAT, because Windows 95 has its own 32-bit device driver for accessing the CD-ROM drive. One reason for activating real-mode device drivers is so that older hardware for which 32-bit device drivers don't exist can still work with Windows 95. Another reason is that users who run DOS programs using the Windows 95 special *MS-DOS Mode*, which removes Windows 95 from memory, need the real-mode device driver in order to run a DOS program from the CD-ROM drive. However, the Registry doesn't store any information about the real-mode, DOS-level CD-ROM device driver. It *does* store information about the 32-bit device driver that Windows 95 programs use. (Windows 95 programs ignore the real-mode device driver in memory.)

The Registry's Role

Now that we've cleared up what the Registry is, what's its role in a Windows 95 machine? What does it actually *do?* Go ahead and refill the coffee cup now, because the list is a long one!

Recording installation choices

The Registry fires up and gets working during the Windows 95 installation program. When a user — either an *end user* (the person who purchases a computer) or a *PC vendor* (a computer retailer) — first installs Windows 95, the user can specify information about devices connected to the computer or installed in the computer. The setup program stores that information in the Registry. The user also can choose what pieces of Windows 95 to install: a minimal setup (which leaves off games, wallpaper, and so on), a typical setup, or a custom setup. Again, the setup program records those choices in the Registry.

Setting up hardware

Your Windows 95 PC is likely different than ours, because Windows 95 supports a great many hardware devices such as graphics accelerator cards, CD-ROM drives, modems, hard disks, and so on. When Windows 95 starts, it must set up all those devices by assigning them the *resources* that they need to function. These resources include *interrupts* that devices use to request the PC's attention, *memory* areas that they use to communicate with the PC, software *drivers* that form the link between the device and Windows 95, and so on.

Windows 95 permits you to define different *hardware configurations,* or *profiles.* For example, you may work with a notebook computer on the road, but you can attach that notebook to a docking station with a different display, keyboard, and network connection when you're in the office. The Registry stores these hardware profiles so that Windows 95 can configure itself properly depending on the hardware configuration that you need at the time. Chapter 7 discusses hardware profiles in more detail.

Setting up Windows 95

You can change many of Windows 95's operating system settings, so Windows 95 needs to know how to set itself up for operation when it starts. Here are a few examples of Windows 95 startup information contained in the Registry:

- What time zone to use
- How the Windows 95 PC is to be used: as a typical desktop, as a portable with limited memory, or as a server machine sharing files and printers with other users
- How quickly Windows 95 can access the PC's CD-ROM drive

And here are some examples of Registry settings that apply to a Windows 95 PC in a network environment:

- ✔ The computer's network name
- ✔ The server that Windows 95 should look for when the user logs on to the network
- ✔ The order in which to load different network components, if the PC connects to more than one kind of network

Running startup programs

The Registry maintains a list of programs to run when Windows 95 starts, independent of the list that you can create by manually modifying the Start menu. The Registry's run list typically includes programs that absolutely, positively must run every time Windows 95 starts, such as network communication programs and antivirus utilities.

The Registry can also run certain programs one time only. This option typically comes into play after a user installs a new application program, and the software vendor provides a utility that should only run once in order to set up the application for its maiden voyage.

Defining how Windows 95 appears

The Registry tells Windows 95 how to get dressed in the morning. It specifies all the user-settable display options, such as screen resolution, how many colors to display, what wallpaper to use, what fonts and sizes to use for icon titles, and so on. It also tells Windows 95 what icons and folders to put onto the desktop, and what icons to place in the *system tray* (the little box at the opposite end of the taskbar from the Start button).

If you set up the PC for use by multiple different individuals, the Registry keeps track of each person's preferences so that when someone logs on, Windows 95 displays the desktop designed by that person. If users roam from machine to machine in a PC network, the Registry maintains desktop preferences on a network server, so that when the user logs on to the network, Windows 95 fetches the user's preferences from the server. Chapter 10 discusses these features, which go by the name of *user profiles*.

Specifying what double-clicking does

You can run a program in Windows 95 by double-clicking a data file that's associated with that program. Double-click a file with the TXT suffix, and you typically run Notepad. The Registry tells Windows 95 which program to run when a particular type of data file is double-clicked. (Yes, you can change this behavior!)

Specifying what drag and drop does

Windows 95 and its programs enable you to do all manner of things by dragging and dropping icons from point A to point B: You can print a file, graft a chunk of data into a different document, compress or decompress a file, and much more. The Registry controls all the drag-and-drop behavior for the various types of data files that it knows about.

Defining right-click behavior

The right mouse button, which in Windows 3.*x* had about as much to do as an American vice president, is a very busy little rodent appendage in Windows 95. When you right-click a file of any kind in Windows 95, a *context menu* appears listing the choices available for that file: open, print, delete, and so on. The context menu can change depending on what type of file you right-click on. The Registry specifies the appearance and function of the context menu for every data type defined on the system.

Keeping track of application settings

Most Windows 95 programs store *user-definable* settings in the Registry. For example, if you're processing words, you can choose to turn the automatic spell-checking feature off (especially if you're writing about computers and your article has lots of weird abbreviations!). Windows 95 programs also store *user-specific* (as opposed to user-definable) settings in the Registry, such as a list of most recently used files. These sorts of application settings should be kept in the Registry, although in reality, many programs (including some written by Microsoft) use other ways to track user settings, too — such as the time-honored INI files (see "What Does the Registry Replace?" later in this chapter).

Reporting configuration data to administrators

On a network of PCs, administrators and troubleshooters often need to know details of a computer's configuration, but they can't always physically go to the user's computer. The Registry can report a user's PC configuration to a remote administrator, as long as both user and administrator are connected to the same network. That network must be a *client/server* type (such as Novell NetWare or Windows NT Server) that uses a centralized database of users and passwords.

The bottom line is that the Registry handles just about every chore on a Windows 95 PC short of actually running programs and communicating with devices. Now you can begin to understand why the Registry is so important, why every Windows 95 user needs to take steps to protect it, and why you can do so many things to improve the functioning of Windows 95 once you understand it.

Conspiracy theories

Why didn't Microsoft tell you about the Registry if it's so important and if you can do so much with it? Here are our theories:

- ✔ Microsoft's attitude echoes Jack Nicholson's in *A Few Good Men*: "You can't *handle* the Registry!" (We think you can, or we wouldn't have written this book.)

- ✔ Microsoft intended the Registry to be a behind-the-scenes database with which users should never need to directly interact. (In a perfect world, that might be true, but ours isn't.)

- ✔ Microsoft knows that their bare-bones Registry editing tool, REGEDIT, is hastily

assembled, inelegantly designed, and breaks almost every rule of user-friendly software design, so they don't want to call attention to it. (We wouldn't either.)

- ✔ They couldn't figure out how to explain the Registry. (OK, it takes us about 400 pages, so we can sympathize.)

Pick your favorite theory; the truth is probably a combination of all of these. Just remember that Microsoft's scant documentation of the Registry is no indicator of its importance. When you buy a house you don't get a manual describing it, either, but it's probably the most valuable thing you'll ever buy.

What Does the Registry Replace? (For Windows 3.x Veterans)

Many of you reading this book have prior experience with Windows 3.x. You can better understand the Windows 95 Registry by understanding what Windows 3.x files it replaces.

If you've never worked with the combination of Windows 3.x and MS-DOS, feel free to skip this section!

Getting initiated into INI files

Windows 3.x saved the software and hardware settings in various places and forms, but it stored most of these settings in text files having the extension .INI, such as WIN.INI. (For details on other INI files, see the sidebar, "History 310: INI files in Windows 3.x.") The INI stands for initialization, because Windows looks at these files when it starts up. (Windows and Windows programs also look at some of the INI files after startup, too.)

All INI files follow the same simple formatting rules: section headings in square brackets, items underneath section headings can appear in any order, items under the wrong heading don't work, a leading semicolon "comments out" a line so that Windows doesn't process it, and so on. You can (with rare exceptions) edit any INI file with a simple text editor, such as Windows Notepad. Figure 1-2 shows an excerpt from a fairly typical INI file, SYSTEM.INI.

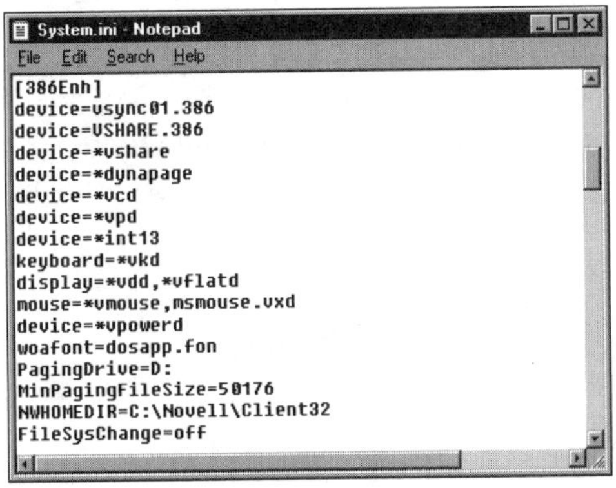

Figure 1-2:
Windows
3.*x* relies
almost
exclusively
on INI files
to record
software
and
hardware
information.

```
[386Enh]
device=vsync01.386
device=USHARE.386
device=*vshare
device=*dynapage
device=*vcd
device=*vpd
device=*int13
keyboard=*vkd
display=*vdd,*vflatd
mouse=*vmouse,msmouse.vxd
device=*vpowerd
woafont=dosapp.fon
PagingDrive=D:
MinPagingFileSize=50176
NWHOMEDIR=C:\Novell\Client32
FileSysChange=off
```

History 310: INI files in Windows 3.*x*

The INI files that Windows 3.*x* used are as follow:

✓ **WIN.INI** includes a variety of desktop appearance information, as well as file type associations — what happens when a user double-clicks a BMP file, for example.

✓ **SYSTEM.INI** contains primarily hardware information, including the names of the specific device drivers that Windows must use to speak to the display, mouse, and so on.

✓ **CONTROL.INI** contains information pertaining to the Windows control panel, including multimedia device drivers, as well as certain desktop appearance settings.

✓ **PROGMAN.INI** contains settings that affect the Program Manager shell, including a few optional restrictions on what users can do within Program Manager.

✓ **Private INI files** contain information that allows individual programs to run and can appear in various places on the hard drive, such as C:\WINDOWS, C:\WINDOWS\ SYSTEM, or in the application's own directory. EXCEL.INI is an example of a private INI file. These files exist because WIN.INI has a 64K limitation and can't hold every setting for every program without bursting its belt.

Yes, Virginia, there is a Windows 3.x Registry

The first attempt to address some of the INI file shortcomings mentioned in the sidebar ("What's wrong with INI files?") was the Windows 3.x Registry, although Microsoft actually called it the *Registration Database* (see Figure 1-3). Much narrower in scope than the Windows 95 Registry, the Registration Database limited itself to file type associations (which data files go with which programs), compound document creation (embedding or linking a chunk of spreadsheet data into a word processing program), and drag-and-drop behavior.

Figure 1-3:
The
Windows
3.11
Registration
Database,
as viewed
by the 3.x
REGEDIT
utility.

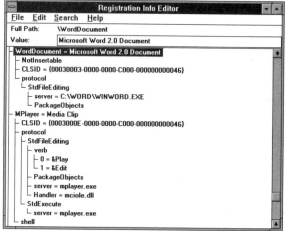

As a practical matter, the Registration Database isn't sufficient to store all the various settings a program may need to keep track of, so it didn't make WIN.INI and private INI files obsolete. However, it represented a good first step toward consolidating at least certain categories of Windows information, and it did a good enough job to encourage Microsoft to extend the concept dramatically in Windows 95.

INI files that Windows 95 needs

So are the INI files now obsolete in Windows 95, given that the new Registry is much more comprehensive than the Windows 3.x Registration Database? It's a nice thought, but unfortunately far from reality.

While you can run Windows 95 without the DOS startup files CONFIG.SYS and AUTOEXEC.BAT, you can't run Windows 95 without at least WIN.INI and SYSTEM.INI, yet. In fact, if you try deleting WIN.INI, Windows 95 thumbs its nose at you by rebuilding a minimalist WIN.INI file the next time it starts (see Figure 1-4). If WIN.INI didn't exist, the setup program for most Windows 3.*x* applications would fail.

SYSTEM.INI still exists, too, on a standard Windows 95 PC. Microsoft was able to migrate most SYSTEM.INI settings to the Registry, but not all. As a result, you still need SYSTEM.INI around, even though it's much smaller than it was under Windows 3.*x*.

WIN.INI and SYSTEM.INI are also important to ensure compatibility with the 16-bit Windows 3.*x* applications that use them. When a user makes a change to the desktop via one of the Windows 95 control panels, that change may very well occur in two places: WIN.INI and the Registry. (Try changing the desktop wallpaper, for example; you'll find the new BMP file listed both places.) Windows 3.*x* applications look to WIN.INI for desktop information and Windows 95 applications look to the Registry.

What's wrong with INI files?

What's the problem with INI files? Why replace the INI file structure with the new Registry system? Well, the INI file system has never been ideal. Here's a short list of its shortcomings:

✔ **Flat structure.** You couldn't have a subsection underneath a main section; one level of structure is all that was available, limiting the ability of Microsoft and application developers to organize INI file settings more finely.

✔ **Size limit.** Each INI file can be no larger than 64K. (This became a big problem for Windows 3.*x* users who had tons of installed fonts; WIN.INI would get too large, and Windows would refuse to start!) It resulted in individual applications installing private INI files to keep WIN.INI under 64K.

✔ **Scattered locations.** Although you can say with certainty where the core Windows INI files are (they all have to be together), you never know where programs might put their private INI files.

✔ **Poor separability.** Some INI files contain both machine-specific settings and user-specific settings. As a result, it's difficult to have all the user settings — wallpaper, program groups, and so on — follow a "roaming user" who may work on different networked PCs at different times.

✔ **No remote administration.** Without third-party add-ons to Windows 3.*x*, no way exists for an administrator to connect to a Windows 3.*x* PC and access its INI files.

Figure 1-4:
Windows 95
insists on a
minimalist
WIN.INI
even if you
delete it.

INI files that other programs need

Many other private INI files still exist on any given Windows 95 machine, too. You can quickly check the INI files on a given machine using Start⇨Find⇨Files or Folders and type *.INI in the Named field (Glenn counts 199 separate INI files on his main Windows 95 PC!).

While we could understand 16-bit Windows 3.*x* programs using private INI files, Microsoft breaks its own rules by using private INI files for some of its own Windows 95 applications. Clearly, private INI files are going to be with us for some time. However, the same is not true of the DOS startup files, as the next section explains.

Goodbye to two old friends

Although WIN.INI and SYSTEM.INI still have a place in Windows 95, granted a much less important place than they enjoyed in Windows 3.*x,* two other system files that date back to the original have become dispensable on most Windows 95 PCs. These are the DOS startup files, CONFIG.SYS and AUTOEXEC.BAT.

You may still need these files (as we mentioned in the "All hardware" section toward the beginning of this chapter) if you still use old devices or if you run DOS programs in Windows 95's special MS-DOS Mode. However, most DOS programs run well the usual way (that is, as a separate window executing within the Windows 95 user interface). If you run all Windows programs on a given PC, chances are good that you can simply delete CONFIG.SYS and AUTOEXEC.BAT and never worry about them again. A quick way to find out is to simply rename these files to names such as CONFIG.SAV and AUTOEXEC.SAV, restart the computer, and see if all your programs seem to work normally. If not, renaming the files back to their original names is a simple matter.

What Does the Windows 95 Registry Add?

Okay, so the Windows 95 Registry replaces a lot of information that the DOS and Windows 3.x startup files used to contain. Does the Registry store any new information that DOS and Windows 3.x never needed to track? (You can tell by the fact we're asking the question that the answer is yes.)

User profiles

Because the Windows 95 Registry divides user specific settings into a separate file, it's now possible for user preferences (desktop color, wallpaper, icons, and so on) to travel with users who roam around a network. It's also possible for a Windows 95 PC to allow multiple individuals to log on to a single machine and see their own preferences. Chapter 10 deals with these *user profiles*.

Plug-and-Play info

The Plug-and-Play standard helps make installing new hardware easier. It also makes it easier to rip out old hardware you no longer want. Plug-and-Play maintains a database of hardware settings that helps automate the process of assigning and unassigning computer resources to specific devices. Guess what? That database is in the Registry! Chapter 7 looks at it in depth.

Access restrictions

The Registry adds settings to support the great variety of access restrictions that Windows 95 can impose. It also adds a nifty mechanism for setting up multiple Windows 95 PCs to all use the same set of restrictions: the policy file, which is an optional Registry file that you can create with the System Policy Editor utility (POLEDIT.EXE). Chapter 9 tells you all about policy files.

Rule #1: Saving the Registry

By now, if you've been reading this chapter from the start, you've probably begun to realize that Windows 95 depends upon the Registry to much the same extent that Congress depends on campaign contributions from special interest groups. If anything happens to the Registry, Windows 95 becomes a boat without a sail. The First Rule of the Registry, therefore, is as follows:

> *Periodically save a "known good" copy of the Registry where it's out of harm's way.*

Chapter 2 gives you details on various ways to save the Registry, but here's what you absolutely must know in a nutshell.

How to save

You have several choices as to how you save the Registry. Here, we just mention one: the Emergency Recovery Utility. Although you may expect a program with such an important name would be at the top of the Start menu's program list, Windows 95 doesn't even install it for you during setup; you have to install it yourself from the Windows 95 CD-ROM. (Chapter 2 gives you the step-by-step procedure.)

Once you install ERU, running it is simply a matter of double-clicking the ERU.EXE icon and specifying a target location that's big enough to store all the files. If your Registry is even moderately large, a single diskette can't hold it, so you should specify another directory on the hard disk, a directory on a second hard disk (if the PC has one), a removable magnetic disk (such as ZIP), a writable optical disk (such as CD-R), or a network directory. When ERU completes successfully, you see the screen shown in Figure 1-6.

Figure 1-6:
The
Emergency
Recovery
Utility
provides an
encouraging
message
after it
copies the
Registry
files to a
clean, dry
place.

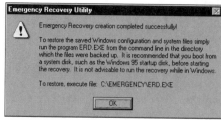

When to save

Always save a copy of the Registry at the following times:

- ✔ As soon as you finish a Windows 95 installation and everything seems to work

- ✔ As soon as you fire up a new PC that came with Windows 95, and (again) everything seems to be working fine

- ✔ Before you install or remove any program, except perhaps the minor *applets* (such as Calculator and Notepad) that come with Windows 95

- ✔ After you install or remove any program and everything looks like it's working right

- ✔ Before you make any significant changes with the Control Panel (for example, installing network software is significant, but changing the time and date is not)

- ✔ Before you make changes with the System Policy Editor, which is a Registry-editing wolf in sheep's clothing

- ✔ Before you even think about running REGEDIT or any similar utility (such as the Norton Registry Editor that comes with Symantec Norton Utilities 2.0 for Windows 95)

Finding Out What You Can Do with the Registry

So what can you *do* with the Registry, besides make backup copies of it to ensure against future problems? Quite a lot. Chapters 8, 9, 10, and 11 provide many examples of how you can use the Registry to customize a Windows 95 PC. For now, here's a sampling of five useful things you can do once you understand the Registry's ins and outs.

Fixing Windows 95 bugs

Windows 95 comes with a few bugs that range from the cosmetic to the serious. An example of a serious bug is a problem with *file system profiles,* the settings you can make on the System control panel's Performance tab to optimize Windows 95's performance for a portable, desktop, or server PC (see Figure 1-7). In the first two versions of Windows 95 (which you can check in the System control panel), 4.00.950 and 4.00.950a, the only choice that works correctly is the desktop choice. If you change the file system

profile to either of the other two settings, Windows 95 actually slows down!
The culprit is two pairs of incorrect entries in the Registry; fix those with
REGEDIT, and the file system profiles work properly, making your PC run
faster. (Chapter 14 provides all the details under the heading "File system
profiles don't work right.")

Figure 1-7:
Two of
Windows
95's three
file system
profiles
don't work
correctly
without a
Registry fix.

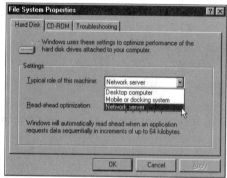

Recovering from crashes

Microsoft didn't write Windows 95 with reliability as the number one design
goal. Compatibility was the prime directive: Microsoft wanted Windows 95
to work with as wide a variety of software and hardware as possible. In
many cases, Microsoft had to sacrifice the goat of reliability on the altar of
compatibility. End result: Windows 95 can crash. Further end result: Windows 95 can damage the Registry when it crashes. The situation gets worse
when you consider that many (all?) application software vendors don't write
perfectly reliable programs. Third-party programs can crash Windows 95,
too, and they can also damage the Registry.

You can recover gracefully from a Windows 95 system with a damaged
Registry if you heeded the previous section on backing up the Registry. For
example, if you use a utility such as ERU, you can simply run its counterpart,
ERD (Emergncy Recovery Disk), to get the Registry back to where it was the
last time that you ran ERU. ERD isn't the only way to get out of trouble,
though. Chapter 16 goes into some depth on various step-by-step procedures for restoring a damaged Registry, and when to use them.

Making the desktop easier to use

You can customize the Registry to make the Windows 95 desktop more user-friendly. For example, when you right-click a data file, a *context menu* pops up and gives you the option to "Open" the file. The file type association stored in the Registry determines the program that runs: BMP with Windows Paint, for example. In many situations, however, users may use more than one program to work with a given type of file. Windows Paint may be fine for casual editing of a BMP graphic — changing a couple of pixels here and there — but a user may need to use a more powerful tool, such as Adobe Photoshop, for more serious editing, such as applying color corrections to a scanned photograph. By using the Registry, you can change the context menu so that it offers a convenient list of all the programs the user might need (see Figure 1-8, and Chapter 11).

Speeding up Windows 95

Various user interface settings in Windows 95 tend to slow down how fast the operating system feels in daily use. For example, the animated way that windows minimize and maximize — with a sort of visual "whoosh" — is slick and fun for about five minutes, after which it becomes merely a slightly annoying delay factor. For another example, the hesitation that Windows 95 makes on the Start menu when the user points at an entry that leads to a subsidiary menu is also a "feature" that makes the desktop feel more sluggish than it needs to. You can use your knowledge of the Registry to eliminate the animated window behavior and to reduce the menu display lag time. Chapter 11 tells you how to perform these customizations as well as several others.

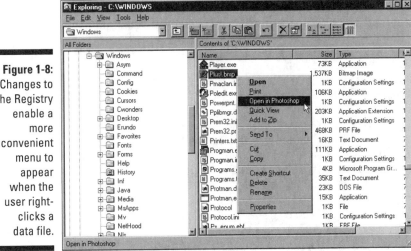

Figure 1-8: Changes to the Registry enable a more convenient menu to appear when the user right-clicks a data file.

Increasing security

Windows 3.*x* offered practically no tools for limiting user access to the operating system. By contrast, Windows 95 lets you secure the desktop seven ways to Sunday, and all the security features happen via the Registry. Security is very important in a business environment, but it also can be convenient on a home PC (you don't want your six-year-old making direct Registry edits!). A great security feature is the ability to run the System Policy Editor program, which comes with Windows 95 and which edits the Registry, and disable the REGEDIT program. When you disable REGEDIT, any user who tries to run it sees the screen in Figure 1-9. Chapter 3 gives you the procedure, and Chapter 9 deals with the System Policy Editor in detail.

Figure 1-9:
One Registry security feature prevents users from editing the Registry with REGEDIT.

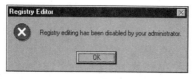

Sailing into the Sunset with the Registry

Microsoft seems highly committed to the Registry concept. This chapter has shown that Windows 3.*x* employed the concept to a limited extent, and that Windows 95 and Windows NT 4.0 rely heavily on the Registry. As it turns out, the Registry is a major part of Windows 98 (see this book's special insert section) and NT 5.0, too. The Registry is therefore going to be important well past the year 2000, assuming that any of our programs still work after January 1 of that year!

The good news is that after you read this book, the knowledge you gain will continue to be useful and applicable for years to come — not always the case with computer books! Even if you move to Windows 98 or NT 5.0, there's enough similarity between the Registries of all these different products so that you'll feel at home — even if you do have to bone up on the aspects of the Registry that are unique to each operating system.

Chapter 2

Backing Up the Registry: How to Sleep at Night

In This Chapter

▶ Discovering the reasons you need to make Registry backups

▶ Understanding what's wrong with CFGBACK and ERU

▶ Using export files as a backup technique

▶ Creating your own custom Registry backup batch file

*M*aking a complete and completely usable Registry backup is not quite as simple as you may think at first (and definitely not as simple as it should be!). However, making a backup isn't difficult at all after you set up your computer to make fast and convenient backups.

In Chapter 1, we introduce the First Rule of the Registry, restated here:

> *Periodically save a "known good" copy of the Registry where it's out of harm's way.*

The most important action that many of you can perform as a result of reading this book is to back up the Registry. If we can help you get into the habit of backing up your Registry successfully, then this book has paid for itself in one chapter. (Think of the other 17 chapters as a bonus!)

However, nowhere in Microsoft's standard documentation for Windows 95 can you find information on how to save a copy of the Registry so that you can safely restore it (copy it back) in case of mishap. Most of the Registry books currently available treat this subject incompletely, and sometimes downright inaccurately. Furthermore, the tools that Microsoft supplies for Registry backup are seriously flawed. Rely on them blindly, and you may find your backup against a wall. (Groan.)

Our job here, then, is to present the why, when, where, and how of Registry backups and describe enough alternatives so that you can choose a method — or, more likely, a combination of methods — that works best for you. After you set up a Registry backup plan and adhere to it, you can relax a little whenever you need to modify the Registry. Even if you do make a mistake, and at some point mistakes are inevitable, you can always get back to where you were before. (If only life in general could work that way!)

This chapter focuses on *creating* backups, and Chapter 15 looks more closely at *restoring* from your backups. The later chapter discusses some of the same programs that we discuss here, in the context of disaster recovery.

Why Backups Matter

Here's why you really do need to back up the Registry:

- ✔ The Registry is at the center of everything that Windows 95 does, as Chapter 1 explains. Problems with your Registry can affect every program on your PC and even prevent Windows 95 from starting properly.

- ✔ In severe cases, a damaged Registry may require you to completely reinstall Windows 95 and all Windows 95 applications, if you don't have a good Registry backup.

- ✔ The Registry is vulnerable to damage from disk media failure (hard drives, like milk, eventually go bad) and from buggy software install and uninstall programs.

- ✔ The Registry files have characteristics, or *attributes,* that exclude them from processing by commands, such as COPY, that you may use to back up other key files.

- ✔ Damaging the Registry during a session with the Registry Editor is easier than overeating at Thanksgiving.

- ✔ The Registry files aren't text files. Unlike a Windows 3.1 INI file, if something goes wrong with the Registry, you can't fix it by loading it in a simple program like Notepad.

When to Back Up the Registry

A solid Registry backup plan includes both *landmark* and *scheduled* backups.

Landmark backups

A *landmark backup* is a backup that you perform at an unscheduled time, when backing up seems prudent. In this book, we usually display the *Safety First!* icon to point out when a landmark backup makes sense, but here's a general list of situations that call for a Registry backup:

✔ As soon as you finish a Windows 95 installation, and everything seems to work

✔ As soon as you fire up a new PC that came with Windows 95, and (again) everything seems to be working fine

✔ Before you install or remove any program, except perhaps the minor *applets* (such as Calculator and Notepad) that come with Windows 95

✔ After you install or remove any program, and everything appears to be working right

✔ Before you make any significant changes with the Control Panel (for example, installing network software is significant, but changing the time and date is not)

✔ Before you make changes with the System Policy Editor, which is a Registry-editing wolf in sheep's clothing

✔ Before you run REGEDIT or any similar Registry-editing utility

If you're reading this book start to finish, the preceding list may seem familiar (that's because we present it in Chapter 1, too). Sorry, but certain points bear repeating, and you may be the kind of reader who always skips a book's first chapter. (We usually do!)

Scheduled backups

A *scheduled backup* (also known as *recurring backup*) is a backup that occurs on a regular basis. For example, many computer users back up everything on their hard drives to a tape drive once a month; that's called a full backup.

Scheduled backups come in two flavors: ones you have to remember to do, and ones the computer remembers for you. The second option is usually better but takes a bit more planning. You need a scheduling program, such as the System Agent utility that comes with the Microsoft Plus! package or the Norton Scheduler that comes with Norton Antivirus, if you want to run regularly scheduled Registry backups (for example, via a batch file that you create; see "Batch file solutions" later in this chapter). The documentation or online help for your scheduling program tells you how to specify the file you want to run (say, REGBAK.BAT) and how often you want to run it (every Friday night at 2:00 a.m.).

If you're on a network, you may be able to use a server-based backup program, in combination with a *backup agent* program running on your PC, to set up periodic, unattended Registry backups over the network. Your server-based backup software should document the steps in detail. This type of backup is a very slick solution!

Scheduled backups that include Registry files can be risky if they overwrite older scheduled backups. Sometimes you don't notice a Registry-related problem right away, and if a scheduled backup wipes out an earlier scheduled backup, it may create a backup with the same problems that your current active Registry files have. If you use scheduled Registry backups, which is a great idea, save the files in a location different from the location that you use for your landmark backups.

Where to Back Up

Here are the places that you can back up your Registry files to, in approximate order of desirability:

- ✔ **A network drive.** You're likely to have plenty of space on a network drive, and you're protected if your hard drive fails totally.

- ✔ **A removable cartridge drive.** The popular Iomega ZIP and Jaz drives are examples. Norton Utilities version 3.0 for Windows 95 includes a diskette-plus-ZIP-disk option for creating a Rescue Disk set that boots Windows 95 into graphical mode instead of command-prompt mode. Again, a hard drive crash doesn't trash your backup.

- ✔ **A diskette drive.** This method is slower than network or cartridge drive backups, and you should only use it with software (such as the WinZip program provided on this book's CD-ROM) that can create a multiple-diskette set containing your entire Registry. Note that neither the Windows 95 startup disk program nor the Norton Rescue Disk program back up Registry files that are too large to fit on a single diskette!

- ✔ **A tape drive.** Even slower than a diskette drive, but again, you still protect yourself against a hard drive failure.

- ✔ **A different directory on your local hard drive.** Very fast, but hard drive failure wipes out your backup.

If you're fortunate enough to have two hard drives in your PC, your best option is to back up Registry files to the second hard drive. This method is fast and safe.

Backing Up the Registry with Freebie Software

You don't have to buy any software in order to make Registry backups. You just have to know about the tools and techniques that are available to you already, and what their advantages and disadvantages are.

The behind-the-scenes backup

Windows 95 makes an automatic Registry backup every time it starts. It creates the hidden files USER.DA0 and SYSTEM.DA0 in the C:\WINDOWS directory based on the original Registry files USER.DAT and SYSTEM.DAT. Although you may be able to use these backups in certain troubleshooting situations, these files take on the same problems as the original Registry after one reboot, and you can't tell Windows 95 to make a new set any time you like.

Configuration Backup

One of the more popular Registry backup tools is another hidden freebie on the Windows 95 CD-ROM: Microsoft Configuration Backup, or CFGBACK for short (that's also the name of the EXE file that you run). We've seen at least a dozen articles and books (some written by people a lot more famous than we are) that recommend this utility. Unfortunately, CFGBACK is so badly flawed that we don't even waste your time telling you how to install and run it. (If you happen to inherit a PC that has used CFGBACK, we do tell you how to attempt a restore operation in Chapter 15.)

CFGBACK doesn't run in Safe Mode, which may be the only way that you can run Windows 95 after severe Registry damage. Also, it uses a special data file format (*.RBK) that no other program can understand, so if you can't run Windows 95, then you can't run CFGBACK, which renders your backups useless. The program doesn't work unless the backup files are in C:\WINDOWS, which doesn't help you much if your hard disk fails. But the most damning fact is that Microsoft itself suggests you not use this tool. Here's an excerpt from Microsoft technical note Q142572:

> SYMPTOMS: When you restore a backup of the Windows 95 registry by using the Configuration Backup tool (CFGBACK.EXE), some settings are not properly restored.

RESOLUTION: Rather than using the Configuration Backup tool, use another method to back up and restore the registry.

Hey, that's all we need to hear, and we hope it's enough for you, too. If the vendor doesn't recommend this program, we sure don't. Why Microsoft didn't pull this buggy utility off the Windows 95 CD-ROM years ago beats the heck out of us.

Emergency Recovery Utility

The ill-conceived CFGBACK is luckily not the only utility that you can use to back up your Registry. Microsoft provides another Registry backup tool called Emergency Recovery Utility (ERU for short). You can download this program from www.microsoft.com/windows/download/eruzip.exe, but installing it from the Windows 95 CD-ROM is easier.

Don't install ERU through the Add/Remove Programs control panel wizard. Just copy the files from the CD-ROM's \OTHER\MISC\ERU directory into a directory of your choosing on your hard drive. (We suggest C:\Program Files\ERU.)

To create a Registry backup with ERU, follow these steps:

1. **Run the program by double-clicking the ERU.EXE file in My Computer or Explorer.**

   You see a short message describing the program.

2. **Click Next and select a target location for your backup.**

   We suggest that you choose Other Directory rather than Drive A: because the Registry normally can't fit onto a single diskette, and ERU doesn't make multiple-diskette backups. If you choose Other Directory, click Next again to specify that directory.

3. **Click Next again to see the screen as shown in Figure 2-1.**

   If you don't see ten files listed here, ERU won't make a complete system file backup.

4. **If you want to change the file list, click the Custom button to display the screen shown in Figure 2-2. Make sure that you check the USER.DAT and SYSTEM.DAT check boxes if you intend to back up the Registry. Click OK when done.**

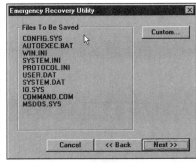

Figure 2-1:
The list of
files that
ERU backs
up, if they
exist and if
the target
location
has room.

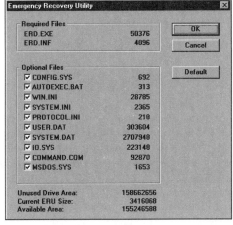

Figure 2-2:
You can
pick and
choose
which files
you want
ERU to
back up.

5. Click Next to begin the backup process.

ERU displays a progress window and finishes with a dialog box explaining briefly how to restore the files if you ever need to.

We like ERU for its inclusion of several important system files above and beyond the core Registry files, for its ability to restore backed-up files when Windows 95 can't boot to its graphical mode, and for its ability to save backup files onto any directory, hard drive, or network drive.

ERU is a much better choice than CFGBACK, but it has its flaws. You can use ERU — we do — as long as you know about the flaws and keep a watchful eye out for them.

✔ If any of the files that ERU expects to find on your system are absent, then ERU may not work. (So much for the claim that Windows 95 no longer needs AUTOEXEC.BAT and CONFIG.SYS!) If the Registry backup isn't successful, ERU doesn't warn you, either.

✔ ERU wants to back up your system files to a diskette, but a diskette probably doesn't have room for SYSTEM.DAT — one of the two critical Registry files — so ERU blithely omits it, without so much as a tiny computer beep to let you know anything's amiss.

✔ ERU doesn't back up all the individual user settings on a PC that's set up for multiple users. (These settings are the various USER.DAT files in C:\WINDOWS\PROFILES — see Chapter 10 for the details.)

You start Windows 95 in command prompt mode to restore an ERU backup. Chapter 15 provides the details.

Windows 95 startup disk

You can create a Windows 95 startup disk (or, as Microsoft sometimes calls it, an Emergency Boot Disk) by using the Control Panel's Add/Remove Programs wizard. Just click the Startup Disk tab, pop a fresh floppy into drive A:, and click the Create Disk button. However, although you can boot with such a diskette, *it doesn't contain your Registry files!* (Try this method and see whether you can find USER.DAT and SYSTEM.DAT on the diskette.)

Go ahead and make a startup disk; as Martha Stewart might say, it's a good thing. Just don't expect to back up your Registry there.

Export and import

One of the simpler and more frequently recommended ways to back up your Registry is to run REGEDIT (or a similar program, such as Norton Registry Editor) and export the entire Registry to a text file. The procedure with REGEDIT is as follows:

1. **Run the Registry Editor, for example by choosing Start⇨Run⇨REGEDIT and clicking OK.**

2. **Choose Registry⇨Export Registry File to display the dialog box shown in Figure 2-3.**

3. **Specify the target directory in the Save In field and name the file in the File Name field.**

   REGEDIT defaults to creating a file with the suffix .REG.

4. **Click the All radio button under Export Range and click Save.**

Figure 2-3:
Backing up
the entire
Registry
to a text
file with
REGEDIT.

Although very easy, this procedure has some problems.

✔ As Chapter 15 explains in greater detail, you can't restore a full Registry backup when Windows 95 is running in its graphical mode and be completely certain that the resulting Registry is identical to the one you backed up. The reason is that a REG file import can't delete existing Registry entries, it can only modify them or add new entries.

✔ When Windows 95 runs in its command prompt mode, the import operation doesn't always work if you use the version of REGEDIT that comes with Windows 95 Version 4.00.950 or 4.00.950a. (You can check the version number on the General tab of the System control panel.) Microsoft fixed the problem in the version of REGEDIT that comes with Windows 95 Version 4.00.950B, the so-called OEM Service Release 2 (OSR2).

✔ The export procedure doesn't back up user settings for the non-logged-on users of a PC that's set up to handle multiple user profiles. However, the export procedure does back up the settings for the currently logged-on user and the default user.

Because of these problems, the REG file export is more appropriate for partial Registry backups than for full backups if you're running one of the original Windows 95 versions. If you have OSR2, the export method is a more viable solution for full backups, but it's still not perfect.

You can create a REG file export by using REGEDIT even if Windows 95 won't start. Hit the F8 key after you see the Starting Windows 95 message and choose Safe Mode, Command Prompt Only. At the C:\WINDOWS> prompt, you can create a full export of the current Registry by using the following command, where *filename* is the file name that you specify:

```
REGEDIT /E filename.REG
```

Microsoft Backup

The general-purpose backup program that comes with Windows 95, *Microsoft Backup,* can back up your entire disk drive, including the Registry. This program has three big problems:

- ✔ It requires Windows 95 to be running in order to restore files.
- ✔ It doesn't back up the Registry by default when you do a partial disk backup.
- ✔ It doesn't restore your SYSTEM.DAT file if you have to replace a hard drive.

The first problem means that if you experience total, massive, and utter hard disk meltdown and you have to replace the drive, you first have to reinstall Windows 95 onto the drive before you can run Microsoft Backup in order to restore the files you backed up earlier. True, you can specify a minimum install and save some time, but doing so is still a pain and adds a half hour to your recovery time.

The second problem is fairly serious. Many users of Microsoft Backup assume that when they use it to back up the contents of C:\WINDOWS, the Registry files are included. As you can see from Figure 2-4, they're not. The only way to get Microsoft Backup to copy your Registry files is to click File⇨Open File Set and choose Full System Backup.set. Then, remove the directories and files that you don't want to back up, leaving C:\WINDOWS selected. Microsoft Backup makes copies of USER.DAT and SYSTEM.DAT into files that it names HKUBACK and HKLMBACK, respectively. (Incidentally, Microsoft Backup doesn't always delete these files after it exits, so you may have to manually tidy up after running Microsoft Backup.)

The third problem probably stems from concern on Microsoft's part that you may install a different sort of hard drive than was present before. The SYSTEM.DAT file contains hardware information, including information about your hard drive. If SYSTEM.DAT looks for one kind of hard drive (say, EIDE) and finds another (say, SCSI), the PC may not even boot to Windows 95. So, the Windows 95 Backup program doesn't restore SYSTEM.DAT. The practical reality is that you are 99 percent likely to replace a dead hard drive with one of a similar type, but you can't tell that to Microsoft Backup, which steadfastly refuses to restore SYSTEM.DAT no matter what.

Using Microsoft Backup for Registry backups and for full-disk backups is okay. Just remember to always use the Full System Backup file set, regardless of whether you're backing up the entire drive or just the Registry directory. And you may want to make a separate, manual backup copy of SYSTEM.DAT in case you need to restore a complete hard drive. And don't

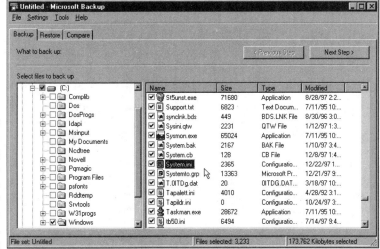

Figure 2-4:
Windows 95
Backup
skips the
Registry
unless you
dance a jig.

forget to clean up HKUBACK and HKLMBACK. If that's too much for you to remember, we sympathize. A better way does exist, and we've been saving the best for last.

Batch file solutions

Our favorite free solution for making Registry backups is to write a *batch file* that handles the job for you. A batch file is simply a text file containing a sequence of DOS commands that run one after another. Creating a batch file is the only way we know that you can avoid all the pitfalls and problems that plague the previously discussed methods. Writing a batch file involves a little bit of the "P" word — programming — but the programming is easy, and we give you a substantial head start.

If you're not comfortable with writing batch files, consider hiring (or bribing) someone who is and getting them to help you set up a batch file that works for you, based on our examples.

Most batch files that we've seen for making Registry backups use the plain old COPY command and the ATTRIB command to remove the Read-only attribute so that COPY can see the files. However, a simpler approach is to use the XCOPY command, which has a qualifier (/H) that copies hidden and system files. If you're backing your Registry up to the REG directory on a removable cartridge drive (drive letter E:), you may write a simple batch file that looks like this:

```
XCOPY C:\WINDOWS\USER.DAT E:\REG\ /H /Y /R
XCOPY C:\WINDOWS\SYSTEM.DAT E:\REG\ /H /Y /R
```

In the previous commands,

- ✔ /H instructs XCOPY to copy hidden and system files.

- ✔ /Y means that XCOPY doesn't ask you if it's overwriting an old file (necessary if you want to run your batch file in unattended mode by using a scheduling utility, such as Microsoft System Agent).

- ✔ /R means that XCOPY can overwrite any read-only files in the target location that are left over from an earlier backup. You don't even have to create the REG directory on the E: drive; XCOPY does that for you if it doesn't already exist.

Now, if you want to get a little fancier, you can make sure that any user-specific parts of the Registry also get backed up if you have a system set up for multiple users (see Chapter 10 for a complete treatment of user profiles). Just add the following line to your batch file:

```
XCOPY C:\WINDOWS\PROFILES E:\REG\PROFILES\ /H /Y /R /S
```

The /S at the end tells XCOPY to include all nonempty subdirectories underneath C:\WINDOWS\PROFILES, ensuring that all user-specific versions of USER.DAT get backed up. You don't even have to know the user names; XCOPY moves every user directory under the PROFILES directory.

As icing on the cake, create a desktop shortcut that points to this batch file, so the batch file is easily accessible. Right-click the desktop, choose New⇨Shortcut, browse to locate the BAT file that you created with Notepad, and name the shortcut something like **Back Up Registry**. Then, right-click the new icon, choose Properties, click the Program tab, select Minimized in the Run field drop-down list, and click the Close on Exit check box.

If you really want to be on the safe side, close all your Windows programs before running your Registry backup batch file. A Windows program may possibly be writing to the Registry files at the same moment that your batch file is backing them up, which can cause USER.DAT and SYSTEM.DAT to get out of synch. You can put a few lines at the start of your batch file to remind you of this caution, like this:

```
@ECHO OFF
ECHO Please close all Windows programs before proceeding.
PAUSE
```

Backing Up the Registry with Non-Freebie Software

Okay, if you're willing to fork over a little cash in order to get a great Registry backup utility, what are your options?

Norton Utilities rescue disks

Norton Utilities for Windows 95 has a rescue diskette creation program that's far superior to the built-in Windows 95 startup disk feature. The big differences are that the Norton program creates a multiple-diskette set containing some of the Norton recovery utilities, and that the program creates a Registry backup on the hard drive. (If you want to back up the Registry to a separate disk, you need Norton Utilities 3.0 and a ZIP drive.)

✔ The Rescue Disk program in Norton Utilities 2.0 does *not* back up the critical SYSTEM.DAT file to diskette if it exceeds 1.44MB. Instead, Rescue Disk creates the file C:\WINDOWS\NUSYSTEM.REG, which you can manually use to rebuild the Registry (with the command REGEDIT / C NUSYSTEM.REG) after restarting.

✔ Rescue Disk version 3.0 creates the combined file C:\WINDOWS\ REGISTRY.RSC (see Figure 2-5), which basically contains the entire Registry (USER.DAT and SYSTEM.DAT). Also, version 3.0 permits the use of a ZIP disk and floppy diskette combination.

If you have Norton Utilities, use its rescue diskette procedure (Start⇨ Programs⇨Norton Utilities⇨Rescue Disk) rather than the Windows 95 startup disk procedure.

Tell Norton to include the Windows 95 INI files (WIN.INI, SYSTEM.INI, and CONTROL.INI) in your rescue diskette set for a more complete backup. The command for including your Windows 95 INI files is Options⇨Add New Item (version 2.0) or Options⇨Add Files (version 3.0). Use this same command to add C:\WINDOWS\USER.DAT and C:\WINDOWS\SYSTEM.DAT to the Rescue disk set if you use the ZIP disk option in version 3.0 and you want your Registry backed up to a separate device, which we recommend.

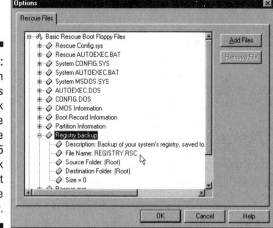

Figure 2-5:
The Norton
Utilities
rescue disk
feature
blows the
Windows 95
startup disk
program out
of the
water.

Norton Registry Editor

We have mixed feelings about the Norton Registry Editor's backup features.
(The command for a total backup is File⇨Backup Entire Registry.) This
program comes with Norton Utilities 2.0 and subsequent versions, so we're
inclined to think highly of it. However, Norton Registry Editor turns out to
work just like the REGEDIT export method, except for the fact that it's much
slower. In Norton, the export occurs as a background task, so you can
continue working while the export occurs; however, the time to complete the
backup is much longer. We therefore prefer REGEDIT's export to Norton's.

Norton Registry Editor enables you to back up portions of the Registry by
using a nonstandard binary format called *.SRG, or Symantec ReGistry
archive. (The command is File⇨Save Symantec Registry Archive.) Why you
would want to do this is a little unclear to us. No other program can read
these files, and you can easily and accidentally restore the files' contents to
the wrong place in the Registry.

Shareware

You can find a variety of shareware Registry backup utilities, including
Safety Net, RegBackup, and so on. To be honest, we have yet to find one that
works well in all circumstances. For example, Safety Net can back up all DAT
files, but if you have multiple copies of USER.DAT beneath your C:\WINDOWS\
PROFILES directory, Safety Net doesn't keep them apart for you. It just
writes each new USER.DAT over the previous one. That's a problem for
systems with multiple user profiles.

General-purpose backup programs

A variety of programs improve on Microsoft Backup for Windows 95. You have to pay for them, but they are so much better than the general-purpose backup program that Microsoft supplies that you may find one of them worth owning.

Our favorite general-purpose backup programs (see Appendix B for contact information) are Backup Exec for Windows 95 from Seagate Software and Cheyenne Backup for Windows 95 from Cheyenne Software, now a division of Computer Associates. These programs work with a wide variety of backup devices (tape drives and so on), and you can choose from many options to find the best balance of speed and security. Cheyenne Backup even enables you to restore to a brand-new hard drive by booting to a diskette, so you don't have to reinstall Windows 95 — something that Microsoft Backup can't do.

Be sure to check out NovaBACKUP, an up-and-coming backup program that we feature on this book's CD-ROM. NovaBACKUP is a multiplatform, multilanguage program that you can use to back up and restore your files to any disk drive and more than 400 tape drives.

The Bottom Line

Here's a summary of the key points in this important chapter, with our recommendations in italics:

- ✔ Windows 95 makes automatic backups of Registry files, but they can easily become damaged themselves. These backups only occur at startup, and they live on the same hard drive as your original files. *Don't rely solely on the behind-the-scenes backup.*

- ✔ The Configuration Backup program is fatally flawed, and even its parents have disowned it. *Don't use this method.*

- ✔ The Emergency Recovery Utility is a functional choice as long as: you don't use it to back up to diskette, you have all the files on your PC that ERU thinks you should have, and you don't set up Windows 95 for multiple users. *Use ERU if you want, but look over its shoulder to make sure it works right.*

- ✔ The Windows 95 startup diskette is okay for starting your PC in some situations, but it doesn't contain your entire Registry because it can't make a multiple-diskette set. *Don't use this method to back up your Registry.*

✔ The Registry Editor's export feature is useful for backing up parts of the Registry, and you can restore your backups even if Windows 95 can't start. However, a full Registry backup and restore may not work unless you have the latest version of Windows 95. *Use this method for partial Registry backups (selected keys only) but not for full Registry backups, unless you have OSR2 (Windows 4.00.950B).*

✔ Microsoft Backup can back up your Registry, but you must use the Full Backup Set template. *Use this method if you want to save Registry files to tape and you don't have a better general-purpose backup program.*

✔ Creating your own batch files works well. This method is convenient, and you can restore your backups even when Windows 95 can't start. Using batch files is the only method we know that enables you to back up your complete Registry even if you set up your PC to work with multiple users. However, creating batch files requires a little up-front work and maybe some expert help. *Use this method if you're familiar with batch file programming or you know someone who is.*

✔ The rescue diskette method in Norton Utilities 2.0 and newer makes a Registry backup on your hard drive, but can only back up the Registry to a separate drive if you have version 3.0 and a ZIP drive. *Use this method for general system recovery and (in version 3.0) to protect against total disk failure, but supplement it with another, faster method for daily use.*

✔ Explore shareware Registry backup utilities with caution; most are flawed in one way or another. *Use a shareware or freeware utility only after you research and test it thoroughly.*

✔ Industrial-strength backup programs such as Cheyenne and Backup Exec work very well for everything from Registry-only backups to full-disk backups. *Use this method for your regular, full hard drive backups, but consider a simpler method for day-to-day landmark Registry backups.*

We know that this chapter has been a little bit complicated, but if you go through it carefully and choose the options that work for your situation, you'll thank us for going into as much detail as we have. Choose a method or a combination of methods that's as easy and convenient as possible, so you'll actually make your Registry backups as often as you should. Happiness, to paraphrase The Beatles, is a warm backup.

Chapter 3

Editing the Registry without a Registry Editor

* *

In This Chapter

▶ Discovering why the Registry Editor is a risky utility

▶ Finding out why other alternatives to editing the Registry are safer

▶ Getting familiar with the Windows 95 control panels

▶ Using My Computer and Open With to manage file type associations

▶ Uncovering the secret use of the System Policy Editor

* *

*M*any Windows 95 features allow you to edit the Registry without using the Registry Editor utility. In this chapter, we introduce you to these features and explain why they're preferable to REGEDIT.

Some books about the Windows 95 Registry focus single-mindedly on the Registry Editor program, REGEDIT. We certainly give REGEDIT its due in Chapter 3, and we use it a lot in the chapters that follow (as well as to perform one cool trick in this chapter). It's the only tool available for making many of the changes you may want to make. However, if the First Rule of the Registry is to save it frequently, the Second Rule is as follows:

> *Never use the Registry Editor unless no safer alternative is available.*

Or, stated another way:

> *If you want to cut butter, a butter knife is better than a chainsaw.*

 Whereas every other tool that Windows 95 provides for modifying the Registry has some safeguards (even if they're minimal), the Registry Editor has no safeguards at all. We're all for using the chainsaw when no other tool will do but, fortunately, Windows 95 provides a variety of butter knives.

You have to know what the "safer alternatives" are and what they do in order to follow this Second Rule of the Registry. For example, if you're aware that a Windows 95 control panel can make a certain setting for you, then you can use the control panel instead of REGEDIT — and run much less risk of making a mistake that could ruin your whole day.

What's So Risky about REGEDIT?

Why is a control panel, for example, safer than REGEDIT? Well, if you take as your starting point that almost nothing is more dangerous than REGEDIT, just about *any* alternative is safer by default. Here's why:

- **REGEDIT changes occur immediately.** Most programs let you make whatever changes you want without committing them to disk until you choose File⇨Save. But take a look at the REGEDIT menus. No File menu! Changes that you make in REGEDIT head straight for the Registry as soon as you make them (even though some don't actually take visible effect until Windows 95 restarts). As a result, if you're just horsing around with REGEDIT when the system crashes or experiences a power cut, you may be stuck with a damaged Registry.

- **REGEDIT offers no undo feature.** Want to reverse yourself and nullify your last change? You'd better have a great memory, because REGEDIT doesn't help you retrace your steps. REGEDIT's lack of an Undo feature can be a major pain. For example, imagine that you accidentally delete the value {25336920-03F9-11cf-8FD0-00AA00686F13}. This is a real Registry value identifying the file MSHTML.DLL, which can display Web graphics within Internet Explorer. Think you can remember it well enough to correct your mistake? We know *we* can't. There go all those lovely Web page graphics. (Okay, some of them are just annoying ads, but you get our drift.)

The Norton Registry Editor that comes with Norton Utilities 2.0 (and newer) for Windows 95 by Symantec *has* an undo feature. The availability of the Undo feature alone warrants using the Norton Registry Editor over REGEDIT.

- **REGEDIT offers no warnings.** If you're about to do something that could really damage the Registry, such as delete a whole bunch of essential values, REGEDIT presents the same brief warning message that it presents when you delete a single, trivial value (see Figure 3-1). The program has no built-in warnings to help the user distinguish between minor and major changes.

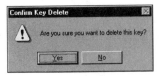

✔ **REGEDIT's help needs some.** The online help for REGEDIT should be a major embarrassment to Microsoft. For the company to provide such an important utility with practically no information in the help file is appalling. (Windows 3.*x* at least shipped with some "read me" files explaining core features of the INI files.) Want to know the purpose of the Registry's six primary branches? The help file doesn't even mention them! In fact, as Figure 3-2 shows, the REGEDIT help file consists of a total of nine (count 'em, nine) little windows' worth of information — about the same amount of text as two pages of this book.

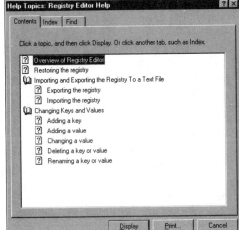

What's So Safe about Alternatives?

Most of the Windows 95 alternatives to REGEDIT give the user more guidance to warn of certain potentially harmful actions and make complex tasks much easier; it can also modify the Windows 95 INI files when necessary.

Extending a helpful hand

As an example, consider the issue of giving a Windows 95 computer a network name. The network name identifies the computer to other computers on a local area network. In the Microsoft naming scheme, a computer name may not include a blank space. If you work with the Network control panel, you can receive this advice by clicking the **?** help icon on the control panel's menu bar and pointing-and-clicking on the Computer Name field, as shown in Figure 3-3.

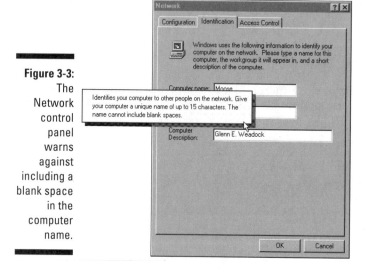

Figure 3-3:
The
Network
control
panel
warns
against
including a
blank space
in the
computer
name.

If you use REGEDIT to change a computer name, however, you have no way of finding out that you can't include spaces in the name. The control panel method isn't perfect, because keying in a name with a blank space in it doesn't generate an error message. In fact, you won't even know there's a problem until someone tries to access the wrongly named computer over the network. But if you're cautious enough to use the control panel and check the online help before making the change, you'll see the warning.

Simplifying complex changes

Some of the chores you need to perform with Windows 95 are mind-numbingly complex if you attempt to perform them by directly editing the Registry. For example, adding new network software to the system can involve dozens of changes to the Registry. For example, take a look at Figure 3-4, which shows a small subset of all the Registry entries that Windows 95 creates when a user installs the Novell NetWare client software via the Network control panel.

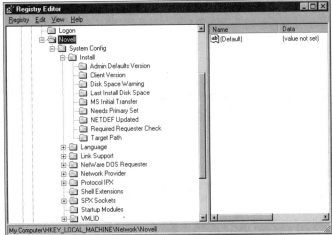

Figure 3-4: Adding what appears to be a single software component in a control panel can add or change dozens of Registry entries.

Admittedly, we're giving you an extreme example: Certain control panel settings only change one or two Registry entries. Even in those cases, however, you can make the change using the control panel more easily than you can figure out precisely which Registry entries correspond to the change and precisely what to type into REGEDIT to accomplish it.

Taking care of INI files

Sometimes, Windows 95 settings reside in the Registry and also in one of the INI initialization files, which are holdovers from the Windows 3.*x* world. Windows 3.*x* programs may look for a given setting in an INI file rather than in the Registry, so keeping the Registry and INI files in synch is necessary for your Windows 3.*x* programs to work happily. If you make a change using REGEDIT, you don't necessarily know whether a corresponding change needs to occur in WIN.INI or SYSTEM.INI. If you make the same change with a control panel, however, Windows 95 knows to update the INI file or files.

See Chapter 1 for more discussion of INI files.

Some Windows 95 settings don't even exist in the Registry. For example, the *swapfile* settings reside in SYSTEM.INI alone. (The *swapfile* is the mechanism that Windows 95 uses to run programs and load data files that don't fit into available Random Access Memory, or RAM.) As long as you use the System control panel to change swapfile settings (see Figure 3-5), you don't have to worry about where Windows 95 stores the data — the control panel knows.

If you have two hard drives and your D: drive is faster than your C: drive, you may want to change the swapfile settings from C: to D:.

Figure 3-5:
Some
control
panel
settings
don't even
modify the
Registry,
such as
these
swapfile
settings,
which
modify only
SYSTEM.INI.

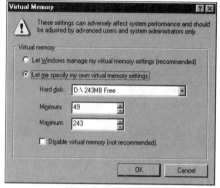

In general, we save the nitty-gritty details of Registry settings for situations where you can't change or view a setting more safely or conveniently any other way. For example, we don't tell you exactly which Registry settings get modified when you change the desktop wallpaper, because it's easier and safer to change it in the Display control panel. We figure that you don't want to know the difficult and risky way to do things unless no better option is available.

Having said that, there may be times when you legitimately need to see what effect a control panel (or any other action, for that matter) has on the Registry, or when you're just curious and want to understand more about what the control panels actually do. Chapter 12 presents some tools and techniques for tracking Registry changes (wherever they may come from) and the list of control panels in the next section gives you clues as to which control panels affect which Registry branches.

Control Panels

The Windows 95 control panels are the most common and useful alternatives to the Registry Editor for making changes to the Windows 95 configuration. Most of the control panels modify the Registry; but some also modify various INI files on the disk, too, as with the swapfile settings we discuss in the section, "Taking care of INI files."

Which control panel icons appear depend on which control panel files (they have the suffix .CPL) are present in the C:\WINDOWS\SYSTEM directory. In fact, one way to hide a particular control panel is to remove or rename the associated .CPL file, but take care: Some CPL files, such as MMSYS.CPL, handle more than one control panel icon. A better way to control access to control panels is to use the System Policy Editor, as described in Chapter 9.

We don't go into all the details of every control panel here — that would take a book in itself — but we do mention the more common ones. Spend some time, if you haven't already, getting familiar with these control panels and using their online help features (usually a little **?** on the menu bar that then lets you click on individual settings) so that you get an idea of what the control panels do for you. The goal is to become aware of when you can use a control panel instead of the Registry Editor to make a change to Windows 95.

Primary control panels

The primary control panels are those that appear on just about every Windows 95 PC. You can fire up the control panel main screen by choosing Start⇨Settings⇨Control Panel (see Figure 3-6).

Figure 3-6: The Windows 95 main control panel window.

The last column of Table 3-1 tells you the more important part or parts of the Registry that the particular control panel modifies. We explain the structure of the Registry in Chapters 4 and 6, so check those chapters out to figure out what a *Registry key* is and where it lives in the Registry.

Table 3-1	Control Panel Effects on the System and Registry		
Control Panel	*Filename*	*Description*	*Registry Keys Affected*
Add New Hardware	SYSDM.CPL	Activates the Add New Hardware wizard, a series of question-and-answer dialog boxes that guide you through the process of installing a new device (such as a sound card). The wizard modifies the hardware-related Registry settings by reading INF files supplied by the device manufacturer; see Chapter 7 for more on INF files.	*HKLM\Enum, HKLM\hardware, HKLM\System\ CurrentControl Set\Services\Class*
Add/Remove Programs	APPWIZ.CPL	Enables you to conveniently install and uninstall components of Windows 95 as well as 32-bit Windows 95 applications that supply their own installation and deinstallation programs.	*HKLM\SOFTWARE* for settings affecting all users, *HKCU\ Software* for settings affecting individual users, *HKLM\SOFTWARE\ Microsoft\Windows\ CurrentVersion\ Uninstall* for the deinstallation info
Date/Time	TIMEDATE.CPL	Enables you to set the clock and time zone. Access it quickly by double-clicking the clock on the taskbar.	*HKLM\System\ CurrentControlSet\ Control\ TimeZone- Information*

Control Panel	Filename	Description	Registry Keys Affected
Display	DESK.CPL	Enables you to change screen size, color options, screen saver settings, and the desktop color scheme. (You have to use the System control panel to change display accelera- tion settings, however.) Varies in appearance on depending the kind of video card the PC has and whether the PC has the Microsoft Plus! software installed. Easily accessible by right-clicking any empty area of the desktop and choosing Properties.	*HKCC\Display\ Settings, HKCU\ Control Panel\Desktop, HKCU\Control Panel\Colors, HKU* for each user (if user profiles are being used). Can also modify SYSTEM.INI and WIN.INI
Fonts	*n/a*	Functions a little differently from most other control panels. Opens a window showing all the TrueType fonts installed on the system. You can add or delete TrueType fonts from this window. If you use Adobe Type Manager to provide PostScript fonts, you can't add or delete them from here; you have to use the PostScript control panel that Adobe supplies separately.	*HKLM\SOFTWARE\ Microsoft\ Windows\ CurrentVersion\ Fonts*
Joystick	JOY.CPL	Changes joystick settings for (usually) computer games.	*HKLM\System\ CurrentControlSet\ control\ MediaResources*
Keyboard	MAIN.CPL	Handles key repeat delay and repeat speed, as well as the text insertion cursor blink rate (don't ask us why that last one is a keyboard setting).	*HKCU\Control Panel\Keyboard*

(continued)

Table 3-1 *(continued)*

Control Panel	Filename	Description	Registry Keys Affected
Modems	MODEM.CPL	Runs the Install New Modem wizard if no modem is set up, or the Modems control panel otherwise. Set modem speeds, dialing properties, and communications options here.	HKLM\System\ CurrentControlSet\ Services\Class\ Modem, HKLM\Enum
Mouse	MAIN.CPL	Enables you to set not only mouse preferences but also cursors (mouse pointers).	HKCU\Control Panel\Cursors, HKCC\Display\ Settings, and (typically) HCKU\Control Panel\Microsoft Input Devices\Mouse, HKU for each user (if user profiles are being used)
Multimedia	MMSYS.CPL	Enables you to set audio and video preferences, such as whether to play back video clips at original size or full screen.	HKCU\Software\ Microsoft\ Multimedia, HKCU\Software\ Microsoft\ Windows\ CurrentVersion\ Multimedia, HKU for each user (if user profiles are being used)
Network	NETCPL.CPL	Functions as the nerve center for all your network settings, such as which network communications language you want the PC to use. Get here quickly by right-clicking the Network Neighborhood desktop icon and choosing Properties.	HKLM\Enum\ Network, HKLM\Network, HKLM\System\ CurrentControlSet\ Services\Class\Net (and . . .~\NetClient, . . .~\NetService, and . . .~\NetTrans)

Control Panel	Filename	Description	Registry Keys Affected
Password	PASSWORD.CPL	Enables you to set up the PC for remote administration (for example with the Remote Registry Editor), set up user profiles so multiple people can use the same PC, and change the Windows logon password.	*HKLM\System\ CurrentControlSet\ Control\ PwdProvider, HKU* for each user (if user profiles are being used)
Printers	*n/a*	Opens a special folder called the Printers folder, where you can adjust settings such as resolution, print darkness, and so on. (Functions similarly to the Fonts control panel.)	*HKLM\System\ CurrentControlSet\ control\Print\ Printers, HKCC\ System\ CurrentControlSet\ Control\Print\ Printers*
Regional Settings	INTL.CPL	Enables you to set location-specific preferences for how Windows 95 displays numbers, currency, and time-and-date information.	*HKCU\Control Panel\International*
Sounds	MMSYS.CPL	Enables you to associate sounds (for Windows 95 and certain applications) with particular events, such as minimizing a window or closing a program.	*HKCU\AppEvents, HKU* for each user (if user profiles are being used)
System	SYSDM.CPL	Enables you to tune Windows 95 performance (the Performance tab), run down hardware problems (Device Manager tab), and set up multiple hardware configurations (Hardware Profiles tab).	*HKLM\System\ CurrentControlSet\ Control\FileSystem, HKCC\Config\ Display, HKLM\Enum,* and *HKLM\Config.* Can also modify SYSTEM.INI

Secondary control panels

We define secondary control panels as those that may or may not appear on a given PC: control panels that pertain to specific applications you may install or that you obtain from other sources (such as the Microsoft PowerToys). Here is a list of some common secondary control panels, but many others exist:

- **32-Bit ODBC.** (File: ODBCCP32.CPL) You may see this one if you use Microsoft Access or any other database program that speaks the Structured Query Language (SQL).

- **Accessibility Options.** (File: ACCESS.CPL) Here's a control panel with a variety of helpful desktop modifications for users with disabilities.

- **Desktop Themes.** (File: THEMES.CPL) If you have Microsoft Plus!, you can dress up your desktop with custom setting groups including wallpaper, colors, sounds, screen savers, animated cursors, desktop icons, fonts, and so on.

- **Find Fast.** (File: FINDFAST.CPL) This control panel comes with Microsoft Office 95 and 97 and is supposed to make opening Office documents faster. It seems to slow down our machines, though, so we usually turn it off.

- **Internet.** (File: INETCPL.CPL) You see the Internet control panel if you installed Microsoft Internet Explorer or if the software came with your PC. A quick way to get to this control panel is to right-click the Internet icon on the desktop and choose Properties.

- **Mail and Fax.** (File: MLCFG32.CPL) If you have Microsoft Exchange or its successor, Outlook, installed on the PC, this control panel lets you set e-mail and related options. You can right-click the Inbox icon on the desktop and choose Properties as a quick way to get to this control panel.

- **Microsoft Mail Postoffice.** (File: WGPOCPL.CPL) Again, if you run Exchange or Microsoft Mail, this control panel lets you set up a post office facility on the PC.

- **Power.** (File: Varies) This control panel sets power management options for the computer.

- **QuickTime 32.** (File: QT32.CPL) Here's where you can set preferences for playing digital movies (*.MOV) that use Apple's QuickTime format.

- **TweakUI.** (File: TWEAKUI.CPL) This control panel is a freebie download from Microsoft and comes with the PowerToys package assembled by Microsoft programmers. TweakUI is so handy that we look at it further in Chapter 10.

Showing your control panel who's boss

If you're like us, you're always looking for ways to reduce the number of clicks, double-clicks, and keystrokes that common Windows 95 procedures require. One way to save clicks when using the control panels is to put them onto the Start menu in such a way that you can pluck the particular control panel you need from a cascading menu (see Figure 3-7), instead of having to double-click the icon in the main control panel window. Coincidentally, doing so introduces an important Registry concept: the *Class ID*.

You can't just drag-and-drop the Control Panel icon from the My Computer window to the Start menu button and get the cascading effect in Figure 3-7. Instead, you have to create a Start menu item that points to the Windows 95 control panel object with its unique identifier, called a *Class ID* (or CLSID, as it appears in the Registry). This identifier needs a word or two of explanation. Every kind of object in a Windows 95 system, including data file types (such as a PowerPoint slide show) and program modules (such as the code that displays and processes dialog box radio buttons), has a special Class ID all to itself. Notice that we say every "*kind* of object" has its own unique identifier, not every *object*. That is, if you create three different PowerPoint slide shows, they don't have three different Class IDs; all three are part of the same "class" and share the same Class ID.

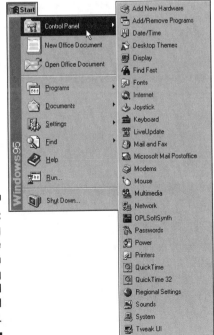

Figure 3-7:
Saving
mouse
clicks with
a cascading
Control
Panel
menu.

First, you have to figure out which Class ID runs the control panel. You won't be modifying the Registry to do this, but it's still a good idea to make a backup before you run REGEDIT (see Chapter 2 for details if you're not sure how to back up the Registry). Once you've made a Registry backup, follow these steps:

1. **Choose Start⇨Run, type** REGEDIT **in the Open field, and click OK.**

   The Registry Editor window appears.

2. **Hit the F3 key to bring up the Find dialog box.**

3. **Type** control panel **in the Find what field, make sure all three check boxes are checked, and click the Find Next button.**

   In a few seconds, the Registry Editor finds the Class ID for the control panel object. It appears as a long string of seemingly random letters and numbers next to an opened folder in the left window pane (see Figure 3-8). You could jot this long Class ID down on a piece of paper, but you might make a mistake, and there's an easier way: copy the Class ID to the invisible Windows Clipboard using the following four steps.

4. **Right-click the opened folder in the left window pane.**

5. **Click Rename to highlight the Class ID.**

6. **Type Ctrl+C to copy the Class ID to the Windows Clipboard.**

7. **Close the Registry Editor by clicking the close box in the upper right corner (it looks like an X).**

   Now it's time to create the Control Panel item on the Start menu in Steps 8 through 14.

8. **Choose Start⇨Settings⇨Taskbar, click the Start Menu Programs tab, and click the Advanced button.**

   You should see an Explorer window showing the structure of the Start menu.

Figure 3-8: Finding the control panel's class identifier using the Registry Editor.

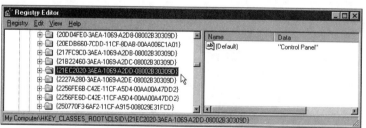

9. **Click the Start Menu folder at the top of the left window pane to highlight it.**

10. **Choose File⇨New⇨Folder to create the new menu entry for the control panel.**

11. **In the highlighted area for the new folder's name, type** Control Panel. **(including the final period).**

12. **With the folder name still highlighted, type Ctrl+V to paste the Class ID from the Windows Clipboard into the space right after the period.**

    Putting the Class ID right after the period in the folder name tells Windows 95 to make this new folder work just like the control panel object. You can use this little trick with other Class IDs, as we'll show you later in the book.

13. **Close the Explorer window by clicking the close box in the upper-right corner.**

14. **Click OK to close the Taskbar Properties dialog box.**

You're done! Now, click the Start button to see your new menu, with the Control Panel entry on it. Move the mouse up to highlight Control Panel, hold it there for a second or so, and Windows 95 displays a cascading menu showing each individual control panel. You've just made your control panel easier to use, and you've discovered that every Windows 95 object has a unique identifying number in the Registry.

SETUP

The Windows 95 setup program, SETUP.EXE, is responsible for copying Windows 95 files onto a PC and for building the very first version of the Registry on that PC. As a matter of fact, a big chunk of that first Registry remains on your system as the file C:\SYSTEM.1ST.

If you're reading this book because you already have a Windows 95 PC and you want to make it work better, what actually happens during setup doesn't concern you a great deal. You probably never plan to run it again, and you shouldn't need to. However, if you're responsible for other Windows 95 PCs, you may be interested to know how you can customize SETUP to build a Registry that's more nearly the way you want it from the very start. Chapter 8 provides all the details.

Deciding *not* to reinstall Windows 95 to fix your Registry

From the "olden" days of Windows 3.*x* to the present, reinstalling Windows has been a favorite suggestion of technical support staff who can't figure out any other way to fix a given problem. At some point in your experience with Windows 95, you may encounter a technician or Help Desk analyst who tells you to rerun SETUP. Be very cautious before accepting such advice!

When you reinstall Windows 95, SETUP creates a brand new Registry for you from scratch. It's possible that doing so will fix the particular problem you've run into, but the cure may be worse than the disease. SETUP zaps all the customizations you've made to the Windows 95 desktop. All the Registry entries for application software you've installed also get zapped. You end up having to reinstall all your software and reenter all your software-specific configuration settings. Yes, you can back up your Registry, reinstall Windows 95, and then restore your Registry; but doing so is also highly likely to restore the problem you're trying to solve.

If you have experience with Windows 3.*x,* you may think we're exaggerating. After all, you could reinstall Windows 3.*x* and most of your application programs would still work fine. That's because they used private INI files to store their settings, and reinstalling Windows 3.*x* would leave many of those private INI files in place. Not so with Windows 95! Windows 95 programs are *supposed* to store their settings and user preferences in the Registry, and most do.

We're here to tell you that reinstalling Windows 95 is almost never truly necessary to fix a problem. We've both run Windows 95 computers for over two years, running an amazing variety of software, without ever having to reinstall the operating system. If a software vendor tech support person (including Microsoft) tells you to rerun SETUP, politely ask to speak to a senior tech support analyst who may be able to give you more specific and less drastic advice.

My Computer and Explorer

My Computer, which displays a single-paned window into the computer, is supposedly for the "typical" Windows 95 user, while Explorer, which displays a double-paned window, is for "advanced" users. Most Windows 95 users get frustrated with the limitations of My Computer and end up using Explorer. Whichever you prefer, you can use it to edit the Registry!

As long as we're discussing Explorer, we should mention a terminology *gotcha* that confuses many Windows 95 uses. The term *Explorer* actually means two entirely different things in Windows 95: the file management program (Start⇨Programs⇨Windows Explorer), and the Windows 95 desktop shell itself. Try this experiment: type Ctrl+Alt+Delete with no programs running. See the entry for Explorer? It's not referring to the file management program, because you're not running it. The Explorer entry refers to the Windows 95 *shell,* or graphical user interface. Now click the entry for Explorer and then click End Task. You should see the system shutdown dialog box — exactly what you expect when you shut down the Windows 95 user interface. Yes, it's confusing, but when you think of how many hundreds of people worked on Windows 95, a little left-hand-right-hand syndrome is probably inevitable.

Most people don't think of either My Computer or Explorer as making changes to the Registry, but they can, and they're very convenient tools for certain kinds of changes. Open either program and choose View⇨Options, and then click the File Types tab. You should see the screen in Figure 3-9.

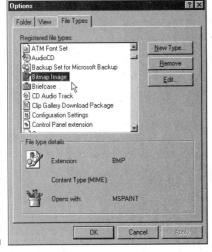

Figure 3-9:
The File Types tab is a miniature Registry editor for file type associations.

Figure 3-9 shows a window into the branch of the Registry that handles file type associations. (See the little line of text that says `Registered file types`, just above the scrolling list? The word *Registered* clues you in to the fact that you're looking into the Registry.) For example, in Figure 3-9, you can see that the BMP file type associates with the MSPAINT program. When the user double-clicks a file with the suffix .BMP, Windows 95 runs Microsoft Paint — the little graphic editor that comes with Windows 95 as an accessory program. Typically, when you install a new application program, that program registers one or more new file types, and they appear on the list in Figure 3-9 after installation.

Don't make any changes to this list just yet. Chapter 11 explores (pardon the pun) how you can use this property sheet as a user-friendly Registry editor in order to make the Windows 95 desktop more convenient. For now, we'll just mention that you may want to make a different program run when you double-click on a particular kind of file — or even change the menu that appears when you right-click on that file type. It's much nicer to make such changes here than in REGEDIT.

Opening a Program with Another Application

At some point you may have bumped into the tip that you can hold down the Shift key when right-clicking any data file in My Computer or Explorer, and a new option, Open With, appears on the context menu that pops up. If you select Open With, you see the dialog box in Figure 3-10. You can then scroll through the list of registered program types and choose which one you want to use to open the selected data file.

Figure 3-10: The Open With dialog box lets you open a data file with any program.

Notice the little check box at the bottom of the scrolling list, with the label Always use this program to open this type of file. If you check the box, then from that moment on, any time you double-click on a data file with the same suffix as the one you originally right-clicked, the program you've chosen will run the data file.

You've figured it out by now: The Open With dialog box lets you modify the list of file type associations that we looked at in the preceding section. Open With is a miniature Registry editor, too!

System Policy Editor

The System Policy Editor, POLEDIT.EXE, has two roles in life. Its main job is to create *policy files* that become part of the Registry and restrict what users can do on a Windows 95 PC. However, the System Policy Editor can also work like a Registry editor — and a much more user-friendly one than REGEDIT, at that.

Chapter 9 discusses the installation and use of the Policy Editor in detail.

Just to give you a taste for how you can use the System Policy Editor to modify the Registry, here's how you would turn off the user's ability to run REGEDIT on a given Windows 95 PC.

1. **Run the System Policy Editor by choosing Start⇨Programs⇨ Accessories⇨System Tools⇨System Policy Editor.**

   Windows 95 doesn't install the System Policy Editor in a typical installation, so if you don't see it listed, refer to Chapter 9 on how to install it.

2. **Choose File⇨Open Registry.**

   Two icons appear in the System Policy Editor window, corresponding to the two main files of the Registry: USER.DAT and SYSTEM.DAT.

3. **Double-click the icon labeled Local User.**

   The Local User Properties window appears.

4. **Click the + sign to the left of the book icon labeled** System**.**

   The System book opens, and a new book labeled Restrictions appears underneath it.

5. **Click the + sign to the left of the book icon labeled** Restrictions**.**

   The screen should now look like Figure 3-11.

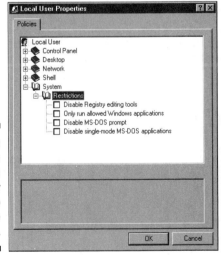

Figure 3-11:
Using the
System
Policy
Editor to
disable
REGEDIT.

6. **Select the Disable Registry Editing Tools check box.**

7. **Click OK in the Local User Properties window.**

8. **Close the System Policy Editor by clicking the close box in the menu bar's upper-right corner.**

9. **Click Yes in the dialog box that asks you if you want to save changes to the Registry.**

Now, try to run the Registry Editor by choosing Start➪Run and typing **REGEDIT** in the Open field. Access to REGEDIT is now *verboten*.

For those of you who are interested, you've just changed the Registry entry *HKCU\Software\Microsoft\Windows\CurrentVersion\Policies\System\ DisableRegistryTools*. We explain the structure of the Registry in Chapter 6 if this looks a bit hairy to you right now.

Fortunately, access to the System Policy Editor is not *verboten* by the change you just made, so you can run POLEDIT again and change the setting back to its original value. We should also mention in passing that disabling REGEDIT doesn't disable the Norton Registry Editor, if it's present. Not exactly ironclad security, but good enough for many situations, and we'll show you how to tighten up policy restrictions in Chapter 9 so that they're very difficult to sidestep.

Application Software

Last but not least, application software programs modify the Registry, both when installed and when users modify program settings to suit their own preferences. Here are the typical ways users can modify application program settings:

✔ **Choosing Tools➪Options or View➪Options from the program's menu bar.**

Microsoft is not consistent in where it places the Options choice, and other software vendors sometimes choose other locations. You might say the location of the Options command is optional.

✔ **Running a wizard.**

Wizards are little automated programs that lead you step-by-step through a procedure such as setting up an application program's user preferences. Microsoft's Internet Connection Wizard is an example: It runs the first time the user double-clicks the Internet desktop icon.

✔ **Modifying an application's private INI file with Notepad.**

This method is considered clumsy and *passé*, but many programs still use it.

✔ **Right-clicking the program icon and choosing Properties.**

This method often produces the same results as selecting Options from within a program menu, as in Microsoft Outlook and Microsoft Internet Explorer 3.

An application program doesn't always let you change every setting that you may want to change. For example, the Microsoft Web browser, Internet Explorer, always opens a file called C:\WINDOWS\SYSTEM\BLANK.HTM if a user runs the program without establishing an actual Internet communications link. You may prefer a different file to run in this situation — say, a file on a network server that displays helpful information on how the user can create an Internet link. That setting requires delving into the Registry with REGEDIT. (The precise location is *HKCU\Software\Microsoft\Internet Explorer\Main\Local Page,* but if that doesn't mean anything to you, don't worry — we explain it all in Chapters 4 and 6.)

The main point to remember is that if you can make an application setting via a menu option, wizard, INI file, or property sheet, do so. Save your Registry editing for cases that require it.

Chapter 4

The Tools You'll Use: Registry Editors from Stem to Stern

In This Chapter

▶ Letting REGEDIT know who's boss (you are!)

▶ Editing elegantly with Peter Norton

▶ Adding shareware and freeware to your toolkit

*K*nowing your tools makes working with the Registry safer, easier, faster, and more fun. This chapter lays out the fundamental features of Microsoft REGEDIT, as well as a few other less well-known but valuable tools.

The Windows 95 Registry isn't a simple text file, so you can't use a program like Notepad to view or edit it. Also, the Registry consists of more than one file, so you need a program to bring these files together into a single view. The most common tool for viewing and modifying the Registry is the Registry Editor program that comes with Windows 95: REGEDIT.

Mark Twain once said that Wagner's music isn't as bad as it sounds. In the same vein, REGEDIT isn't as difficult as it looks — the complicated underlying structure of the Registry just makes it *feel* difficult. Think of REGEDIT like a magnifying glass that you use to examine an intricate fingerprint. Understanding the fingerprint's details may take some time, but the magnifying glass itself isn't hard to use.

If you've already learned your way around any modern word processor or spreadsheet program, you'll find, as we did, that REGEDIT is much less complicated and much easier to master than those applications. Getting familiar with the ins and outs of the Registry is worth your while before doing any serious Registry tinkering.

Any good sailor travels with a few handy tools rather than just one. The software industry has provided a few utilities that make up for REGEDIT's shortcomings, and we've picked out a handful of the better ones. We even include some of these utilities on the CD-ROM that comes with this book, so you can try them on for size.

Cautions and Alerts

Before we get going with REGEDIT, we restate the First and Second Rules of the Registry, which appear first in Chapters 1 and 3.

Registry Rule #1

Periodically save a "known good" copy of the Registry where it's out of harm's way.

Before you even think about possibly coming close to running REGEDIT, save your current Registry contents to a cool, dry place. Read Chapter 2, reread it, pick your favorite backup method, and then practice it a couple of times.

We aren't harping on this because we're the type of guys who always do things "by the book." We're harping on it because, on the contrary, we tend to think we're macho computer studs who can sail by the seat of our pants and navigate out of any predicament — and because we've ended up aground on the rocks more than once because of it. Take it from us: Don't screw up, back up.

Registry Rule #2

Never use the Registry Editor unless no safer alternative is available.

If you haven't read Chapter 3, now is a good time to skim it over at least. To recap briefly here: If you can make a desired system change by using a control panel, the Explorer, the System Policy Editor, or a specific application program, do it there — not in the Registry. Reserve REGEDIT for those cases when no other method is available — because REGEDIT is a risky tool. The Registry Editor makes changes immediately; it doesn't offer an "undo" feature; it doesn't offer much in the way of warnings or cautions; and its built-in help is minimal.

REGEDIT Is from Mars

With apologies to John Gray, REGEDIT is from Mars. What we mean is that REGEDIT has many of the typical masculine virtues and shortcomings: It's direct and muscular but also uncommunicative and unrefined. The only way to use it successfully is to understand it inside and out. Fortunately, it's much less complex than the male psyche (or the female psyche for that matter). Spend an hour with REGEDIT and this chapter, and you've got it down cold. Try saying *that* about most computer programs!

The first point to get out in the open is that REGEDIT has different versions and different operating modes within those versions.

A tale of two versions

Windows 95 comes in two primary flavors these days, and you get a different version of REGEDIT depending on which flavor you have. Check your version by choosing Start⇨Settings⇨Control Panel, double-clicking the System icon, and looking at the line right underneath *Microsoft Windows 95,* toward the upper-right corner of the General property tab (see Figure 4-1).

Figure 4-1:
The System
control
panel
shows the
Windows 95
version
number.

✔ The original Windows 95, the so-called *gold release* that came out in August 1995, is version 4.00.950. Within a few months of the product's debut, Microsoft released a free *Service Pack* (dubbed *Service Pack 1,* or *SP1*) that fixed some bugs in the gold release. If a computer has the SP1 fixes, the version number becomes 4.00.950a, but the product isn't much different — just more reliable.

✔ Starting in late 1996, Microsoft started selling a substantially enhanced version of Windows 95 — but only to PC manufacturers. Joe End User couldn't buy it without buying a new PC. This new version goes by the name *OEM Service Release 2,* or *OSR2* for short (OEM stands for Original Equipment Manufacturer — that is, a PC maker). Most important in a long laundry list of some two dozen new features and enhancements is a new file system that makes more efficient use of disk space. If a computer is running OSR2.0 or 2.1, the version number is 4.00.950B and if it's running OSR2.5, the version is 4.00.950C.

It turns out that the version of REGEDIT that you get with Windows 95 versions 4.00.950 and 4.00.950a is different from the version that you get with 4.00.950B and C. The only differences we've found are as follows:

✔ The new Edit menu has an extra command, Copy Key Name.

✔ Running the new REGEDIT from a DOS prompt permits a new command, Delete a Key.

✔ The new REGEDIT can handle a larger Registry without crashing when run from a DOS prompt.

Trouble is, if you only have one PC and it's running the earlier version of Windows 95, you can't get the new REGEDIT — unless you're rich and can just go out and buy a new computer. As we write this, the new REGEDIT isn't available on the Microsoft Web site.

If, however, you *do* have access to more than one PC, you may be tempted to get the new REGEDIT off an OSR2 machine and copy it to an older Windows 95 PC. The trouble with doing so is that the new REGEDIT checks for DOS version 7.1, which is the version OSR2 reports, and older Windows 95 PCs report DOS version 7.0. The new REGEDIT detects the "wrong" DOS version and stubbornly refuses to run.

DOS veterans may recognize this situation, and you can remedy it with a nifty little program called SETVER. The SETVER utility, which incidentally Windows 95 loads automatically at startup, fools a program into thinking it's running on a different version of DOS than it really is. All you have to do is open a DOS Prompt window under Windows 95 and type:

```
SETVER REGEDIT.EXE 7.10
```

From now on, as long as you boot from your hard drive, you can run the new version of REGEDIT on your old Windows 95 PC.

We've tried this experiment and it seems to work fine, but you have a slim chance that running the newer REGEDIT on an older version of Windows 95 will do something weird. (You may notice the "Don't call us if you get yourself into a jam with this program" message from Microsoft when you run the SETVER command.) We therefore recommend that you try the above procedure only if the old REGEDIT gives you an error message when you try to import the Registry by using REGEDIT /C (see "REGEDIT à la mode, part 2: Getting real" later in this chapter).

REGEDIT à la mode, part 1: Getting GUI

Whether you have the new and improved REGEDIT or the old standby, you can run the program from Windows 95 *(protected mode)* or from DOS *(real mode)*. You normally run REGEDIT in protected mode, which is a lot easier because of the graphical user interface (or GUI, pronounced *gooey*).

Adding REGEDIT to your desktop

Windows 95 doesn't put an icon for REGEDIT on your desktop or your Start menu after a typical installation, but it does copy the file REGEDIT.EXE to the C:\WINDOWS directory (or whatever you name your Windows 95 directory). You can start the program by choosing Start⇨Run, typing **REGEDIT**, and clicking OK.

If you plan to spend a fair amount of time with REGEDIT, you probably don't want to use the Start⇨Run⇨**REGEDIT**⇨OK method several hundred times. You can create a desktop icon for REGEDIT by right-clicking the desktop, choosing New⇨Shortcut, typing **REGEDIT** on the Command field, and typing whatever label you like in the Select a Name for the Shortcut field. If you'd rather bury the command a little deeper, so that other people who may use your PC aren't as easily tempted to run REGEDIT, you can put the program on your Start menu along with other system tools. Here's the procedure:

1. **Choose Start⇨Settings⇨Taskbar, click the Start Menu Programs tab, and click the Advanced button.**

2. **Click the + to the left of the Programs folder in the left window pane to expand it.**

3. **Click the + to the left of the Accessories folder in the left window pane to expand it.**

4. **Click the System Tools folder in the left window pane.**

5. **Choose File⇨New⇨Shortcut to create the new menu entry for REGEDIT.**

6. **Type C:\WINDOWS\REGEDIT.EXE in the Command Line field in the Create Shortcut dialog box. (If Windows 95 resides in a directory other than WINDOWS, substitute the correct directory name.)**

7. **Type** Registry Editor **in the Select a Name for the Shortcut field in the Select a Title for the Program dialog box.**

8. **Close the Explorer window by clicking the close box in the upper-right corner.**

9. **Click OK to close the Taskbar Properties dialog box.**

You can now run REGEDIT by clicking Start⇨Programs⇨Accessories⇨ System Tools⇨Registry Editor.

If you're in charge of a bunch of Windows 95 PCs, put this book down right away and run around from machine to machine deleting REGEDIT.EXE. Leaving this program where novice users can get to it is an invitation to trouble. You can carry your copy around on diskette or put it up onto a network directory that only you and your fellow administrators can use.

Anatomy of the REGEDIT window

Figure 4-2 shows the REGEDIT window, which has many of the usual Windows program features: a *menu bar* at the top, a *status bar* at the bottom (which shows the full Registry path of the currently active selection), and *scroll bars* to help you navigate up, down, and side to side. The REGEDIT window has two panes: the *key pane* to the left presents an Explorer-like hierarchical view of the Registry database, and the *value pane* to the right shows the contents of whatever key you highlight in the key pane. (*Key pane* and *value pane* are our terms, not Microsoft's. Other writers use different terms; key pane and value pane make the most sense to us.) You can use the Tab key to jump quickly between the key pane and the value pane.

Each folder icon in the key pane represents a Registry *key,* which is a location for storing data. (A key isn't the same as a folder in Explorer, although the icon is the same. We wish Microsoft had used a different icon — making the REGEDIT window look like an innocent Explorer window is a little risky.) Many keys (the ones with a + sign to their left) contain other keys, which may be called *subkeys* — much the same way directories on your hard disk may be called subdirectories if they reside inside another directory.

You can expand the tree-like structure of the key pane by clicking the + sign to the left of any key that has one or more subkeys, and you can collapse the structure by clicking the - sign. Or, if you prefer, you can expand and collapse the structure by double-clicking the folder icon itself (it's a bigger target!). You can even right-click the folder icon and choose Expand or Contract from the context menu. If you have good hand-to-mouse coordination, clicking the + and – symbols is your fastest method.

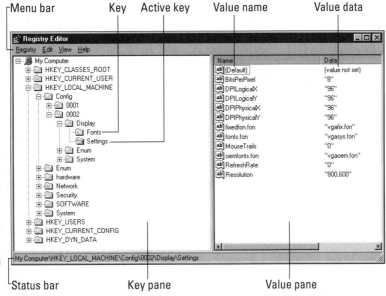

Menu bar   Key   Active key   Value name   Value data

Status bar   Key pane   Value pane

Figure 4-2:
The anatomy of REGEDIT's graphical mode.

The active (selected) key in the key pane displays an open-folder icon, while all the other keys display a closed-folder icon. The key contents, called *values,* appear in the value pane to the right; every value has both a *name* field, which identifies the value, and a *data* field, which contains the value's setting. Every key contains at least one value, named *Default,* but a key can contain a whole bunch of values, and many do. These values have three types: *string, binary,* and *DWORD.* We explain these value types more in Chapter 6, but for now we just mention that the string type (indicated by a tiny icon in the value pane's Name column containing the letters *ab*) is usually for text, and the binary and DWORD types (indicated by a tiny icon containing some 1s and 0s) are usually for numeric information. Demonically, string values can contain numbers, but you can almost always tell a string value because it appears enclosed in double quotes.

Note: Key names aren't unique in the Registry, and the same key name may crop up in several different places. So, when we describe a particular key in this book, we usually give its complete location, such as *HKCR\Drive* or *HKLM\SOFTWARE\Classes\Drive.* In these examples, we use abbreviations for the *branches,* or top-level keys: for example, *HKCR* is short for *HKey_Classes_Root.* Chapter 6 discusses these primary keys in more detail.

The menu bar in REGEDIT has four menus, but two of these menus are barely worth a glance:

- ✔ **The Registry menu** enables you to print, import, and export Registry data from and to text files, and connect to a remote user's Registry (see "Where's the remote?" later in this chapter).

- ✔ **The Edit menu** lets you create, delete, rename, and hunt for keys (in the left window pane) or values (in the right pane). You can also copy a key name if you have the newer version of REGEDIT that comes with OSR2 (see "A tale of two versions" earlier in this chapter), a capability annoyingly absent from the earlier REGEDIT.

If you have the older REGEDIT, you can usually select a key, choose Rename, and use the standard Windows Ctrl+C command to copy the key name, and then use Ctrl+V to paste it somewhere else. (Microsoft chose Ctrl+V because Ctrl+P is already taken: It usually means *print*.) To copy a value's data field, double-click the value name and then hit Ctrl+C to copy the data field.

- ✔ **The View menu** lets you turn the status bar on or off (why you'd ever want it off is a mystery to us), move the split bar separating the two panes (which you can do much more easily with the mouse), and refresh the display (which just re-sorts the current window contents alphabetically; you can do this more easily by pressing F5). In other words, if you use a mouse, forget about the View menu.

- ✔ **The Help menu** provides, alas, very little. Go ahead and take five minutes to read the help screens at least once through, then you can forget about this menu, too.

Sometimes, REGEDIT "grays out" a menu option if it isn't available for the selected item. For example, you can't delete or rename any of the six main Registry keys. (Good thing, too — you'd crash the whole system.)

Changing stuff

Most of the changes you make to the Registry involve modifying a value that already exists. REGEDIT makes this job pretty simple. The basic method is to hunt around in the left window pane (the *key pane*) until you find the key containing the value you need to change. (If you don't know exactly where that key is, see "Finding" later in this section.) Make a particular key active by clicking it. Then, change the value in the right window pane (the *value pane*) by double-clicking the value name (fastest method), by right-clicking the value name and selecting Modify (slower method), or by clicking the value name and choosing Edit⇨Modify from the menu bar (slowest method).

Which dialog box appears next depends on the type of value you selected. The Edit String, Edit Binary Value, and Edit DWORD Value dialog boxes that you work with are shown in Figure 4-3. Chapter 6 describes the number format for binary and DWORD values. Make whatever change is necessary in the Value Data field and click OK. You may notice that in each case the Value Name field is grayed out, meaning that you can't change the information in this field. (Go ahead, try. We dare you.) The reason that you can't change this info is that while you may have a legitimate reason to change a value's *data,* you're less likely to need to change a value's *name,* and doing so runs the risk that Windows 95 or an application program can't find your renamed value. If you're really certain that you do need to rename a value, right-click the value name in REGEDIT's value pane, and choose Rename.

If you need to change a value's type, for example from binary to string, REGEDIT doesn't offer a command to do so. You have to delete the existing value and create a new one with the same name. This situation doesn't come up often, but we've occasionally created new values that use the incorrect type.

When changing a string value, don't put double quotes around it, even though you saw quotes when you looked at the value before you double-clicked it. REGEDIT puts the double quotes around string values automatically.

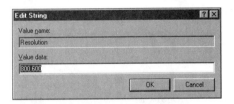

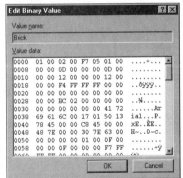

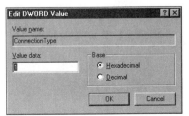

Figure 4-3:
Use the Edit dialog boxes to change a string value, a binary value, or a DWORD value.

Sometimes a key appears in more than one place, as we describe in Chapter 6. If you've set up *user profiles,* that is, multiple user accounts on the same Windows 95 PC, changing a setting for the current user doesn't change that setting for all other users. Chapter 10 explains user profiles in detail.

Adding keys and values

You can add two things to the Registry: a key or a value. Adding a key is simpler than adding a value. You can add a new key in a few different ways, but the way that makes the most sense to us is to follow these general steps:

1. **In the key pane (on the left), right-click the key that you want the new key to appear beneath, in the hierarchy.**

   For example, if you have the Windows 95 Quick View accessory installed, here's a tip that adds a Quick View command to the right-click menu of the REG file type (see "Exporting and importing" later in this chapter for more on REG files). Find *HKCR\regfile* and right-click it.

2. **Choose New⇨Key from the context menu and type in the key name over the text** New Key #1.

   In our example, the name of the new key you should type is **Quickview.**

3. **Press Enter.**

REGEDIT automatically adds the famous Default string value that every key must contain; the word (Default) appears in the value pane, to the right. To complete the Quick View example, double-click the (Default) value name and type * (an asterisk) in the Value Data field, and close REGEDIT. Now you can right-click any file with the REG suffix and choose Quick View from the context menu to safely view the file's contents.

(If you want, as an alternative method to add a new key, you can single-click the key under which you want the new key to appear, and use the menu bar to choose Edit⇨New⇨Key.)

Adding a value to a key is almost as easy as adding a new key; you just have to know a little more information ahead of time. In addition to the value name, you need to be able to specify what type the value should be (string, binary, or DWORD) and what data it should contain. Follow these general steps to add a value to a key:

1. **In the key pane, highlight the key in which you want to add the value.**

   For example, if you want to hide a particular file type so that it doesn't show up in My Computer's View⇨Options⇨File Types list, you can do so by adding a Registry value. We'll hide the REG file type ("Registration entries") by first highlighting the key *HKCR\regfile.*

2. **In the value pane, right-click anywhere within the pane except on an occupied entry in the Name column.**

3. **Choose New⇨String Value, New⇨Binary Value, or New⇨DWORD Value from the context menu.**

   In our example, you'd choose Binary Value.

4. **Type in the value name over the text** New Value #1 **and press Enter.**

   In our example, type **Editflags**. This is a special value that controls what actions you can perform from the File Type list.

5. **Press Enter again.**

   The Edit String, Edit Binary Value, or Edit DWORD Value dialog box appears, depending on the value type you're editing.

6. **Type in the value data in the Value Data: field, and then click OK.**

   To complete our example, type the hexadecimal values 01 00 00 00. After you close REGEDIT, open the File Types list; "Registration entries" no longer shows up, which is handy if you don't want a user to be able to change how REG files behave. You usually add a Registry value at the direction of a tech note, a tech support person, a book like this one, and so on. So you can expect to have some guidance from these sources as to what value type and data to enter.

Adding keys and values to the Registry isn't as common as modifying keys and values that already exist, but you will perform these tasks occasionally. Sometimes you add keys and values for your own purposes, without affecting Windows 95 or application programs (see Chapter 17, "Annotate the Registry"). Other times, as in the examples in this section, you may have to be careful that whatever keys and values you add meet the formatting requirements that Windows 95 or an application expects (see also Chapter 11, "Opening unknown file types"). As always, when in doubt, back up the Registry before you add new entries to it.

Deleting keys and values

Destroying is always easier than creating, and REGEDIT is no exception. To delete pretty much anything — a key (as long as it's not one of the six main ones), or a value of any type — just display it, right-click it, and choose Delete. (Left-clicking the key or value and hitting the Delete key may be faster, although some people prefer the mouse-only method.) You have to answer Yes in the ensuing dialog box to complete the deletion, so you always have an out if you chose Delete by accident or in haste.

Good thing you have an out because after you delete something in REGEDIT, you don't have an easy way to get it back. (Chapter 14 gives you a fairly painstaking method that you can use in a pinch.) If you use Norton Registry Editor, you get a nifty Undo command, but REGEDIT doesn't have one. Contrary to what *some* books say — we won't mention any names, but Microsoft Press should really be more careful — rebooting Windows 95 in Safe Mode does *not* restore the Registry's previous settings.

When you delete a key in the Registry, you also delete every value in that key and every subkey underneath that key. Deleting a key is like sawing a big branch off a tree: In doing so, you also remove every smaller branch that grows from the big branch, and every leaf on all those smaller branches.

Before you delete a Registry key or value, save it by using REGEDIT's Export Registry File command (see the section later in this chapter called "Exporting and importing"). You may even want to designate a special directory on your hard drive (C:\TEMPREG or something similar) for these exports. If everything works fine for a few days after you delete the key or value, you can delete the export file from your hard disk.

If you want to delete several values in a particular key, you can select a bunch of adjacent keys by clicking the first one, holding down the Shift key, and clicking the last. If you want to delete several nonadjacent values, hold down the Ctrl key and click each value that you want to delete. Then right-click any highlighted value and choose Delete from the context menu that appears.

Finding

Many times, especially when you're just getting your Registry sea legs, you may know what a key is called or what a value name is, but you don't know precisely where something lives within the maze-like Registry structure. REGEDIT's Find command, limited though it is, comes in mighty handy in such situations.

Fire up the Find command by choosing Edit⇨Find from the menu, typing Ctrl+F, or (our favorite method, and the fastest) pressing the F3 key. REGEDIT displays the Find dialog box shown in Figure 4-4.

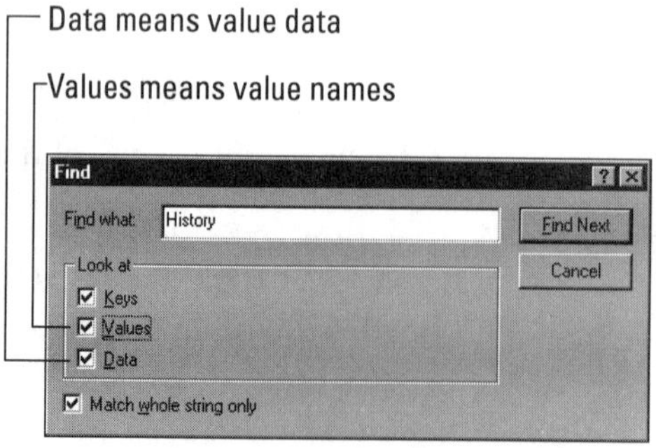

┌─ Data means value data

┌─Values means value names

Figure 4-4:
The Find
dialog box
in REGEDIT
with
imprecise
labels
and all.

You can type in the value you're looking for in the Find What field and tell REGEDIT where to look by checking the appropriate check boxes in the Look at area. Microsoft isn't precise with its wording here: the Keys check box is self-explanatory and correct, but the Values check box really means *value names* (the left column in the value pane), and the Data check box really means *value data* (the right column in the value pane). If you know whether the data you're searching for resides in a key name, value name, or value data field, you can uncheck the other two boxes to speed your search a little. If you want to find a string fragment and you're not sure you know the entire string, uncheck the check box labeled Match Whole String Only.

Click the Find Next button to start your hunt. When REGEDIT locates a match, it highlights the appropriate entry in the key and value panes. If you suspect that you'll have multiple matches, hit F3 again to resume the search. When REGEDIT can't find any more matches, or if it didn't find any in the first place, it displays a dialog box saying that it has `Finished searching through the Registry.` (Yes, it *would* be nice if REGEDIT said "No matches found" if that's the case, but we *told* you the program is an uncommunicative little rascal.)

Neither REGEDIT nor Norton Registry Editor can find data in DWORD or binary values; they can only find data in key or string values. If you want to search for DWORD or binary values, export the key that you think contains the values (see "Exporting and importing" later in this section) and use your favorite word processor's Find command.

Printing

You may think that the best way to print all or part of the Registry is to choose REGEDIT's Registry➪Print option (or press the shortcut, Ctrl+P). The naked truth is that this command is fine for a quick-and-dirty printing of little chunks of the Registry, but that's about it. Here's the procedure for this quick-and-dirty method:

1. **In the key pane, navigate to the key you want to print and then click it. The folder icon opens.**

2. **Choose Registry➪Print to bring up the dialog box in Figure 4-5.**

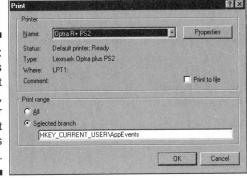

Figure 4-5: REGEDIT's Print dialog box, suitable for short printouts only.

   3. Choose the printer you want in the Name field, and click the Selected branch radio button in the Print Range area.

   4. Click OK, and fetch your hard copy.

TIP

REGEDIT doesn't go in for niceties such as margin settings or other output formatting options. (This program is from Mars, remember?) If you want to print a serious chunk (a big key or, if you've lost your mind, the whole Registry, which can require several hundred pages), export the desired chunk to a text file, as described in the next section. You can then pull that text file into a bona fide word processing program, where you can play with the page margins, font style, font size, and so on, before you actually print. You can also delete chunks that you don't want to print, saving trees and speeding print time.

Exporting and importing

Exporting and importing is the last subject we need to touch on in this overview of REGEDIT's graphical *modus operandi*. Exporting and importing have very specific meanings in the context of the Registry, and the commands that you use to export and import are ones that you use often if you read very much of this book.

Exporting a Registry key (or the whole Registry, for that matter) creates a text file on disk with the suffix .REG. The text file contains the contents of the specified key, plus any subkeys under that key, plus all the associated values contained in those keys. (The original information stays in the Registry.) You can view an exported REG file in any text editor (Notepad, for example) or word processor. You can also double-click a REG file in order to merge its contents into the current Registry, so exporting is a popular way of backing up a particular key before making changes to it. However, exporting the entire Registry can take a pretty long time, so this method isn't the most convenient way to back up your whole Registry database.

The procedure for exporting a Registry key is simple, although not quite as elegant as we might like:

   1. Click the key you want to export in the key pane to make it active, and choose Registry⇨Export Registry File.

   It would be slicker if you could just right-click the key and export it from the context menu, but that's an enhancement that you need Norton Registry Editor to enjoy. The Export Registry File dialog box appears, as shown in Figure 4-6.

   2. Give your export file a destination in the Save In field.

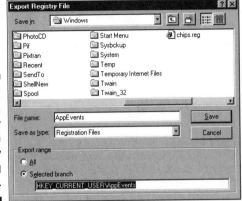

Figure 4-6:
You can
export a key
or the entire
Registry
by using
REGEDIT.

3. **Give your export file a name in the File _N_ame field.**

You don't need to specify the REG suffix. Avoid spaces in both the path and file name and keep the main filename to eight characters or less for convenience when using REG files at the DOS command prompt.

4. **Check that the S_e_lected Branch radio button is selected in the Export Range area. (Click the _A_ll radio button in this box if you want to export the whole Registry.)**

5. **Click the Save button.**

Importing from a REG file is a similar process. Choose _R_egistry⇨_I_mport Registry File from the menu bar and specify the REG file that you want to import in the Import Registry File dialog box. Alternatively, you can just open Windows Explorer, find the REG file, and double-click it — or right-click the file and choose Merge from the context menu.

Importing a REG file can create new Registry entries and modify existing ones. REGEDIT doesn't warn you if the REG file that you're importing is about to overwrite existing values. _Always_ back up the Registry before importing a REG file.

Here's a _gotcha_ that caught us with our virtual pants down when we were first getting to know Windows 95. Importing a REG file works flawlessly as long as you're adding values to the current Registry or changing existing values. The problem comes up when you want to import a REG file with less information: Importing a REG file doesn't delete existing keys or values. Suppose, for example, that you export your Registry to a REG file because you want to add some keys and values that you think will have a given effect. When you find out that the files don't have the desired effect, importing your old REG file _doesn't_ remove the bogus keys and values. The only way that you can be sure that the Import operation correctly restores the Registry is to delete the keys from the Registry _before_ you import them from the REG file.

After you realize that REG files are the primary way that new programs add keys and values to the Registry, you can appreciate the good sense of this arrangement. You don't want new programs to be able to accidentally trash Registry entries created (and relied upon) by other programs. We take a closer look at REG files and their cousins, the INF files, in Chapter 8.

REGEDIT à la mode, part 2: Getting real

You may have times when you need to run REGEDIT in its so-called *real mode,* that is, from a DOS prompt rather than from the graphical Windows 95 environment. For example, you may find yourself in a situation where Windows 95 doesn't boot properly, and you can't even get to the graphical protected-mode environment. This may be the case if your Registry is FUBAR. (FUBAR is a famous computer acronym standing for — at least in polite society — Fouled Up Beyond All Recognition.)

Note: You don't actually run a different program file when you run REGEDIT in real mode. It's the same REGEDIT.EXE; the program just senses whether you're at the DOS prompt or running Windows 95 and starts accordingly.

Running REGEDIT in real mode is riskier than running it in graphical protected mode because you can accidentally and easily type one wrong letter and destroy the entire Registry. Only run REGEDIT in real mode if no other option is available, or if this book advises you to do so in a particular situation.

You can't run REGEDIT in real mode by simply opening a DOS prompt under Windows 95 and typing the command; all this does is open a graphical REGEDIT window. Here's how to get to the real-mode command prompt:

- ✔ If you're already running Windows 95, choose Start⇨Sh<u>u</u>tdown, select the Restart the Computer in MS-DOS Mode radio button, and then click Yes.
- ✔ If you can't get to Windows 95, try hitting the F8 key when you first see the Starting Windows 95 message; then select the Safe Mode Command Prompt Only menu option.
- ✔ If all else fails, you can boot the PC with the Windows 95 emergency startup disk that you created when you installed Windows 95. (If you didn't make one then, you can make one anytime using the Add/ Remove Programs control panel's Startup Disk tab.) The emergency startup disk includes a copy of REGEDIT.EXE.

However you get to the DOS command prompt, change to the C: drive and the \WINDOWS directory, and you can then type **REGEDIT** and see a fairly cryptic listing of the command line options:

```
REGEDIT [/L:system] [/R:user] filename1
REGEDIT [/L:system] [/R:user] /C filename2
REGEDIT [/L:system] [/R:user] /D [regpath]
REGEDIT [/L:system] [/R:user] /E filename3 [regpath]
```

- **The /L and /R options** allow you to specify the location of the SYSTEM.DAT and USER.DAT files, respectively, but usually you work with the files in the C:\WINDOWS directory, so you don't need these options. To merge the contents of an existing REG file into the Registry, you just type **REGEDIT filename1.REG**.

- **The /C option** is the dangerous one: It creates a brand-new Registry from scratch, importing the contents of filename2 — which must end in the suffix .REG and which should contain a full Registry export. REGEDIT doesn't look at filename2 to verify that filename2 contains a full Registry, and if filename2 doesn't, you can end up worse off than before.

- **The /D option** lets you delete a Registry key, but you only get this option if you have the newer version of REGEDIT that comes with Windows 95 OSR2. This option is potentially dangerous, too. An example command to remove a key left over from a program uninstall may be

```
REGEDIT /D HKEY_CURRENT_USER\Software\VendorX\ProgramY
```

- **The /E option** exports the Registry to filename3. If you only want to export a portion of the Registry, you can specify the starting key as the *regpath*. (The *regpath* is just the key location, as in the /D example in the previous bullet item.)

How can you use REGEDIT in real mode to fix a problem? Chapters 14 and 16 offer some ideas, but the most common technique is to use REGEDIT /E to export the Registry (or a particular key), run a text editor to load the exported REG file, fix what's wrong, save the REG file, and then use REGEDIT again to reimport it. If that sounds like a pain, it is!

You're much better off making Registry backups whenever you make a change because restoring a backed-up Registry is much easier than troubleshooting with the real-mode REGEDIT program.

Where's the remote?

Say you're using Windows 95 on a network and, because of your skills, your job description, or both, other network users look to you for technical support. Now, say a novice Windows user calls you for help, and it becomes clear that some Registry editing is necessary — but you would no more trust that user with REGEDIT than give a 13-year-old the keys to a Corvette. You can always walk over to the user's PC, but if you do a lot of technical support work, you don't want to spend your life walking around the building — and besides, all your handy reference books are in your own office. Good news: With the right sort of network and a bit of foresight, you can run REGEDIT on your machine and edit the distressed user's Registry remotely, over the wire.

For those of you who aren't running Windows 95 on a network or who don't plan to offer technical support to others, feel free to skip this section.

Getting set up for remote Registry editing

You can only use REGEDIT remotely if all the following conditions are met:

- ✔ Your network is a *client/server* type, that is, you have a dedicated central server running a network operating system like Novell IntranetWare or Windows NT Server. In other words, you can't run REGEDIT over a peer-to-peer network like LANtastic or the peer-to-peer network that's built in to Windows 95.

- ✔ The Windows 95 PCs all use 32-bit protected mode software to communicate over the network (this is the usual setup). In other words, the PCs can't be running real-mode network software that loads via AUTOEXEC.BAT.

- ✔ The Windows 95 PCs you want to connect over the network share at least one common *protocol* (that is, the network language, usually TCP/IP, IPX, or NetBEUI).

- ✔ The Windows 95 PCs are set up for *user-level security* on the Network control panel's Access Control tab. (This is also the usual setup in a client/server network, where each user has a single ID and password. The alternative, *share-level security,* is common in a peer-to-peer network, where each shared resource has its own password.)

Remote editing also requires a little foresight: You have to install a bit of software on both your machine and the machine you want to access remotely so that REGEDIT can find the remote machine's Registry over the network. This software goes by the name *Microsoft Remote Registry* (some books and magazines call it the *Remote Registry Service*). You may want to go ahead and install this software on every PC on the network. Here's how:

1. **Pop the Windows 95 disc into the PC's CD-ROM drive; or if Windows 95 was installed from a network drive, make sure that you're logged on to the network and that the network server drive containing the Windows 95 setup files is available.**

2. **Click Start➪Settings➪Control Panel and double-click the Network icon.**

3. Click **Add** to display in the Select Network Component Type dialog box.

4. Double-click the Service option to display the Select Network Service dialog box.

5. Click the **Have Disk** button to display the Install From Disk dialog box.

6. Type **X:\ADMIN\NETTOOLS\REMOTREG into the Copy Manufacturer's Files From text box (where** *X:* **is the drive letter of the CD-ROM or network drive containing the Windows 95 files) and click OK.**

7. Click OK again in the Install From Disk dialog box.

8. Click **Microsoft Remote Registry in the Select Network Service dialog box, and click OK.**

Now that the remote registry software is on the system, a few final steps enable the PC to be administered from afar. You have to tell the computer exactly who is empowered to perform remote administration.

1. Click **Start⇨Settings⇨Control Panel.**

2. Double-click the Passwords icon.

3. Click the Remote Administration tab.

4. Select the **Enable Remote Administration of This Server check box.**

   In the Administrators list, if you run an NT Server network, Domain admins appears automatically; if you run a Novell network, the Supervisor (NetWare 3.x) or Admin (NetWare 4.x) account appears. You can add people to the list with (you guessed it) the Add button — for example, if you're not a network administrator but you're the one who may be doing the remote Registry editing, add your logon name to the list. When you're done, click OK.

Running REGEDIT remotely

After you complete setting up a Windows 95 PC for remote editing (see preceding section), using REGEDIT to modify a remote user's Registry is a piece o' cake:

1. **Run REGEDIT.**

2. Click **Registry⇨Connect Network Registry.**

3. Type in the name of the computer you want to connect to in the **Computer Name field of the Connect Network Registry box, or select the computer you want from a list by clicking the Browse button.**

4. Click OK in the Connect Network Registry dialog box. You see a screen like Figure 4-7, showing your local machine's Registry at the top of the left window pane and the remote machine's Registry at the bottom.

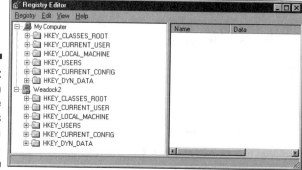

Figure 4-7:
Viewing a
remote
user's
Registry in
REGEDIT.

You can follow a similar procedure to edit a remote Registry with the System
Policy Editor, which Chapter 9 discusses in more detail.

Norton Registry Editor Is from Venus

The Norton Registry Editor (NRE) that comes with Norton Utilities for
Windows 95 version 2.0 and above is a kinder, gentler REGEDIT (see Figure 4-8).
The advantages of NRE include a much better Find command, bookmarks,
safety features, and greatly improved online help.

Take an advance look at NRE by installing the Norton Utilities trialware
program included on this book's CD-ROM.

Figure 4-8:
The Norton
Registry
Editor adds
a third
window
pane
beneath the
usual two
and also
provides
access to
Windows 95
INI files.

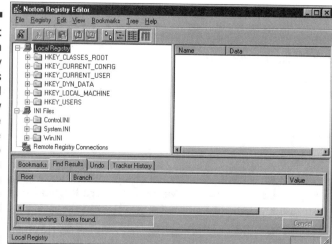

Enhanced Find command

Instead of REGEDIT's tedious one-at-a-time find feature, the Edit⇨Find command in NRE lists all the results of a find operation in the lower window's Find Results tab. There, you can scroll up or down to see what your search turned up, and then double-click the entry you want to see. NRE takes you to the selected entry by resetting the two upper window panes to show that entry. The NRE Find method lets you ignore irrelevant find results more easily.

The Find dialog box in NRE Version 2.0 lets you specify orphans instead of particular text strings. (Symantec has moved this feature out of NRE and into the WinDoctor utility in Version 3.0.) *Orphans* are file path names in the Registry that no longer point to files or directories that exist on your computer's hard drive. Usually, orphans occur when a user incompletely uninstalls an application program. Chapter 13 takes a closer look at Registry orphans.

NRE's Edit⇨Replace command lets you perform a global search-and-replace throughout the entire Registry. You may want to use this feature, for example, if you move a program's files to a different directory but don't want to reinstall the program from scratch. You can simply replace all references to the old directory with a reference to the new one.

Bookmarks

One of our favorite additions in NRE is the ability to create *bookmarks*. A bookmark is a Registry location that you create by right-clicking a key and choosing Bookmark from the context menu. NRE then puts a little red dot on the bookmarked key. After you create one or more bookmarks, you can instantly go back to a marked location by double-clicking the bookmark in the Bookmarks tab in NRE's lower window pane. You can save your bookmarks in a file, retrieve a set of bookmarks that you saved previously, and even create multiple bookmark sets that you can use for different purposes: fun tips, security settings, bug fixes, and so on.

Safety features

NRE offers a couple of good safety features that are absent from REGEDIT:

  ✔ **Undo.** You can choose Edit⇨Undo to undo your last action, and the Undo tab in the lower window pane displays a list of all the actions you've taken in the current session (that is, since you opened NRE).

✔ **Read only.** You can choose Registry⇨Read Only to prohibit any changes to the Registry. This is a great idea when you're exploring the Registry structure and want to make sure that you don't inadvertently change something. Microsoft included this feature in the Windows NT Registry editor REGEDT32, but left it out of the Windows 95 utility.

Help that helps

Finally, NRE Version 2.0 has a functional and fairly useful online help feature — unlike REGEDIT, which comes with an embarrassingly spartan help file. Click the Advisor tab in the lower window, and NRE tells you a little about the key that's highlighted in the key pane at the top left. If NRE doesn't include help about a specific key, it navigates its way up the structure and offers help about the nearest key above the highlighted one that it knows something about. That's a nice user-oriented touch. (Incidentally, if the help screens look vaguely familiar, that's because they use the same formatting that Internet Web files use: HTML, or HyperText Markup Language.)

Alas, NRE version 3.0 does away with this feature. We lament that Symantec removed what was one of NRE 2.0's best features. Maybe they'll bring it back in NRE 4.0.

The NRE help system makes use of the Registry itself. The key *HKLM\ SOFTWARE\Symantec\Norton Utilities\Norton Registry Advisor* helps NRE know what part of the consolidated help file ADVISOR.HTM to display for each Registry key.

Shareware and Freeware Utilities

In addition to Norton Registry Editor, a few other free and shareware programs deserve consideration for inclusion in your bag of Registry editing tricks.

We haven't yet seen the perfect Registry editing tool — or the perfect Registry backup utility, for that matter. (We'd love to see those capabilities combined into one killer product.) Meanwhile, throw a few programs into your Registry duffel bag; some are good for some tasks, others for others.

SCANREG

This little command-line program hails from the Microsoft Windows NT Resource Kit and enables you to search for a particular string within the Windows 95 or NT Registry (either local or remote). You can specify whether you want to search keys, value names, or value data; whether you want your search to be case-sensitive (that is, match uppercase and lowercase precisely); and which primary Registry branch you want to search. Figure 4-9 shows the results of a SCANREG search for the text string *PageMill*.

SCANREG isn't as slick as the REGEDIT Find command or the shareware programs we mention later in this section. However, it's handy if you can't boot to Windows 95 due to a damaged Registry, and it's free as long as you or someone in your company has the Windows NT Resource Kit. SCANREG.EXE resides on the Windows NT Resource Kit CD-ROM under \I386\REGISTRY. The README file is oddly located in \COMMON\REGISTRY.

Note: SCANREG was written by a Microsoft programmer but isn't supported by Microsoft, so if you call with a question about it, Microsoft will pretend they've never heard of the program. Also, don't confuse this program with the SCANREG utility that comes with Windows 98 and that also goes by the name of *Registry Checker* (see the Windows 98 insert in this book); these are two different animals. (Hey, Microsoft is a big company, it's bound to duplicate program names occasionally.)

COMPREG

Another program from the Microsoft Windows NT Resource Kit, COMPREG.EXE, allows you to compare two Registry branches — for example, on two different computers. As with SCANREG, COMPREG works with local or remote Registries, and it works with Windows 95 or NT. This little utility can be handy when troubleshooting — you can see what's different between a machine that works and one that doesn't.

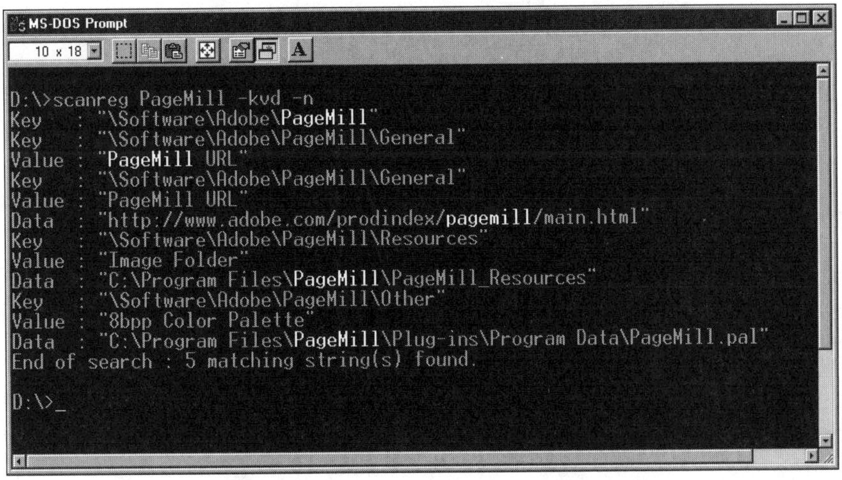

Figure 4-9:
SCANREG
is a Registry
find utility
that works
from a
command
prompt.

Registry Search and Replace

This $20 shareware utility from Steven J. Hoek Software Development adds to REGEDIT's Find command by including the ability to replace one chunk of text with another. If you have Norton Registry Editor, you already have better and safer search-and-replace capabilities, but if you don't have NRE, take a look at Registry Search and Replace (RS&R).

RS&R can log your search or search-and-replace session to a file. It works with remote Registries as long as the usual conditions are met (see the section "Where's the remote?" earlier in this chapter). You can use RS&R with Windows NT as well as Windows 95. RS&R adds a new option to the Start⇔Find command. The In the Registry option is a quick way to run the program. You don't have to open REGEDIT to run RS&R, and you can save your settings as a *search profile* so you don't have to enter them each time you run the program. Finally, you can choose to look at and approve each replacement separately *(prompted replacement),* which is safer than blindly performing all replacements at once *(specified replacement).*

The program is good but not perfect. Version 2.10 can't search for both value names and value data in the same pass, and it doesn't have an undo feature. (Back up the Registry before you use this program!) Also, like REGEDIT and NRE, RS&R can't find data in DWORD or binary values.

Figure 4-10 shows a screen that's set up to replace every occurrence of C:\PROGRAM FILES\LOCATIONA with C:\PROGRAM FILES\LOCATIONB and to log all your results to a file (always a smart idea in case something goes wrong and you need to reverse one or more changes).

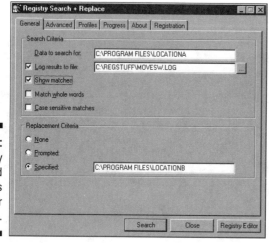

Figure 4-10:
Registry
Search and
Replace is
primed for
action.

Whether you use RS&R or Norton Registry Editor, search-and-replace operations can produce unintended results if you allow partial matches (changing *nut* to *bolt* also changes *doughnut* to *doughbolt*). To be safe, select the Match Whole Words option in RS&R or the Match Whole String Only option in Norton.

RegSurf

RegSurf, a $28 shareware program from ISES Inc., doesn't do search-and-replace, but it does have the ability to search every Registry key (see Figure 4-11), something that Registry Search and Replace doesn't do. RegSurf also includes a handy option to print the results of your search. It works with the Windows NT Registry as well as the Windows 95 Registry, and it's pretty fast (especially if you choose the Minimize While Surfing option).

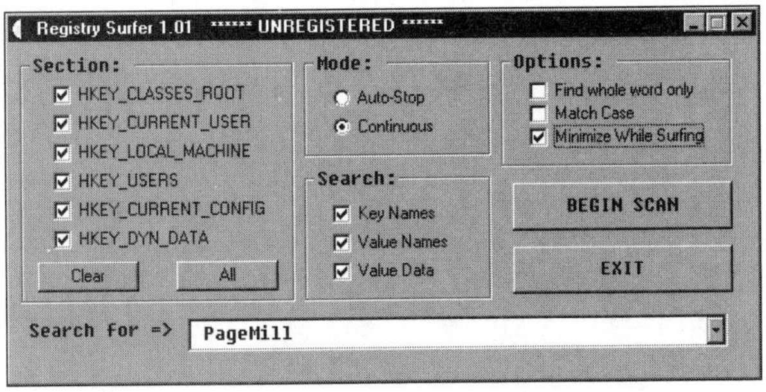

Figure 4-11:
RegSurf lets
you search
every
Registry key.

Other stuff we discuss later

Other tools make handy additions to your Registry arsenal, but we save discussion of them for later on in the book. For example, Chapter 9 discusses the System Policy Editor, Chapter 11 explores TweakUI, MTUSpeed, and TweakDUN, and Chapter 12 looks at REGMON and FILEMON. We've covered enough stuff here for one chapter. (Maybe more than enough!)

Part II
Hull, Keel, and Sail: The Registry Structure

In this part . . .

You'd never crew on a sailboat if you didn't have a basic understanding of a boat's working parts ("Grab the tiller? You bet! What's a tiller?" <splash>). In the same way, you shouldn't embark on a journey of Registry discovery without knowing something of the bits and pieces that collectively form the Registry.

In this part, you find out about the two different ways you can view the Registry: You can look at the actual files that constitute the Registry, or you can use the Registry Editor to view the Registry as a unified, multilevel database. Finally, this part explains how the Registry stores information about your PC's hardware in order to work with the Plug and Play standard.

Chapter 5

Where the Files Are

*W*e refer to "The Registry" approximately nine zillion times in this book, but what actual files on your hard disk are we talking about? This chapter holds the answer.

You can't take proper care of your Registry unless you know what disk files it contains.

Sure, you can run programs such as the Windows 95 Emergency Recovery Utility (ERU) and Configuration Backup without knowing exactly what files the Registry contains. But if you don't at least know the what and where of the Registry files, you may miss some dangerous little quirks of these programs — such as the fact that ERU usually omits a key file when you use it to back up your Registry to a diskette! Windows 95 also automatically backs up your Registry every time it starts successfully, and knowing where these backup files are located may just save your bacon one day.

If you set up Windows 95 to provide *user profiles* so that multiple users can log on to the same PC or so that users can log on to any network PC and see their own desktop setup, you need to know where these user-specific Registry files live. (Some of those automated Registry backup programs don't back up these user-specific files, so you may need to back them up separately.)

If you ever need to restore your Registry file backups during a troubleshooting session, you need to know where your files are — and which ones to restore. Here again, the automated Registry backup programs don't always give you the flexibility that you may need in specifying which files need to go where.

Finally, Windows 95 contains a few files that aren't strictly part of the Registry but that relate to it in one way or another: REG, INF, and so on. If you don't know where these files are or what they do, you may inadvertently do some Registry damage that isn't easily undoable.

Convinced? (We hope so.) Now, here's the skinny on the Registry files. After you're comfortable with their names, functions, and locations, you're well on your way to qualifying as a Certified Registry Expert Par Excellence and receiving the official certificate of distinction, the CREPE Paper. (Okay, we're sorry, but if we didn't throw in a bad joke from time to time, you might quit reading.)

Let's Get Physical

You can look at the Registry in two ways: as a logical entity, in which you look at how the Registry's information is organized, or as a physical entity, in which you look at the actual locations of Registry files.

Chapter 6 explores the Registry's *logical structure*, which is the tree-like organization you see when you open the Registry Editor. (Okay, it doesn't always seem all that logical, but that's the term nevertheless.)

The actual files on disk that make up the Registry constitute its *physical structure*. In this chapter, we look at the Registry's *physical structure,* the actual files on disk that make up the Registry. We discuss the physical structure first mainly because it's a little simpler than the logical structure. Figure 5-1 shows the physical structure of the Registry, and the rest of this chapter explains the various files and what they do.

Before you drop your jaw looking at the figure, please understand that your Windows 95 PC may not use all these files on a regular basis, or at all. The main files we're concerned with are SYSTEM.DAT and USER.DAT, but you may need to know about the other ones depending on how you've set up your machine and whether your machine is on a network. If you have a simple, single-user, stand-alone PC, you don't have to worry about many of the files this chapter discusses — just SYSTEM.DAT and USER.DAT.

SYSTEM.DAT and USER.DAT divide your PC into system-specific and user-specific settings, respectively. Why divide the Registry like this? Doing so enables multiple users to work on the same PC, to roam a network, and to see their own settings when they log on. The SYSTEM.DAT file stays with the PC, but the USER.DAT file can live on a network server or in separate directories on the local PC hard drive for each user. Splitting the Registry into these two main files is a stroke of genius on Microsoft's part.

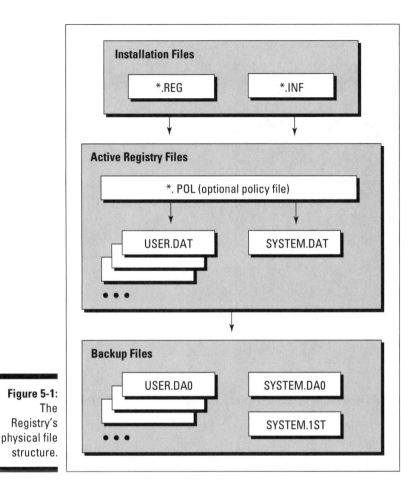

Figure 5-1:
The
Registry's
physical file
structure.

Before looking at SYSTEM.DAT and USER.DAT in depth, however, you need to be able to view and print Registry files, which the following section discusses.

Sharpening your physical skills: Viewing and printing

The first thing to do before wandering around your PC and looking at the Registry's physical structure is to set up Windows 95 so that you can see all the files on your disk with My Computer or Windows Explorer. After a typical Windows 95 installation, many files don't appear in these file management programs because the files have the *Hidden attribute* turned on (see the sidebar entitled, "Windows 95 file attributes"). Here's how to bend Windows 95 to your will and display your hidden files:

1. **Start Windows Explorer the fast way, by right-clicking the My Computer icon and choosing Explore.**

2. **Choose View⇨Options to display the Options dialog box (see Figure 5-2).**

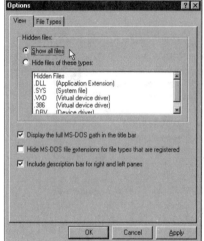

Figure 5-2: Setting up Explorer to show hidden files and file extensions.

3. **In the Hidden Files area, select the Show All Files button.**

   This choice forces Windows 95 to display all files — even files that have the Hidden attribute.

4. **Deselect the Hide MS-DOS File Extensions for File Types That Are Registered check box.**

   This choice forces Windows 95 to display the full file names, including suffixes, for all files.

5. **Click OK and close Windows Explorer.**

At some time, you may want to print a list of files in a particular directory. Sorry! Windows 95 Explorer doesn't have a print command! (Someone at Microsoft must have been asleep at the cyberwheel on this one.) To print a file list, you have to fall back on bad old MS-DOS, and in situations like this one, we're darned glad that it still exists. Here's one method: Open an MS-DOS window and use the ATTRIB command with the /S qualifier, which means "include subdirectories." For example, to display all the files and directories under C:\WINDOWS, type **ATTRIB C:\WINDOWS*.* /S**, and if you want the output to go to a printer connected to your first parallel port, for example, type **ATTRIB C:\WINDOWS*.* /S>LPT1:**

Windows 95 file attributes

PC files have had *attributes* since way back in the days of DOS. Attributes are special settings associated with a particular file. These attributes can be either informational, like the Archive attribute in the following list, or restrictive, like the other three attributes. The Windows 95 file attributes include

>**Read-only (R).** You can't change or delete the file.

>**Hidden (H).** You can't see the file unless Windows Explorer is set up to show all files or unless you know the exact file name.

>**System (S).** The operating system uses the file, and you can't see the file unless Windows Explorer is set up to show all files.

>**Archive (A).** The file has been added or changed since the last backup.

You can view these attributes — and change all but the System attribute — by right-clicking a file, choosing Properties, and viewing the General tab, as shown in the figure. If you need to modify the System attribute, for example during a Registry restore in Windows 95's command-prompt mode, you must use the DOS ATTRIB command.

You can use a couple of grief-saving little tricks while working with the ATTRIB command. If a file, such as SYSTEM.DAT, has both the Hidden and System attributes set, you can't remove one at a time — you have to remove both at once, using a command such as

```
ATTRIB -S -H SYSTEM.DAT
```

Also, if a file has the Read-only attribute set, and you want to remove that attribute so that you can write over the file (as during a Registry restore), you have to either remove the System and Hidden attributes first, or remove all three attributes at once, as follows:

```
ATTRIB -S -H -R SYSTEM.DAT
```

You can restore file attributes with the ATTRIB command by using a + instead of a − in the command.

Finally, Windows 95 adds some new date and time attributes you need to know about for troubleshooting purposes. Windows 95 not only tracks the date and time of file creation, it also tracks the date and time of last modification and of most recent access. You can sometimes use these new date and time attributes, which also appear in the figure, to determine which of two file versions is newer.

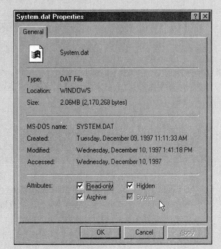

If you don't care about file attributes, and would rather just see a listing of the file names with size, date, and time information, you can use the DIR command like this:

```
DIR C:\WINDOWS\*.* /A /O /S >LPT1:
```

The forward slashes are called *switches* (or *qualifiers*) because they turn different features of the command on or off. The /A switch tells DIR to include files with system and hidden attributes — files that DIR normally omits. The /O part sorts the list into alphabetical order and the /S part makes DIR include the contents of all the subdirectories as well.

The soul of your machine: SYSTEM.DAT

One Registry file that appears on every Windows 95 PC is SYSTEM.DAT, and it's one of the two biggies. You can find it in the C:\WINDOWS directory (or whatever you've named your Windows 95 main directory). If you're running a lobotomized PC with no local disk storage so that it boots from diskette or a remote-boot disk image, SYSTEM.DAT resides in the *machine directory* on the server, along with the other Registry files. We don't cover machine directories in this book because few individuals or companies use them, but if you need this kind of information, check out the *Microsoft Windows 95 Resource Kit* from Microsoft Press.

The SYSTEM.DAT file contains information about the computer on which it resides: mainly hardware configuration data and information about installed software (but not user settings). None of the settings in SYSTEM.DAT change from user to user, if you've set up a Windows 95 PC to accommodate multiple users. SYSTEM.DAT is associated with a particular *computer*, not a particular *user*.

SYSTEM.DAT contains the information in the logical Registry branches *HKEY_Local_Machine, HKEY_Current_Config,* and *HKEY_Classes_Root.* We explain these branches in Chapter 6.

SYSTEM.DAT has the file attributes of System, Hidden, and Read-only (see the sidebar, "Windows 95 file attributes," earlier in this chapter). These attributes help protect the SYSTEM.DAT file. If it's hidden, users running a Windows 95 PC that's set up to hide hidden files from My Computer or Explorer can't see it. If it's a read-only system file, even users who can see a file (by changing the view options for My Computer or Explorer as explained earlier in this chapter) can't delete or change the file.

Now hold the phone. If SYSTEM.DAT is read-only, how can we change its contents by using the Registry Editor? On top of that, how can a new application program add settings for its own use in this file when you install a new program? The sly answer is that Registry Editor bypasses the read-only attribute, and application install programs bypass it, too, typically using REG and INF files. Just about all the Read-only attribute does is prevent users from doing something silly (and dangerous), like deleting or renaming the file in Explorer, or loading the file into a word processor, making a change, and then saving it back. (If you try to do the latter, you see an error message like the one in Figure 5-3.)

Figure 5-3:
Word can't
save a
read-only
SYSTEM.DAT.

Putting the "personal" in "personal computer": USER.DAT

The other Registry file that appears on every Windows 95 PC is USER.DAT, and it's the second biggie. You can find it in the C:\WINDOWS directory along with SYSTEM.DAT. This file contains information about the users who work with the PC: their desktop preferences, Control Panel options they can set, where to find the list of Start menu programs, application-specific settings (such as recently used file lists), and so on.

None of the settings in USER.DAT are machine-specific. If you set up a Windows 95 network so that users can log on from any machine with their own user ID and password, then their USER.DAT files can follow them from machine to machine. USER.DAT is associated with a particular *user,* not a particular *computer.*

USER.DAT contains the information in the logical Registry branches *HKEY_Users* and *HKEY_Current_User.* We explain these branches in Chapter 6.

USER.DAT has the same file attributes that SYSTEM.DAT does: System, Hidden, and Read-only. The same comments we made about these attributes in the preceding section apply here.

If you've turned on the Windows 95 user profiles feature (see Chapter 10), Windows 95 creates multiple copies of USER.DAT in subdirectories underneath the C:\WINDOWS\PROFILES directory. The subdirectory names match the user names that you define when logging on to Windows 95 as a new user. So, on some Windows 95 PCs, you may find many copies of USER.DAT on the machine.

If you use user profiles and you work on a client/server network like NT Server or Novell IntranetWare, Windows 95 stores USER.DAT in a user directory on the server (such as the user's mail directory on a Novell 3.x server, or the user's home directory on a Novell 4.x or Windows NT server). When you log on, if the network copy is newer, Windows 95 copies USER.DAT from the network down to your PC. If your PC copy is newer, Windows 95 copies USER.DAT from your local PC to the network. When you log off, Windows 95 copies USER.DAT back to the network server, just in case you made any changes to your settings.

These multiple copies of USER.DAT are not all the same! Whenever you log on to Windows 95 with a particular name, Windows 95 switches to the USER.DAT file in the C:\WINDOWS\PROFILES\username directory that matches your logon name. If you ever need to restore a USER.DAT file on a PC with user profiles enabled, you must make sure that you use the correct USER.DAT for a particular user. Otherwise, you can create a situation in which Bob logs on and sees Jane's wallpaper (and all Jane's other user-specific settings). Not good — especially if Jane likes a picture of Fabio for wallpaper and Bob prefers Heather Locklear. (The actual problems can be much more significant, of course.)

Many Registry backup utilities just copy the USER.DAT files in the C:\WINDOWS\SYSTEM directory and ignore the ones in C:\WINDOWS\PROFILES. You may want to back up the individual user versions of USER.DAT separately, as Chapter 2 discusses. (If you're wondering what that USER.DAT file in C:\WINDOWS is good for in a multiple-user situation; it's the basis for setting up a new USER.DAT for a new user, and it's also the file that activates if a user skips the Windows 95 logon screen.)

If you run Windows 95 on a client/server network and you enable user profiles, you can create a special version of USER.DAT that users can't change — meaning that they can't modify any Windows 95 or Windows 95 program settings. This version is a *mandatory user profile,* which must have the special name USER.MAN. USER.MAN lives in the user's mail directory on a Novell server or in the user's home directory on a Windows NT Server.

An optional security blanket: *.POL

A third and optional Registry file may exist, and it's a *policy* file. Policy files have the suffix .POL and, even though they're not DAT files, they're still part of the Registry. Policy files act as a sort of security layer, limiting what a user can do with Windows 95. You can also use policy files to customize your desktop and control certain network settings. Windows 95 reads the settings in a policy file and incorporates them into the Registry. That is, a policy file effectively modifies USER.DAT, SYSTEM.DAT, or both. The Registry's overall appearance when you view it with the Registry Editor doesn't change if a policy file is active because the policy file doesn't add any new main branches to the logical structure.

Policy files can govern the user settings in USER.DAT, but only if you set up Windows 95 to activate user profiles. Policy files can govern the computer settings in SYSTEM.DAT, whether you've activated user profiles or not.

You can't necessarily tell in advance what a policy file's full filename is. We see in Chapter 9 that this isn't a drawback; it's a handy feature if you want to get fancy with system policies and control precisely how they behave. The main part of the filename may match a user logon name or a computer name, or it may be CONFIG in the case of the special network-based master policy file, CONFIG.POL. If you're working with Windows 95 on a network, you can place a master policy file on a network server where the user logs on. Windows 95 looks on the server for the file named CONFIG.POL and uses this file if it exists.

Policy files can reside just about anywhere; however, on a client/server network, the usual locations are the NETLOGON directory of a Windows NT Server, or the PUBLIC directory of a NetWare or IntranetWare server. You can set up Windows 95 to look for policy files on your local PC hard disk, too.

Check out Chapter 9 for the full lowdown on system policies.

Backup for a rainy day: *.DA0

Every time Windows 95 starts successfully, it makes an automatic backup copy of SYSTEM.DAT and USER.DAT. The backups go by the name SYSTEM.DA0 and USER.DA0 (that's a zero and not the letter O at the end), and they live in the C:\WINDOWS directory (or whatever you've named it). If you turned on user profiles, then Windows 95 backs up the current user's USER.DAT to USER.DA0 in the directory C:\WINDOWS\PROFILES\username every time the user successfully logs on to Windows 95. If Windows 95 senses at startup that the main DAT files are seriously damaged, it copies the DA0 files over the DAT files in an effort to use the "last known good" Registry.

"Now wait a minute," those of you who pored over Chapter 2 may be saying, "Why the heck did we go to all the trouble of understanding how to back up the Registry if Windows 95 does it for us, automatically?" Here's why:

- You often need to make a Registry backup at times in addition to just when Windows 95 starts. Windows 95 only creates the DA0 files once per work session, when Windows 95 starts up.

- Windows 95 doesn't back up the settings for every user, just the current one, if you're using user profiles to allow multiple people to log on to the same PC with different settings.

- Windows 95 puts the DA0 files on the same disk and in the same directory as the primary DAT Registry files. Lose that disk to hardware failure, and you lose your automatic backups as well as your primary Registry files. (Things are a little better if you're on a client/server network and using user profiles because a copy of the USER.DAT file resides on a network server.)

- Windows 95's definition of a "successful" start is very lenient.

This last bulleted item needs some elaboration. As long as your operating system can start and load its primary device drivers, it *thinks* that it has started successfully. An unsuccessful start is one where Windows 95 can't even get out of bed and you never see the graphical desktop at all. Another kind of unsuccessful start is one where you tell Windows 95 not to load the main device drivers and to start itself in so-called *Safe Mode, Command Prompt Only.* (The graphical Safe Mode start, as opposed to the command prompt only start, is considered to be successful by Windows 95 — contrary to some Microsoft documentation!)

The point to remember here is that a successful start from the standpoint of Windows 95 doesn't mean that your Registry is okay. You may have a serious problem — for example, you may not be able to right-click any icon without getting an error message — but Windows 95 thinks everything is ducky as long as it can load the video and disk drivers properly. So, Windows 95 blithely copies the DAT files to the DA0 files — which now have the same Registry problems that your DAT files have. Your insurance policy has expired.

Backup for a very rainy day: SYSTEM.1ST

Take a gander at the root level of your boot hard drive. One of the files you should see is SYSTEM.1ST, which is the SYSTEM.DAT version that Windows 95 first builds when you (or a hardware manufacturer) install the operating system for the first time.

You can delete SYSTEM.1ST without affecting Windows 95's ability to run, but we suggest you leave this file in place. If you ever find your back up against the wall so hard that it hurts, you can use SYSTEM.1ST to replace SYSTEM.DAT. This approach is a major pain because the original SYSTEM.DAT doesn't have any of the settings for software that you installed after installing Windows 95 itself, but restoring SYSTEM.1ST may be better than not being able to boot Windows 95 at all. After restoring SYSTEM.1ST, you have to reinstall all your application programs to get this file back to where it needs to be.

Windows 95 doesn't create a USER.1ST file after you install the operating system — we're not exactly sure why — so don't waste your time looking for it!

Flotsam and jetsam: Other backup files

You may run across several other Registry backup files with mysterious suffixes. For example, you may find the following files in the C:\WINDOWS directory (or whatever you named the main Windows 95 directory on your PC):

- ✔ **SYSTEM.NU3** and **USER.NU3** are Registry backups that Symantec Norton Utilities creates when you install the program. These files don't change with every successful restart of Windows 95. Symantec documentation advises that you can safely delete these files after you create a set of rescue disks.

- ✔ **SYSTEM.NAV** and **USER.NAV** are copies made by the Symantec Norton AntiVirus (NAV) installation program. Again, these files don't change after you install NAV. As long as you're backing up your Registry regularly, you can delete these files.

- ✔ **SYSTEM.PCA** and **USER.PCA** get created by (you guessed it) Symantec PCAnywhere. The advice from the previous bullet applies.

Other programs are likely to create their own Registry backups for safety's sake. As long as you have a solid plan in place for making Registry backups (see Chapter 2), you probably don't need these files after you make your first "known good" backup. These files can take up a lot of space (10MB on one PC we saw).

Registry-Related Files Not Part of the Registry

You find a certain number of Registry-related files floating around on your hard disk, and we mention them here even though they're not technically part of the Registry.

*.REG

Files with the REG suffix may exist in almost any Windows 95 directory. These special-format text files usually contain partial or full Registry back-ups created with REGEDIT's export command, or application-specific instructions for modifying the Registry during a program installation. You can also use REG files as a convenient way to copy Registry changes to multiple computers. However, REG files are dangerous! If you double-click one by accident, you modify the Registry. We show you in Chapter 11 how to prevent such accidents.

*.INF

Files with the INF suffix, most of which reside in the hidden directory C:\WINDOWS\INF, include instructions for installing new hardware devices and programs. These INF files can modify the Registry, and they do so when you install hardware and software. In one sense, INF files aren't quite as dangerous as REG files because the usual behavior after you double-click an INF file is for Windows Notepad to open the file for editing. Right-click an INF file and choose Install, however, and you're likely to modify the Registry as well as move some files around. In another sense, INF files are even more dangerous than REG files, because INF files can delete Registry keys and values while REG files cannot.

Chapter 12 offers more meat on the subject of REG and INF files.

*.INI

Chapter 1 discusses the fact that Windows 95 still uses Windows 3.x-style INI files for certain operating system settings, such as the location of the swap file (an overflow file Windows 95 uses when it's short on RAM). These files, WIN.INI, SYSTEM.INI, and CONTROL.INI, live in the C:\WINDOWS directory and may be modified by control panels. Because Microsoft didn't move every possible system setting from these INI files into the Registry, backing up INI files whenever you back up the Registry is a smart choice. (We know, we talk forever about backing up the Registry in Chapter 2, but it bears repeating.)

REGEDIT

The Registry Editor, REGEDIT.EXE, typically resides in C:\WINDOWS, although you can put it anywhere you want. The help files, REGEDIT.HLP and REGEDIT.CNT, reside in C:\WINDOWS\HELP. Chapter 4 deals with the Registry Editor.

SHELLICONCACHE

The file SHELLICONCACHE (no suffix) in the C:\WINDOWS directory enables Windows 95 to display desktop icons more rapidly by keeping them all in a single file. When Windows 95 needs to display your desktop, it can get all the icons it needs from SHELLICONCACHE and doesn't have to hunt around for the icons in their various source files. This file is Registry-related because Windows 95 builds it from information contained in the Registry. However, Windows 95 doesn't rebuild the file every time it restarts.

If you're having display problems, such as the wrong icons appearing on the desktop or Control Panel icons appearing all black, you can force Windows 95 to rebuild SHELLICONCACHE with the information contained in the Registry. You can also force a rebuild if you change the icon settings specified in the Registry, for example, with REGEDIT. Here's how to rebuild the file:

1. **In Explorer, copy SHELLICONCACHE to a safe place (such as a diskette or a temporary hard drive directory).**

2. **Select Start⇨Shut Down⇨Restart the computer? and click Yes.**

3. **Hit the F8 key when the computer reboots to display the boot options list.**

4. **Choose Safe Mode, Command Prompt Only.**

   A Microsoft tech memo suggests you choose Safe Mode, but we respectfully disagree. Safe Mode can play havoc with your desktop icons, taskbar settings, and Explorer settings; whereas Safe Mode, Command Prompt Only leaves all this stuff alone.

5. **At the DOS prompt, type the following commands to delete SHELLICONCACHE (don't forget the trailing period in each command):**

```
ATTRIB -H SHELLI~1.
DEL SHELLI~1.
```

6. **Give your computer the three-finger salute, Ctrl+Alt+Del.**

   Let Windows 95 restart normally.

7. **Choose Start⇨Sh<u>u</u>t Down⇨<u>R</u>estart the computer? and click <u>Y</u>es.**

   Let Windows 95 restart normally a second time.

You can now see the newly created SHELLICONCACHE in Windows Explorer, and your icon problems should disappear. After using your PC for a few days, you can delete the backup copy you made in Step 1. Note that some books and magazine articles recommend that you rebuild the file in order to decrease the size of SHELLICONCACHE. In our experience, it's equally likely that rebuilding the file increases its size (on our test system, the file grew from 723K to 895K), so don't be surprised!

Chapter 6

What You Must Know to Use REGEDIT: The Registry's Logical Structure

In This Chapter

▶ Discovering the Registry's three basic components

▶ Why some Registry branches point to other branches

▶ Using string, DWORD, and binary values

▶ Getting comfortable with the Registry map

Knowing where the Registry files are is important for backup and recovery purposes. However, if you want to sail the Registry seas with Microsoft's REGEDIT Registry Editor program, you need to spend a little time with the navigational charts describing the Registry's internal structure.

In Chapter 5, we explain that the Registry is contained in two files, SYSTEM.DAT and USER.DAT (and maybe an optional third file called a "policy" file, like CONFIG.POL). These files represent the Registry's *physical structure* — files that you can back up or copy. However, you can't view or edit these files individually. They're stored in an encrypted binary format, and you need a special viewer to decode their contents.

That viewer, the Registry Editor, integrates the files into a single "logical" structure — much as a typical e-mail program integrates its various data files (MAILBOX.PST and MAILBOX.PAB, for example) and presents them in a logical structure (inbox, outbox, sent items, address book, and so on). You need to understand the e-mail program's logical structure in order to use the program, and you need to understand the physical structure (the files) in order to make backups for safekeeping.

The Basic Components

The Registry's organizational structure is like an upside-down tree (see Figure 6-1). Just like a real tree consists of branches, twigs, and leaves, the Registry consists of *branches, keys,* and *values.* The whole complicated Registry tree becomes much more comprehensible after you look at the basic components, so that's a great place for us to start. We look at how the branches and twigs actually fan out a little later in the chapter.

If you only find three different basic kinds of components, how many total components exist in a typical Registry? All Windows 95 Registries have six branches. Glenn's Registry has about 18,000 keys and about 33,000 values. For a complete list of each of these keys and values, see Appendix E of this book. (Just kidding!) Seriously, don't let the big numbers concern you. A botanist can understand everything that's important about a tree without knowing where every single branch and leaf goes.

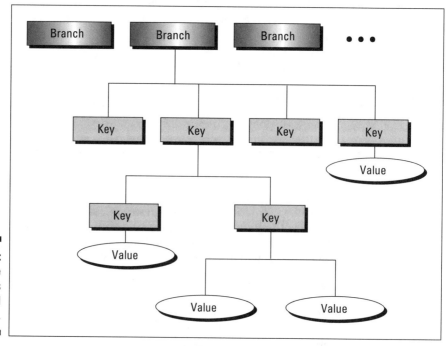

Figure 6-1:
The
Registry is
an inverted
tree.

Branching out

The Windows 95 Registry has six *branches,* listed in Table 6-1, which are the main organizational structures at the top level of the Registry's inverted-tree layout. You can't delete a branch itself, although the Registry Editor typically lets you delete most of a branch's contents.

These branches all start with the quirky notation "HKEY." The "H" stands for *handle,* and so these branch names act as *handles* to particular *keys* (specific Registry entries) that you need to view, change, or delete. People who program in C++ tell us that this notation makes perfect sense; we take their word for it. You can pronounce HKEY different ways; we've heard "high-key" and "aytche-key," but we tend to prefer "hickey," which brings back fond memories of high school.

Table 6-1	Windows 95 Registry Branches	
Branch Name	*Is an Alias for*	*Abbreviation*
HKEY_LOCAL_MACHINE		HKLM
HKEY_CURRENT_CONFIG	HKLM\CONFIG\number	HKCC
HKEY_CLASSES_ROOT	HKLM\SOFTWARE\Classes	HKCR
HKEY_USERS		HKU
HKEY_CURRENT_USER	HKU\username	HKCU
HKEY_DYN_DATA		HKDD

Unlike a real tree, where each main branch is completely separate and distinct from every other main branch, some of the Registry branches are really nothing more than *aliases,* or pointers, to specific keys located elsewhere. These particular keys are chosen because you use them frequently, so using a shorthand notation to refer to them is handy.

For example, you often spend time in *HKEY_CLASSES_ROOT* (abbreviated *HKCR*) because it contains information about how different file types behave. Saying (and writing) *HKCR* is easier than *HKLM\SOFTWARE\Classes.* The two locations contain the same exact information, though. Check it out yourself. If you're familiar with the Registry Editor, look at *HKCR\AVIFile* and compare it to *HKLM\SOFTWARE\Classes\AVIFile.*

So, *HKCC, HKCR,* and *HKCU* just point to other places in *HKLM* and *HKU.* The "core" branches *HKLM* and *HKU* actually contain the entire Registry contents, except for *HKDD,* which is a special branch that Windows 95 recreates in memory at each startup. (For the curious, the physical file SYSTEM.DAT contains *HKLM,* and the physical file USER.DAT contains *HKU.*)

The strategy of using aliases is confusing at first, but it's really just for convenience. You'll appreciate aliases as you begin spending some time with the Registry. Unfortunately, no visual clues tell you which branches are aliases and which aren't; you just have to get familiar with Table 6-1 (or keep this book near your computer!).

Figure 6-2 provides a more graphical way of looking at the Registry's branch organization.

Getting keyed up

A Registry *key* is nothing more complex than a location for storing data. A key is a container, and it can contain a *value* (see next section), another key, or any number of both. You can think of a key as similar to a directory or folder in Windows Explorer. In fact, the icon that the Registry Editor uses is the same for both keys and directories. Or, if you like the upside-down-tree analogy, a key is like a twig or a branch. (In fact, a Registry branch is just a key that happens to live at the top organizational layer.)

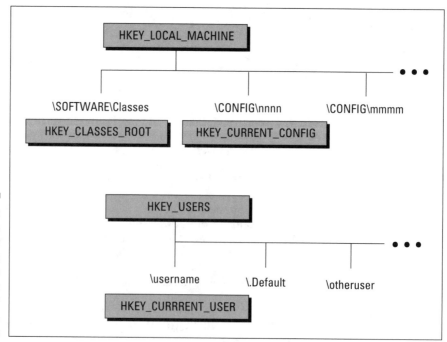

Figure 6-2:
Some Registry branches point to keys on other branches.

Many keys (the ones with a + sign to their left in the Registry Editor window) contain other keys, or *subkeys* — in the same way that you can call certain directories on your hard disk *subdirectories* if they reside inside another directory. In this book, *subkey* and *key* really mean the same thing, just in a slightly different context. If we talk about a subkey of Key X, we're just emphasizing the subkey's location in the logical structure.

Complete key names can be fairly long because a key can reside several subkeys deep in the Registry structure. We separate keys in a complete key name with the backslash character (\), and we usually abbreviate the branch name according to Table 6-1. Even so, we sometimes have to break complete key names across lines, in which case we try to make the break at a syllable so you don't have to worry about any invisible spaces at the end of the first line in which the key name appears. Just remember not to include the hyphen.

Adding value

Most of the useful information in the Registry resides in values. A *value* is like a leaf on a tree branch: You can't have anything else hanging off a leaf. It's the end of the line in the organizational chain: "The chlorophyll stops here." Or, if you prefer to think of keys as directories in Windows Explorer, then think of values as individual files.

The Registry uses three types of values: *string*, *binary*, and *DWORD*. In all cases, the maximum size of a single value is 64K. (In fact, the sum of the sizes of all the values within a single key can't exceed 64K. Not that you ever bump into that limitation, but it's worth knowing so you understand why the Registry often points to a file's location on disk, instead of just including all that file's information in a Registry key.)

String

The string value type (indicated by a tiny icon in the value pane's Name column containing the letters *ab*) usually contains text, but may also contain numbers. (As with many aspects of the Registry, the rules are sometimes soft and slow rather than hard and fast.) String values almost always appear enclosed in double quotes. Here are some examples:

```
"C:\WINDOWS\SYSTEM"
"Oh Canada, My Canada"
"1024"
```

Binary

The binary value type (indicated by a tiny icon containing some 1's and 0's) is usually for numeric information. True binary numbers contain nothing but ones and zeroes, but binary values in the Registry show up as hexadecimal numbers (base sixteen) where each digit ranges from 0 to F. (A is the same as decimal 10, B is the same as 11, and so on.)

It takes a two-digit hexadecimal number to make a *byte*. For example, *FF* represents a byte with the decimal equivalent of 255, and *00* represents a byte with the decimal equivalent of 0. In the Registry, binary values appear as a succession of two-digit, single-byte hexadecimal numbers separated by spaces. Figure 6-3 shows a Registry key containing a single string value (Default) and a bunch of binary values. A binary value can have as few as 4 bytes and as many as 65,536.

Figure 6-3:
The "ab"
icon
denotes a
string value,
and the
"011110"
icon
denotes a
binary or
DWORD
value.

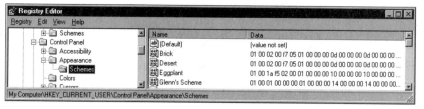

Sometimes you may want to convert quickly between hexadecimal, decimal, and binary values. For example, if you see in the Registry the hexadecimal value *d7 0a*, you probably don't immediately know that this value is the same number as decimal 55,050 or binary 1101011100001010. (If you *do* immediately realize this, then you'll have no trouble finding gainful employment in the computer industry, should you desire it.) Fortunately, you have a nifty conversion tool in the form of the Windows 95 calculator! Open the calculator and choose View⇨Scientific to unveil the "hidden" calculator in Figure 6-4. You can enter a number in any format you like, and then instantly convert it by clicking the Hex, Dec, or Bin radio buttons (we skip Oct because the Registry doesn't use octal numbers).

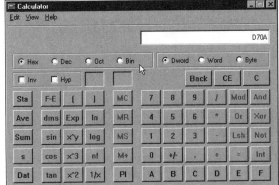

Figure 6-4:
The
Windows 95
calculator,
in its high-
tech mode.

DWORD

The DWORD value type (which uses the same icon as the binary value type) is also almost always for numeric information. You can think of DWORD as a special kind of binary value that's always the same size: four bytes. That translates to eight hexadecimal digits. (*DWORD* is short for *double word*. In computer lingo, two bytes make a word, so a double word is four bytes long.)

The Registry format for a DWORD value is "0x" plus eightnumbersallrun-together plus the decimal equivalent of the number in parentheses — like this:

```
0x00000001(1)
```

Caveat Registry user: Just because a value has four hexadecimal bytes doesn't mean it's a DWORD value. It can be a plain-old binary value that happens to be the same length as a DWORD value. (Hey, we just write about this stuff, we don't invent it.)

Chapter 4 offers specific information on how to create, change, and delete Registry keys and values with the Registry Editor.

Gross Registry Anatomy

This section presents an overview of the primary branches and keys near the upper levels of the Registry's inverted-tree organization. We could go several layers deeper in this section, but we won't because doing so would take a hundred pages, no one besides a chronic insomniac would read it, and 99 percent of the material would be info that you'll never need to know about the more obscure keys.

We think giving you a fairly high-level view here and then zeroing in on particular keys as necessary in chapters where they're relevant is a more sensible approach. So, we don't cover every subkey in the pages that follow. If you're the kind who really wants or needs to know what *HKLM\Enum\ Root\Ports\0000\LogConfig* means, you just have to wait for *Windows 95 Registry For Trivia Buffs* (5,700 pages, publication date indeterminate).

HKEY_LOCAL_MACHINE

The *HKLM* branch stores every bit of information that has to do with the computer, rather than any particular computer user. Some people assume that because *HKLM* contains the word "machine," it's all about hardware information. Not so! *HKLM* contains lots of software information, too. Whatever details about the computer that apply to every user of the computer go in this branch. These details include hardware devices, device drivers, installed programs, and user-independent program settings.

HKLM also contains the keys that form aliases to *HKCC* and *HKCR* (as you can see from Table 6-1). *HKLM* is definitely one of the two Big Kahunas of Registry branches, *HKEY_USERS* being the other.

HKLM contains at least seven major keys, as described in the following sections.

Config

Here's where the Registry stores the details of one or more hardware configurations. Most Windows 95 PCs don't use multiple configurations. For more on the subject, see "HKEY_CURRENT_CONFIG" later in this chapter.

Enum

This key contains information about every piece of hardware that's ever been installed on your PC since Windows 95 was originally installed. The organization of the subkeys under *HKLM\Enum* is a little hard to follow, but it roughly parallels the computer's bus structure. The precise fields that the Registry stores for each device varies by device and manufacturer, but Figure 6-5 shows a fairly typical entry. You can expect to see the manufacturer's name, product model number, and certain configuration options. Much of this information feeds *HKDD\Config Manager\Enum* at startup to build the Plug and Play "hardware tree" (see Chapter 7).

Hardware

This key has a very logical name, but you just don't seem to use it for anything. It has some minimal serial port information, but the Registry maintains a lot more serial port data elsewhere. We can only guess that

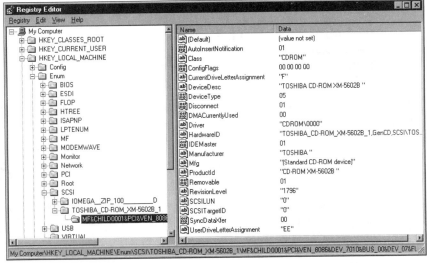

Figure 6-5:
An *HKLM*
entry for an
internal
CD-ROM
drive.

somebody at Microsoft started working away on this key and then got
reassigned to a different project. Or perhaps the key supports applications
designed to work with Windows NT, which makes extensive use of
HKLM\Hardware.

Network

Here the Registry stores various information about your machine's network
account: the previous user to log on, and (potentially) a whole bunch of
details about your computer's network setup that apply regardless of who
logs on. Note that the Novell network client leaves all this stuff in the
Registry even after you remove the client. (Who says Novell and Microsoft
are all that different when it comes to software practices?)

Security

This key contains details about the security provider for a networked
Windows 95 PC — that is, what computer on your network is in charge of
authenticating user logons.

Software

This key is *huge,* both in size and in importance. It contains all the user-
independent settings for Windows 95 and every application installed on
your machine. The Windows 95 settings mostly reside in *HKLM\SOFT-
WARE\Microsoft\Windows\CurrentVersion,* shown in Figure 6-6, a key we visit
several times later in this book.

The general layout is for the software vendor name to appear immediately under *HKLM\SOFTWARE* and the product keys to appear beneath the vendor keys. One exception is the key *HKLM\SOFTWARE\Classes,* which contains all the information about different file types (*.TXT, *.BMP, and so on) and which forms the alias branch *HKCR*.

When you install a new application program, the installation procedure typically creates new Registry entries in *HKLM\SOFTWARE* as well as in *HKCU\Software*. The latter location is for user-specific and user-modifiable settings.

System

Here's where Windows 95 stores the machine-specific details it needs in order to get out of bed in the morning, that is, to boot. *HKLM\System* typically contains a single subkey, *CurrentControlSet,* which in turn contains *Control* and *Services*.

✔ *HKLM\System\CurrentControlSet\Control* contains a wide variety of startup information, including your computer's network name, the order in which to look for types of network connections, what multimedia resources your PC has to offer (printer settings and so on).

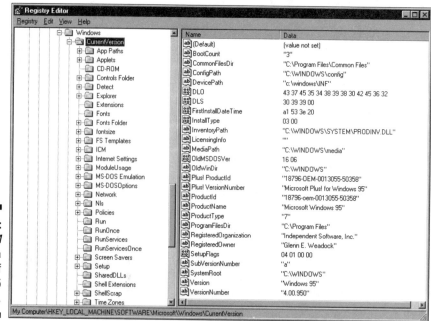

Figure 6-6:
HKLM
stores a
wealth of
Windows 95
settings.

> ➤ *HKLM\System\CurrentControlSet\Services* also contains a wide variety
> of settings, including system resources used (interrupts, memory
> ranges, and so on), hardware device drivers, modem initialization
> settings, and network communication settings. The *Class* subkey and its
> contents are especially important.

HKEY_CURRENT_CONFIG

Most people don't use the feature, but Windows 95 offers something called
hardware configurations or *hardware profiles* (you see both terms in
Microsoft documentation). The idea is that you can define multiple sets of
devices to use in different circumstances.

The classic example is the notebook user who has a docking station at the
office. Such a user would typically define two hardware configurations:
docked and *undocked*. The docked configuration can specify a different
display adapter, printer, and network connection than the undocked configuration. Using the System control panel's Device Manager tab, you can
navigate through the "hardware tree" on a device-by-device basis and
specify which hardware configurations any given device should belong to.

So how does Windows 95 choose a hardware configuration at startup? It
tries to do so automatically, by sniffing around to see what hardware seems
to be connected. If it can't determine which configuration to use, then
Windows 95 asks you to pick one from the list. At that point, Windows 95
copies over the appropriate key from *HKLM\Config* into *HKCC*. *HKCC* is then
an alias that points to *HKLM\Config\000n,* where *n* is a number identifying
the hardware configuration (see Figure 6-7). You rarely, if ever, need to
modify *HKCC* directly.

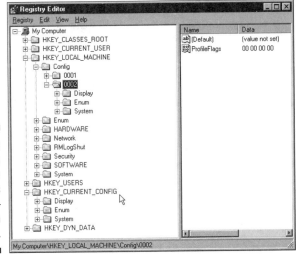

Figure 6-7:
HKCC has
the same
contents as
*HKLM\Con-
fig\0002* on
this PC.

In our experience, hardware configurations can be finicky. Sometimes you can just clear a check box in a Device Manager property sheet to disable a device in a given configuration; other times, you have to right-click the device and delete it from the hardware tree. Some hardware settings don't automatically migrate from one configuration to another, so you end up making these settings twice. The list of quirks goes on and on. This technology seems a little half-baked right now, and we suggest that you not use multiple hardware configurations unless you have a compelling reason — such as a notebook that sometimes uses a docking station.

HKEY_CLASSES_ROOT

The existence of *HKEY_CLASSES_ROOT*, which is an alias to *HKLM\SOFTWARE\Classes*, testifies to Microsoft's dedication in making Windows 95 work with Windows 3.*x* programs. The Windows 3.*x* version of the Registry, the Registration Database, allows programs to "register" file type associations (TXT with Notepad, BMP with Paintbrush, and so on) as well as the drag-and-drop behavior for those file types. If you install a Windows 3.*x* program under Windows 95, the Windows 3.*x* program tries to modify the Registration Database; but through a little sleight-of-hand, it actually modifies the Registry branch *HKCR*. Compatibility, at least at the Registry level, is guaranteed.

We don't mean to imply that Windows 95 doesn't extend the uses that Windows 3.*x* made of the old Registration Database. It does. *HKCR* not only matches up data file suffixes with the appropriate programs, it defines what icons the different file types use; what commands you can apply to file types by right-clicking; and what the files' property sheets look like. *HKCR* also keeps track of the unique numbers that identify each different file type under Windows 95: the *Class IDs*.

Class IDs pop up all through the Registry, especially in *HKCR*. A Class ID, or CLSID for short, is a unique number, such as {25336920-03f9-11cf-8fd0-00aa00686f13}, that identifies an object in Windows 95. *Objects* include data file types (such as a PowerPoint slide show) and program modules (such as the code that displays and processes dialog box radio buttons). Class IDs take the form of a 16-byte number enclosed in curly braces, each byte expressed by a two-digit hexadecimal number, arranged in a 4-2-2-2-6 grouping.

Ignore the first key? You'd be an asterisk it

The asterisk key *HKCR** contains object settings for every sort of Windows 95 file, regardless of type. (You may have guessed this from the common use of the asterisk as a wildcard character in file specifications like "*.*" and so on.) *HKCR** typically contains the single subkey *shellex*, which stands for *shell extensions*.

The Windows 95 graphical user interface goes by the generic name *shell,* meaning that the user interface presents the operating system to you and defines how Windows 95 looks and acts. A shell *extension* is an add-on that defines how the shell deals with a certain file type. That definition appears in the Registry key *shellex,* through its two subkeys, *ContextMenu-Handlers* and *PropertySheetHandlers.* Context menus are the pop-up menus that appear when you right-click files, and property sheets are the tabbed windows that appear when you right-click files and choose Properties.

When you add programs that can work with every file on your computer, such as WinZip, Norton Navigator, or Novell IntranetWare, *HKCR*\shellex* may receive new entries. These new entries are *Class IDs* that usually point to a chunk of program code. The program code handles the job of providing context menu and property sheet choices.

Top half (extensions)

After the *HKCR** key, roughly the top half of all the entries under *HKCR* are *file extension* keys (see Figure 6-8). An entry appears here for every file extension (or suffix, like TXT or BMP) that Windows 95 or a Windows 95 program has defined on the PC.

Many of these file extension keys contain nothing more than a single string value defining the related *file type* key, which appears in the bottom half of *HKCR.* For example, if you look at the *HKCR\.bmp* key, it contains a single value with the data *Paint.Picture* that refers to a later key, *HKCR\Paint.Picture,* which has all the details on how Windows 95 handles such a file.

Why divide up *HKCR* into two halves with extension keys in the top half that point to file type keys in the bottom half — why not just put all the relevant details in the extension key instead of creating an additional file type entry in the bottom half? For example, why not just put all the information under *HKCR\.bmp* instead of having that key just point to *HKCR\Paint.Picture*? For good reason: What if you want the same program to handle a file type that has two different extensions? For example, you want .JPG and .JPEG files to open the same program, as well as HTM and .HTML files to open another program. Using *HKCR's* organizational structure, you can simply have two entries in the file extension key group (the top half) that both point to a single entry in the file type group (bottom half). For example, *HKCR\.JPG* and *HKCR\.JPEG* both point to *HKCR\jpegfile,* and *HKCR\.HTM* and *HKCR\.HTML* both point to *HKCR\htmlfile.*

One detail about file types must appear in the top half, though, and that's what to do if you right-click the desktop and choose New⇨*filetype.* Windows 95 needs to create the file with the proper file extension, so you may find a subkey called *ShellNew* under the file extension key in *HKCR.*

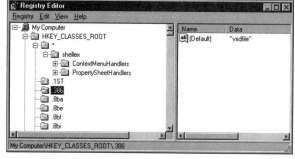

Bottom half (file types)

The bottom half or so of *HKCR* contains file type keys, such as *HKCR\Paint.Picture* or *HKCR\jpegfile*, which the file extension keys in the top half of *HKCR* point to. The file type keys are where all the action is in terms of defining how different file types behave. Figure 6-9 shows an example of the bottom half of *HKCR*.

Some of the subkeys you may find beneath a file type key include the following:

- ✔ *Shell*. Here's where context menu actions unique to a file type appear. For example, *HKCR\filetype\shell\open\command* contains the actual command to run when you double-click a file of the specified *filetype*.

- ✔ *Shellex*. If the file type's property sheet is to display special choices not included on the generic property sheet, here's where the Registry references the Class ID for the program code that provides the property sheet enhancements. The Registry may also include references to a special *ContextMenuHandler* or *DragDropHandler* if special software is required to handle context menus and drag-and-drop desktop behavior.

- ✔ *DefaultIcon*. Here's the location of the icon Windows 95 displays for files of a specified type.

A very special key in *HKCR*'s bottom half, *HKCR\CLSID*, contains a comprehensive list of every CLSID on the system. Underneath each specific CLSID entry, you typically find a subkey named *InProcServer32*, which (again typically) contains the path and filename for the chunk of program code that Windows 95 associates with that CLSID. *HKCR\CLSID* is important to know about if you're troubleshooting problems with a certain kind of file because this key can point you to the DLL file on disk that handles that kind of file.

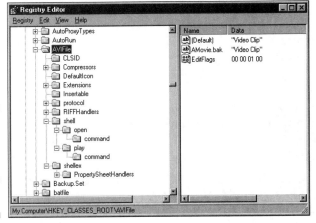

Figure 6-9:
File type
information
in the
bottom half
of *HKCR.*

HKEY_USERS

Any Windows 95 application setting that can conceivably vary from one user to another on a PC set up to support multiple users goes into the *HKU* branch. *HKU* is one of the two Big Kahuna Registry branches, along with *HKLM.*

This key contains at least one primary subkey, *.Default*, and it may contain one additional subkey named after the currently logged-on user. *HKU* never shows more than that, although on a Windows 95 PC with user profiles enabled, the number of different users that can have Registry accounts is practically unlimited.

The contents of each subkey immediately under *HKU* share the same organization and include the following keys, among others.

AppEvents

Here's where the Registry stores user preferences for the sounds that play when specific Windows 95 events occur. (Chapter 17 contains a cool tip to create your own sound events for any program you want.)

Control Panel

Many user-specific control panel settings live here, but watch out. Not all control panel settings can vary from user to user. Remember that modifying control panel settings from a control panel is always better than using the Registry Editor.

Network

Recent and persistent connections to network resources are stored here. (A "persistent" connection is one that Windows 95 tries to reestablish at each logon.)

Software

Here's where all the user-settable and user-specific preferences for installed software applications reside. When you install a new application, it makes entries here and in *HKLM\SOFTWARE* (where settings exist that don't vary from user to user).

HKEY_CURRENT_USER

On a PC set up to support multiple users, *HKCU* contains the subset of settings in *HKU* that pertain to whoever logged on at the Windows 95 startup prompt. *HKCU* is an alias that points to *HKU\username*, where *username* is the logged-on user's name. If your PC hasn't been set up to support multiple users, then *HKCU* contains the same information as *HKU\.Default* — the "default" user is the same as the current user all the time.

HKEY_DYN_DATA

HKDD (the *DYN* is for *dynamic*, or changing) stores information about active hardware, including real-time device status information and performance statistics. It's a unique Registry branch in several ways. Its home isn't USER.DAT or SYSTEM.DAT; *HKDD* lives in main memory, or RAM (Random Access Memory). Windows 95 rebuilds *HKDD* anew at each restart. *HKDD* is also a read-only branch; it's the only Registry branch that neither users nor programs can write information to.

HKDD contains a ton of information, but two keys are of particular interest.

Config Manager

Most of the interesting stuff in *HKDD* resides in the *Config Manager* key. The Configuration Manager is the part of Windows 95 that handles Plug and Play devices — the newer generation of computer components that Windows 95 can set up automatically.

HKDD\Config Manager has a single subkey, *Enum*, under which each active device appears in a key having a unique eight-character identifier. The *HardwareKey* value under a specific device's key in *HKDD\Config Manager\Enum* points back to a key in *HKLM* where the Registry stores static, unchanging details about the device. (No point storing the stuff twice.)

Plug and Play is an important enough subject to get its own chapter. We take a little closer look at the structure of *HKDD\Config Manager\Enum* in Chapter 7.

PerfStats

HKDD\PerfStats contains a huge number of keys and values that point to subprograms that calculate system performance statistics (hence "PerfStats"). It's kind of fun to highlight one of these keys in REGEDIT — say, *StatData* — and hit the F5 key from time to time in order to update the display. For example, *KERNEL\CPUUsage* varies almost every time you hit F5.

Trying to get a good picture of your computer's performance by looking at *HKDD\PerfStats* with REGEDIT is a bit like measuring the acreage of a tropical beach by counting grains of sand. *PerfStats* was never meant for people to look at, just programs — programs like System Monitor, the performance-monitoring accessory that comes with Windows 95.

Some of you may be thinking, "Hey Glenn and Mark, why on earth did Microsoft choose to throw all this stuff into the Registry? Why not just let System Monitor check all the statistics itself, in its own private memory space? And by the way, we're really enjoying your book so far."

First, thanks very much. Second, we asked ourselves the very same question, and the answer appeared to us in a blaze of artificial light when we were writing the part in Chapter 4 about remote Registry editing. Microsoft set up the Registry so that, in the right circumstances (Chapter 4 describes them), an administrator or technician can tinker with another user's Registry over a network link. Now, being able to monitor a remote network PC's performance would probably be equally handy, right? And if all that performance data is in the Registry, then the System Monitor accessory can get to the user's performance data over the network by using the same mechanism that the Registry Editor uses to get to the remote Registry.

After you make a little mental connection like this one, you realize that some pretty clever folks were at work on this stuff, after all. Not that we'll let Microsoft off the hook for some of the boneheaded maneuvers it made in other areas, of course, but we like to give credit where credit is due.

Chapter 7

Making Hardware Work with Plug and Play

*C*ritics of the "Wintel" (Windows plus Intel) PC architecture frequently point to the spastic dance that PC users have had to perform in order to install new hardware. The process can involve manually switching jumper settings or switches on hardware devices, changing arcane-sounding settings like IRQs and DMA channels, and (more often than not) waiting long stretches on the phone for help from overworked and undertrained technical support staff. Before Windows 95, if you came up victorious in the battle to install a sound card into a PC that contained a CD-ROM drive, internal modem, and network card, a bearded old guru would venture down from the Himalayas to award you your fourth-degree computer toolbelt.

Although we tend to focus on its role as a software settings database, the Registry stores all your PC's hardware information, too. Whenever you use the System control panel's powerful Device Manager to fine-tune or troubleshoot hardware settings, you're actually using a Registry editor. The Registry also makes possible one of Windows 95's key advantages (or frustrations, depending on how well it works for you on any given day): *Plug and Play*. Knowing how the Registry and Plug and Play work together may come in handy when you decide to add or remove a device from a Windows 95 PC.

Defining Plug and Play

The ambitious Plug and Play specification tries to set up computer hardware automatically, using the Windows 95 Registry as a central hardware database. The Plug and Play specification was introduced in 1994 by Intel and saw its first commercial application in 1995 when Microsoft released Windows 95.

Plug and Play is a broad hardware and software specification that requires support at all hardware and software levels within a PC — not just the operating system, but also the BIOS (Basic Input/Output System), device driver software, and device hardware. Plug and Play's two main goals are to make setting up your PC hardware as painless and automatic as possible and to reduce support costs for company PCs. It achieves these goals by automatically managing PC hardware resources — such as IRQs, upper memory addresses, and base I/O addresses. If you want to know more about how these resources work, check out the sidebar entitled "The department of PC resources" in this chapter.

The department of PC resources

PC devices, such as network cards, mice, sound cards, and so on, require certain *resources* in order to work. These resources may include one or more of the following:

- **Interrupt number.** A number from 0 to 15 that specifies a dedicated "hot line" to your PC's central processing unit (CPU). If a device needs the computer's attention, the device sends a message to the CPU on its interrupt line.

- **Base I/O address.** A memory range that a device uses to move data between itself and your computer. Four-digit numbers in hexadecimal form express the start and end addresses, for example, 0300 to 030F.

- **Upper memory range.** A chunk of memory between 640K and 1024K that devices use for different and unique purposes. Not all devices need upper memory, but many (such as video cards) do. Like base I/O addresses, four-digit hexadecimal numbers list the range boundaries, such as CC00-CDFF.

- **DMA (Direct Memory Access) channel.** A number from 0 to 7 assigned to devices

that can move data around in memory without bothering your CPU. Sound cards and diskette drives use DMA channels.

The general rule (and you'll find occasional exceptions) is that no two devices can use the same resources. So, when you add a new device to your PC without the aid of Plug and Play, you have to figure out what resources the device needs and assign resources to the new device without overlapping with any existing device's resources.

This resource assignment process can be maddeningly difficult, especially considering that many devices are finicky about which resources they can use. For example, a network card may only work with interrupts 5, 10, or 11. If each of these interrupts is already in use, then the installer must change a setting for an existing device in order to free up an interrupt that the network card can use. However, one change may require another, and another. (Ever stand dominoes in a row and tip the first one?)

Taking the drudgery out of hardware installation

Plug and Play tries to shift the responsibility for assigning computer resources from you to your operating system. When you add a new device and
restart Windows 95, Windows 95 looks at all devices connected to the
machine (a process called *enumeration*) and notices the newcomer.

After recognizing new hardware, Windows 95 swings into action to set up
the new device. Windows first displays the New Hardware Found dialog box,
which asks you whether you want to install software for the device. Normally, you click Yes and insert the diskette or CD-ROM that contains the
manufacturer-supplied device driver software. Windows 95 automatically
installs the device driver software onto your hard drive, assigns any necessary resources to the device based on what the Registry says is available,
and updates the Registry's *HKLM* key to contain essential device information. Everything happens behind the scenes, and you don't have to know an
interrupt from a hole in the ground.

Rating the Plug and Play standard

Plug and Play hasn't gained acceptance as rapidly as Intel and Microsoft
hoped. Part of the problem is that Plug and Play devices must coexist with
non-Plug and Play devices (called *legacy* devices). Another difficulty is that
the success of Plug and Play requires the participation of so many different
players in the PC industry.

Configuration data in the Plug and Play system is shared and communicated
among hardware, the BIOS (Basic Input-Output System; see the "Motherboard BIOS" section later in this chapter), and the operating system. For a
full Plug and Play system, all three levels must support the Plug and Play
standard. Windows 95 provides the operating system support; PC and
device manufacturers must provide hardware support; and BIOS vendors
must provide BIOS support. Getting all three groups to work in concert
hasn't been easy.

Microsoft seems committed to the Plug and Play standard, continuing it into
Windows 98 and bringing it to Windows NT 5.0. Even though Plug and Play
doesn't work perfectly, it does make adding and changing hardware easier
than before. If you follow the tips in the next section, Plug and Play works
even better.

Optimizing Plug and Play

You may run into some snags while adding or changing hardware components, but you needn't sit idly by like a potted plant if Plug and Play doesn't work smoothly for you. The following three tips address some of Plug and Play's more common quirks.

Motherboard BIOS

The *BIOS* (Basic Input/Output System) is an important part of your computer system; it's a set of software code that lives on a chip plugged into the computer's motherboard. At startup, the BIOS looks around your PC and makes a list of the devices it finds, which it then hands off to Windows 95. If your PC's motherboard BIOS conforms to the Plug and Play standard, then Windows 95 can change the BIOS settings itself to make room for new hardware. For example, if your motherboard has a serial port set up to use a particular interrupt, Windows 95 can instruct the BIOS to use a different interrupt for that serial port to accommodate other devices on the system.

Windows 95 can also run with motherboards that don't have a Plug and Play BIOS. In that case, however, Windows 95 must work around the BIOS settings for motherboard devices, which limits its flexibility. That is, Windows 95 can't change resource assignments for motherboard devices in order to accommodate new devices. Also, without a Plug and Play BIOS, Windows 95 can't reliably and automatically detect new Plug and Play hardware, leaving you with only the old method of assigning resources manually ("Plug and Pray").

Periodically check with your PC's manufacturer for BIOS upgrades. These upgrades usually take the form of a program that you can download from the manufacturer's Web site and run once to update the BIOS code. (BIOS code upgradeable in this manner is called *flash BIOS.*) Plug and Play tends to work more reliably with more recent BIOS versions. For example, if the list of devices that the BIOS finds at startup is incorrect, so is the Registry. You can typically see your current BIOS version at the top of the screen when you first power up your PC.

Adapter BIOS

Plug-in circuit boards, or cards, typically come with their own specialized BIOS. If a card's BIOS conforms to Plug and Play, then Windows 95 can change any card setting — interrupt, memory address, and so on — without requiring you to perform PC surgery, flip switches, or juggle jumpers.

When you buy new cards for your PC, by all means get ones that are compatible with Plug and Play — compatibility doesn't cost any more — but also ask whether you have the option to *override* Plug and Play and set up the card manually. You'll be frustrated when Plug and Play doesn't work correctly and you can't get around it. In the worst case, you may be faced with changing resource assignments for every other device in your PC in order to get the card working. Before doing so, we suggest that you trade in the card for one that permits manual resource assignments.

Department of redundancy department

Many times, Windows 95 automatically detects new hardware the first time you install it — and then keeps on redetecting it every time you boot. This situation occurs most commonly with a parallel printer.

To troubleshoot the problem of redundant detection of the same parallel printer over and over, follow these steps:

1. **Run REGEDIT.**

2. **Export the Registry key** *HKLM\Enum\Lptenum,* **just in case.**

   This key is where Windows 95 stores information about Plug and Play devices connected to parallel ports. (If you're unsure as to how to export a Registry key, please see Chapter 4.)

3. **Delete the** *HKLM\Enum\Lptenum* **key and then restart your machine.**

4. **Install the software (that is, the device driver from the manufacturer's diskette or CD) when Windows 95 autodetects the printer.**

   You shouldn't see the New Hardware Found message again.

How Does the Registry Store Plug and Play Data?

What does all this discussion of Plug and Play have to do with the Registry? Everything! The only way a system like Plug and Play can possibly work is if your PC stores all hardware details in one place, so the Plug and Play configuration manager can keep track of all your devices and resources. In Windows 95, that one place is the Registry. In this section, we take a closer look.

HKDD: A special branch

The *HKey_Dyn_Data* branch, *HKDD* for short, is where the list of currently active hardware resides in the Registry. Each device has its own unique eight-character identifier (like C11B3738) in this Registry branch. Windows 95 rebuilds *HKDD* each time it starts, which explains why *HKDD* never appears in any full Registry backups. No need to store *HKDD* if Windows 95 re-creates it at boot time anyway.

HKDD lives entirely in random access memory (RAM), unlike the other disk-based Registry branches. The reasoning behind storing *HKDD* in memory is to enable Windows 95 to respond quickly to what the Plug and Play specification calls *dynamic reconfiguration events:* in English, somebody plugging something in, or somebody unplugging something. If *HKDD* were disk-based, Plug and Play would be much slower in responding to system changes.

Another unique aspect of *HKDD* is that it's a read-only branch. You never use REGEDIT to modify a key in *HKDD*. In fact, you can only make changes to *HKDD* indirectly, by first modifying *HKey_Local_Machine (HKLM)*. The changes that you make to *HKLM* via the System control panel or the Add New Hardware wizard show up at the next reboot in *HKDD*. That's why you usually have to reboot Windows 95 after you add a new device for the first time: Windows 95 needs to rebuild *HKDD*.

HKLM's supporting role

Because *HKDD* lives in RAM and is read-only, you can only make changes to the hardware configuration indirectly, through *HKLM*. So why not just leave all the hardware information in *HKLM* and do away with *HKDD*? We already mentioned the first reason: *HKDD* lives in RAM, so it's fast. Putting *HKLM* in RAM would eat up a lot more memory than necessary because much of the information in *HKLM* doesn't pertain to Plug and Play. Heck, much of the stuff in *HKLM\Enum* may pertain to hardware that's not even in your PC anymore. On the other hand, *HKDD\Config Manager\Enum* contains information about the currently active devices only.

Rather than duplicate all the information about each device in both *HKLM* and *HKDD*, the currently active list in *HKDD\Config Manager\Enum* points back to the appropriate key in *HKLM\Enum*, where the Registry stores most of your device details. Here's a quick example.

The key *HKDD\Config Manager\Enum\C11B3738* includes the values shown in Figure 7-1. The Problem value is all zeroes, which indicates that the device seems to be working okay as far as Windows 95 can tell, and doesn't conflict with any other device. Notice the HardwareKey value, ROOT\NET\0000. This value points us to the subkey underneath *HKLM\Enum* where you can get more details on the device.

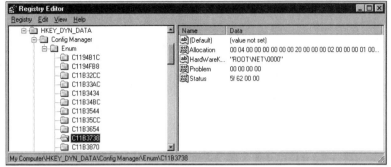

Figure 7-1:
An active
device's
key and
values in
*HKDD\Config
Manager\
Enum.*

So if you mouse on over to *HKLM\Enum\Root\Net\0000*, as shown in Figure 7-2, you see a lot more information about the device. The DeviceDesc value shows that the device is an Intel EtherExpress PRO/10+ network interface card. The Mfg value confirms that Intel makes the device. The presence of the ForcedConfig value suggests that the user told Windows 95 what settings the card needs to use, instead of letting Windows 95 figure them out on its own.

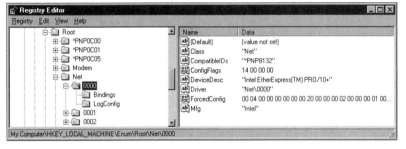

Figure 7-2:
More
information
about the
device
resides in
HKLM\Enum.

Don't waste time looking for hardware information in *HKLM\HARDWARE.* Yes, finding device information in this key does seem logical, but this key is practically empty.

If you had to use REGEDIT to view the details of your PC's hardware configuration — or to change the hardware by adding, removing, or reconfiguring a device — you'd go rapidly bananas. Fortunately, Windows 95 provides two much friendlier programs for accessing the hardware information in the Registry: the Device Manager and the Add New Hardware wizard. The Device Manager, in particular, is worth a closer look.

Swinging from the Hardware Tree

The so-called *hardware tree,* which you display by clicking the Device Manager tab in the System control panel, is a graphical representation of *HKDD\Config Manager\Enum* and various subkeys under *HKLM\Enum*. You're looking at the Registry's hardware database here, but instead of REGEDIT, you're using a much more comprehensible tool (see Figure 7-3).

Figure 7-3:
The Device
Manager,
where the
Registry's
hardware
information
becomes
under-
standable.

In theory, on a completely Plug and Play computer, you never need to look at Device Manager. Windows 95 juggles interrupts and memory addresses for each device in the system, and you've no reason to care what they are. However, not all devices work with Plug and Play. You may have to use Device Manager to assign such devices the PC resources that Windows 95 cannot figure out on its own.

Mousing around Device Manager

The hardware tree in Device Manager expands and contracts just like directories in Windows Explorer: click + to expand a branch, click – to collapse it. After you've expanded a branch to show its individual entries, you can double-click any entry to see its property sheets.

The radio buttons at the top of the Device Manager display enable you to look at your hardware tree from two perspectives: devices grouped by type or devices grouped by hardware connection. The second view matches up more closely with how the Registry organizes devices in *HKLM\Enum,* but most people find the first view a little easier to understand.

Double-click the Computer icon at the very top of the hardware tree, and you get a very handy display with two tabs: View Resources and Reserve Resources. The View Resources tab enables you to see the current device resource assignments by category, as shown in Figure 7-4. (We explain these categories in the sidebar entitled "The department of PC resources" in this chapter.) The Reserve Resources tab enables you to tell Plug and Play not to assign a particular resource because you intend to add a device in the near future that needs it — or because you use a device (such as a scanner card) that Windows 95 doesn't auto-detect, doesn't appear in the hardware tree, and must use a particular hard-wired interrupt number.

Figure 7-4:
Viewing all
resource
assignments
in one
handy
window by
using the
View
Resources
tab.

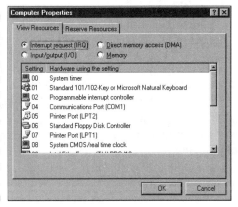

Identifying device conflicts

Device Manager uses three different identifiers to alert you to potential problems:

✔ **A black exclamation point on a yellow field** indicates a device in a problem state — for example, a device using a resource that conflicts with another device, or a device that uses different resources than Windows 95 thinks it uses. This identifier doesn't necessarily mean that the device isn't working, just that it *may not* work, and if it does work, some other device probably doesn't.

✔ **A red "X" mark** indicates a device that's physically present in the system but that is disabled and has no protected-mode device driver loaded. The device may still function, but usually does not.

✔ **A blue "i" on a white field** indicates a device for which you've forced manual settings instead of letting Windows 95 use automatic settings. That is, the Use Automatic Settings check box on the device's Resource property sheet is cleared. The device probably works just fine, but Windows 95 loses some flexibility in configuring other devices because this manually set device is "locked in" to one specific set of resources.

On a 100 percent pure Plug and Play system, you don't see any of these identifiers. However, their presence doesn't mean that you have a conflict — just that you need to take a closer look at the device and its settings, and perhaps change those settings as described in the next section.

Manually assigning resources

You may need to override Windows 95 and its Plug and Play system and manually assign PC resources to a device, in the following situations:

✔ The device doesn't conform to Plug and Play, and Windows 95 doesn't detect the device as one of the 1900 or so devices it knows about already. (Incidentally, Windows 98 knows about even more.)

✔ The device is Plug and Play compatible, but for some reason, Windows 95 can't figure out how to set it up correctly. (This problem often happens with internal modems.)

✔ The device's documentation advises you to make different resource settings than Windows 95 makes on its own.

The Device Manager is very helpful when you set about assigning resources to a device by hand, and you should not use the Registry Editor for this purpose. Editing *HKLM\Enum* with REGEDIT is very rarely necessary.

To manually assign resources in Device Manager, follow these steps:

1. **Expand the hardware tree by clicking + beside the desired device.**

2. **Double-click the device in question and then click the Resources tab (see Figure 7-5).**

   The Resources tab shows all the resource assignments.

Figure 7-5:
The
Resources
tab for a
specific
device
enables you
to edit the
device's
Registry
settings.

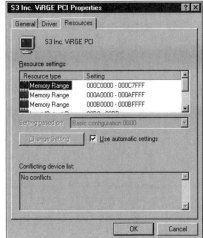

3. **Uncheck the Use Automatic Settings check box.**

   Unchecking this check box tells Windows 95 not to try autoconfiguring the selected device.

4. **Try the predefined configurations listed in the Setting Based On field by choosing them from the list and watch the Conflicting Device list for any messages indicating a resource conflict.**

5. **After you find a configuration that works with no conflicts, click OK.**

   If a configuration doesn't work out, click the Change Setting button and specify the resources individually, again watching for conflict information. You can use trial and error here, or take your cue from the device manufacturer's user manual.

The Registry usually contains a value called *ForcedConfig* for each device that you configure manually. Search the Registry for this value and look at the devices that show up. The more devices with forced configurations, the less flexibility Windows 95 has in configuring new devices because Windows 95 can't change the resources assigned to devices with forced configurations — those assignments are locked down. So, for example, if a new device can only use interrupt 10 and an existing device has a forced configuration that specifies interrupt 10, Windows 95 can't change the existing device to a different number and give 10 to the new device.

Sometimes you don't want to change a device's settings; you just want to shut the durn thing off. Plug and Play can make shutting off a device difficult by automatically redetecting the device at each reboot and adding it to the hardware tree. The trick to forcing Windows 95 not to assign resources to a device is to double-click the device in the hardware tree, choose the device's General property sheet, and clear the check box that reads Original Configuration (current). (In the OSR2 version of Windows 95, you *check* a box that says `Disable in this hardware configuration`.)

Device Manager is a handy way of editing the Registry's hardware database, but it doesn't necessarily show you every device that connects to your PC. It doesn't show printers, for example; that's the job of the Printers control panel. Device Manager also may not show devices that piggyback on other devices, like the tape drives that hook up to a diskette controller cable.

Part III
Rigging for Sea: Registry Customizing

"All right, which one of you clowns has been editing the network Registry?"

In this part . . .

This part is where the fun starts! In Part III, you apply your Registry knowledge to customize Windows 95 to your liking.

With the help of a slick, but nearly unknown, utility called Batch Setup, you can customize the Windows 95 installation program so that the initial Registry looks the way you want it to look. These details are of special interest if you manage Windows 95 on a network.

This part covers customizing Windows 95 for individual computers as well. You can add values to the Registry by using the System Policy Editor in order to restrict what a user can do with Windows 95. By using user profiles, in which multiple users have their own version of the Registry's user-specific half, USER.DAT, you can customize a single Windows 95 computer for several different users.

Finally, this part explains ways you can tune the Registry to squeeze more speed out of Windows 95, change how the operating system looks, and improve how the Registry handles file types.

Chapter 8

Customizing SETUP for Easier, Cleaner Installations

In This Chapter

▶ Putting a network server to work as a Windows 95 installation device

▶ Creating a custom script to control how a user's first Registry is built

▶ Designing a special network account to automatically install Windows 95

*Y*ou can customize the Registry many ways, but one of the slickest is by creating your own custom Windows 95 installation program. In this way, you can modify the Registry's initial contents when a new user installs Windows 95 over a network.

Many people never actually install Windows 95. It appears like a neatly set table on most new PCs, along with a cornucopia of bundled software. Why, then, do so many network managers ruthlessly reinstall Windows 95 afresh whenever a new PC hits the office? Why toss that cornucopia aside and spill perfectly good fruit all over the floor?

Two words: consistency (each machine is set up the same way) and convenience (technicians have fewer changes to make on each machine). This chapter summarizes how you can customize the Windows 95 SETUP program to create a customized Registry that's closer to the way you want it from day one. As it turns out, you can preset most of the Registry changes that this book discusses! Very cool!

If you don't use Windows 95 on a network or if you do but you don't have to worry about taking care of anyone's PC but your own, you can sail right around this chapter.

A LAN with a Plan

Using a network server to install Windows 95, instead of using an installation CD-ROM, is a great example of how to put your Local Area Network (LAN) to productive use. Anyone who must support or troubleshoot multiple Windows 95 PCs knows that the job becomes far easier when all the PCs are set up the same way — fewer troubleshooting variables to consider. And by reinstalling Windows 95 according to a customized script, a technician knows that many necessary options are set correctly in advance, so running around with a notebook full of changes to make on each system is no longer necessary.

These advantages are so compelling that many LAN managers don't care that new PCs usually come with Windows 95 preinstalled. These managers get a new PC, connect it to their network, and then install Windows 95 from their network server, wiping out whatever was already on the system. (Doing so is one way to deal with that pesky problem of some PCs running earlier versions of Windows 95 and some running more recent versions.)

Installing Windows 95 from a central network server works really well in situations where you have a hodgepodge of PC makes, models, and components. Because you're actually running Windows 95 SETUP on each computer, SETUP can still autodetect PC hardware and make adjustments for the fact (for example) that Bob has a 3Com network card while Jane has a Madge network card. The customized script that you create to guide the SETUP program doesn't mandate that everyone's initial Registry looks identical — that doesn't work, for example, with the two different network cards — only that *certain* settings are identical on each PC, such as the time zone, standard networking language, and so on.

If you're lucky enough to work in a network where everyone does have pretty much the same hardware, you may want to consider *disk cloning* as an alternative to a scripted, network-based setup (see the "Cloning around" sidebar).

Copying the Files

The first step in creating a network-based setup procedure is to install a complete copy of the Windows 95 source files onto a server, called a *distribution server,* from which a new user can install Windows 95 across the network onto the workstation. (The server "distributes" Windows 95 to the network users, who use the server as the source for their Windows 95 files instead of the Windows 95 CD-ROM.) Depending on which version of Windows 95 you have, two methods exist: the elegant but elusive NETSETUP program and the brute force file copy technique.

Cloning around

Disk cloning programs, such as GHOST from Innovation Software and DriveImage from PowerQuest, enable network managers to crank out carbon-copy hard drives that include not only Windows 95 but also any desired Windows 95 applications.

The procedure is to set the master PC's hard disk up exactly as you want it, then copy the disk's *image* (its entire contents, including hidden and system files) to the distribution device. The distribution device can be just about anything: a removable cartridge drive, CD-ROM, or network drive. Then, instead of running the normal Windows 95 SETUP procedure for each PC, you use the cloning software to make an exact copy of these master files from the distribution device to the user's hard drive.

This technique only works if all the PCs have the same basic hardware, and you can guess the reason: The Registries on each cloned hard drive are identical. If your network PCs are all very similar, disk cloning may be faster and easier than setting up a network-based setup with a custom script. Cloning a hard drive over a network can take as little as ten minutes.

Cloning software costs around $600 for an unlimited-use, single-technician license.

Warning: Microsoft's official policy is not to support cloned Windows PCs, so if that's a

problem for you or if you have several different PC types on your network, you may have to choose network-based setup instead.

If you choose to go with the network-based setup, here are the basic steps to follow:

1. **Copy the Windows 95 files from a workstation to one or more servers, from which users can later install Windows 95 over the LAN.**

2. **Create a customized script to make Windows 95 SETUP configure the Registry settings that you want to apply to every user.**

   You can use an easy, graphical utility called Batch Setup to create this script, and you can optionally customize the script further by hand if you're feeling your technical oats.

3. **Create a special network account for users to log onto when they're ready to install Windows 95.**

   You can set up the account to run the Windows 95 SETUP program automatically, immediately after logon.

For more information on setting up scripts, check out the sections "Son of a BATCH" and "INFinite Wisdom" in this chapter.

The strange case of NETSETUP

Unlike Windows 3.1, which used the SETUP /A command ("A" for "administrative") for this purpose, Windows 95 has a separate program called NETSETUP.EXE to prepare a server for what Microsoft terms *server-based setup*. If you have the retail Microsoft Windows 95 CD-ROM, full version or upgrade version, you can find NETSETUP and its associated files on the Windows 95 CD-ROM's ADMIN\NETTOOLS\NETSETUP directory.

Using NETSETUP is very simple. You can run it from a Windows 3.1 machine or a Windows 95 machine, and you don't even have to install the program on your hard disk. Just pop the CD-ROM in and follow these steps:

1. **Navigate to ADMIN\NETTOOLS\NETSETUP on the CD-ROM by using Windows Explorer.**

2. **Double-click NETSETUP.EXE to display the screen in Figure 8-1.**

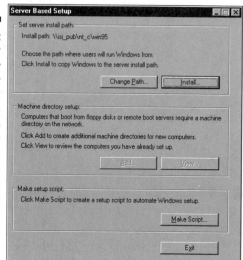

Figure 8-1: NETSETUP is a handy tool for creating a distribution server — but not for OSR2 (the 4.00.950B version, as displayed in the System control panel).

3. **Click the Change Path button to specify the server name and where on the server you want to put the Windows 95 files, and then click Install.**

4. **NETSETUP asks you where your users will run Windows 95; normally you choose Local Hard Drive.**

    Skip the option to create a default script for automating the installation; we do that later in this chapter (see the section "Son of a BATCH") with a much better program, BATCH.EXE. At this point, NETSETUP copies the files from the CD-ROM over the network onto the server.

In the last year or so, we've seen many OEM versions of the Windows 95 CD-ROM that exclude NETSETUP, and Microsoft refuses to put the program up on its Web site (unlike just about every other Windows 95 utility). Furthermore, the program has disappeared from the latest version of Windows 95, OSR2 (version 4.00.950B on the System control panel). A Microsoft tech note even states, without any explanation or justification, that you can't use NETSETUP with OSR2, and that's true (we tried). What's going on here? Did Microsoft suddenly decide networks aren't important anymore?

We suspect that the exclusion of NETSETUP from some OEM versions is all part of Microsoft's somewhat strange behavior regarding OSR2. You can't buy OSR2 except with a new PC, so we're guessing that Microsoft doesn't want you to be able to install OSR2 over a network — even on a fresh, empty hard drive. That's a real disservice to business customers — but fortunately you can work around it by using the brute force approach that the next section discusses.

A brute force approach

If you find yourself with the OSR2 version of Windows 95, you can simply copy the contents of the CD-ROM to a network directory. This approach isn't as efficient as NETSETUP, but it does seem to work. You need to log on to the network as an administrator or supervisor, create a directory that's available to everyone on the network, and use Windows Explorer to copy the CD-ROM files to that network directory. You (or your network manager) may want to flag the files read-only after you copy them over to the server, so that network users can't accidentally delete or modify them.

Note that this "brute force approach" isn't supported by Microsoft and could conceivably put you into technical violation of the OSR2 license agreement. (We're not lawyers, we're technicians, and we don't pretend to understand all the Microsoft legalese.)

Customizing the Install

After you comfortably nestle the Windows 95 files onto your network server, you can exert some control over how future workstation installations from that server behave — specifically, how they create the user's initial Registry.

The really cool part of a server-based installation — and the part where we can start tinkering with the prenatal Registry — is creating a special text file known as the *default batch script*. This script kicks in whenever a user runs the Windows 95 SETUP program (SETUP.EXE) from the server directory, and it controls the Windows 95 installation process.

If SETUP.EXE is the car, the default batch script is the driver. The default batch script's name is MSBATCH.INF, and it lives in the same network directory where you've installed the Windows 95 files. (The file is present whether you customize it or not.)

You customize the batch script with a friendly, graphical utility called Batch Setup (BATCH.EXE). If you want to get *really* fancy, you can even manually customize the MSBATCH.INF file that Batch Setup creates. The next two sections deal with both procedures, the easy one first.

Son of a BATCH

Don't use the clunky old 1995 version of Batch Setup that comes with the Windows 95 CD-ROM and the Windows 95 Resource Kit. (If Batch Setup is already present on your system, run it and choose Help⇨About; if the version number is 1.0, you have the old one.) Use the 1996 version, which is version 2.0 — or, as we affectionately call it, *son of a BATCH*. You can get version 2.0 free from www.microsoft.com/windows/software/servpak1/batch.htm on the World Wide Web.

Install Batch Setup version 2.0 after downloading it by putting the file in its own directory, double-clicking it to extract the files, and then double-clicking the SETUP.EXE installation program. Follow the on-screen instructions.

After you install Batch Setup, running it is simply a matter of navigating with Explorer to the directory where you installed it and double-clicking the BATCH.EXE file. You then see the main screen as shown in Figure 8-2.

You can type in the various identifying names in the top half of the screen. Usually, you just type in the Company name and leave the rest blank. Whatever you leave blank, SETUP asks the user to provide during the Windows 95 installation.

Figure 8-2: Batch Setup's main screen.

The wide button in the center that says Click Here to Retrieve Settings from the Registry is very handy if you want to set up new PCs similar to the PC on which you're running Batch Setup. If you click this button, Batch Setup scans your Registry for the following settings and adds them to the default batch script:

✔ Network clients, protocols, and services

✔ Video resolution settings

✔ Installed printers

✔ Time zone

✔ Security settings

✔ User name, computer name, and description

The three buttons in the Setup Options area at the lower left enable you to make a variety of Registry settings in advance. For example, the Network Options button brings up the tabbed dialog box in Figure 8-3, where you can essentially preset the user's Network control panel. The other buttons enable you to control other aspects of the SETUP program's behavior, including which optional Windows 95 accessories it installs on the user's PC.

When you're finished making your presets, click Done and save the INF file in the same directory where you've copied the Windows 95 files. The default name is BSETUP.INF, but you need to change this name to MSBATCH.INF when you place the file on the network server. If you want to open your INF file in Notepad to take a look at it, go right ahead; it's just a text file. The next section suggests some ways you can change this core installation script to really jump through some hoops, Registry-wise that is.

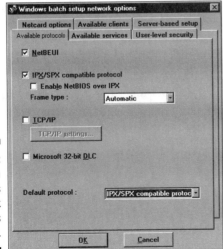

Figure 8-3:
Batch
Setup's
Network
Options
dialog box.

On the Windows 95 CD-ROM, in the area ADMIN\RESKIT\SAMPLES\SCRIPTS, several sample batch scripts reside that illustrate different approaches to a network installation. You can't open the sample scripts directly by using BATCH.EXE; they're commented excerpts for illustration purposes only. View them with Notepad.

If you use the original version of Windows 95 in your shop and you want to include Microsoft's Service Pack 1 update (as we recommend), get the Service Pack administration files, either from the SP1 CD-ROM or Microsoft's Web site. Microsoft explains how to modify MSBATCH.INF to include the SP1 fixes and updates, and how to install the SP1 files onto your distribution server.

The scripts that Batch Setup creates seem to work fine on a distribution server with the Windows 95 OSR2 files. However, because Microsoft doesn't seem interested in supporting server-based setup with OSR2, test your batch script carefully before rolling it out to your full user population.

INFinite wisdom

The MSBATCH.INF file is remarkably powerful when it comes to customizing your Windows 95 installation, and Batch Setup is just a starting point. You can use MSBATCH.INF to put just about any setting you want into the user's initial Registry!

Skip this optional section if it looks as though the graphical Batch Setup program offers all the initial customization you need or want.

If you want to go beyond what Batch Setup lets you do, all you need is your favorite text editor (Notepad works fine), a little patience, and (optionally) a copy of the *Microsoft Windows 95 Resource Kit* — specifically, Appendix D, which provides a wealth of INFormation. Here, we give you a taste of how you can customize the Registry with MSBATCH.INF, so you can decide if the benefits are worth the bit of work required to figure out the ins and outs of INF files.

We also discuss INF files in Chapter 12. They're an extremely versatile method for creating and distributing Registry modifications. INF files can do a lot of the same things as DOS batch files — copy files, delete files, rename files, and so on — with the bonus that INF files can directly modify the Registry and the Windows INI files. INF files also have their own special grammar rules, as you'll see in a minute.

MSBATCH.INF is just one example of an INF file, and it's a great introduction to the subject — partly because the graphical Batch Setup program gives you a head start, and partly because you don't have to do anything special to activate it. Windows 95 SETUP processes MSBATCH.INF automatically when SETUP runs. (You activate other INF files by right-clicking them and selecting the Install option.)

When you start with Batch Setup, you create a basic MSBATCH.INF file to modify (see the earlier section, "Son of a BATCH"). Then, you can run Notepad and open the file to customize it beyond what Batch Setup permits.

The general procedure for customizing MSBATCH.INF is to create an [Install] section heading, including the square brackets, and then add a line such as

```
Addreg=custom.Registry
```

immediately under it. The "Addreg" part has to appear as shown, but the section name after the equals sign can be pretty much whatever you want as long as it's unique within the INF file. This line tells Windows 95 that you have a section in your INF file called [custom.Registry] that contains Registry settings to add. For example, if you want the standard Windows 95 SETUP program to disable the Network Neighborhood icon, you add the following section, below the [Install] section:

```
[custom.Registry]
HKCU,Software\Microsoft\Windows\CurrentVersion\Policies\Ex-
    plorer,"NoNetHood",3,00000001
```

(Notice the way the previous setting works: to turn the Network Neighborhood icon off, you set a "00000001" value, meaning "true," for the "No Network Neighborhood" policy value.) Similarly, you can set up the Registry to forbid file sharing with the line

```
HKLM,SOFTWARE\Microsoft\Windows\CurrentVersion\Policies\Net-
    work,"NoFileSharing",2,"1"
```

In fact, you can place just about any sort of restriction that you can create later with the System Policy Editor, which Chapter 9 discusses in detail.

The general format for a Registry entry in an INF file looks a little odd, but it's not all that complicated. The general format goes like this:

```
Branch, Key, ValueName, ValueDataType, ValueData
```

where *ValueDataType* is 0 for string (*ValueData* in quotes), 1 for binary (*ValueData* expressed as hexadecimal numbers separated by commas), 2 for string (but don't replace an existing value if one exists), and 3 for binary (but don't replace an existing value).

Be very careful when modifying MSBATCH.INF or any INF file, and test your work on a machine you don't care about before making any INF file available to others. INF files are just as powerful as the Registry Editor itself!

Adding the Finishing Touches

Whether you just use the graphical Batch Setup program to create MSBATCH.INF or you take things a step further and edit MSBATCH.INF to include specific Registry settings you want, you can make upgrading PCs to Windows 95 easier for network users by using your customized INF file. Just include the setup command and batch script name in a network logon script. Here's the procedure:

1. **Set up a special user account (say, UPGRADE) for the user who wants to install Windows 95 to log onto.**

2. **Define appropriate security for the UPGRADE account (no changing passwords, rights to the server with Windows 95 on it, and so on).**

3. **Create a logon script and associate it with the UPGRADE user.**

For a Windows NT Server network, your logon script may include lines like the following, where *server**distshare* specifies the server computer directory containing the Windows 95 source files and *sourcedrive* is a drive letter mapping for that directory:

```
net use sourcedrive \\server\distshare
sourcedrive:setup sourcedrive:msbatch.inf
```

For a Novell NetWare or IntranetWare network, the logon script lines look something like this:

```
attach server/distshare:
map sourcedrive:server/distshare
sourcedrive:setup sourcedrive:msbatch.inf
```

The preceding generic script lines are just a guide. If you create a logon script for the Windows 95 UPGRADE account, you need to be familiar with script creation rules for your particular network type and need to try the script on a test PC before unleashing it to the general network population. A mistake in a logon script can create problems for anyone who logs onto the UPGRADE account.

You can create different INF files for different groups of users. For example, BOSS.INF and TECHIE.INF can be used where we've used MSBATCH.INF in the generic script lines. (Technically, you don't even have to specify MSBATCH.INF as long as you use that filename, because SETUP looks for it specifically, but we include the name for clarity.) You could even set up different network upgrade accounts that call the different INF files.

You can use the general procedure we just described for many other purposes besides installing Windows 95. For example, you can create different network accounts that automatically install other application programs. You can even use a system-wide logon script to distribute Registry modifications via INF and REG files, as we look at more closely in Chapter 12.

Chapter 9

Customizing System Policies for Security and Safety

In This Chapter

▶ Discovering the policy file, the Registry's optional third component

▶ Finding out what policies can do for both stand-alone and networked PCs

▶ Policy file caveats

*W*indows 95 doesn't have its own true security system in the sense that Windows NT does. However, Windows 95 does have a feature to restrict and customize user access to the operating system and programs. This feature is the *policy file,* and if you use it, it becomes an integral part of the Windows 95 Registry.

Windows 95 Casual Security

The U.S. Department of Defense assigns security ratings to computer operating systems. However, its ratings are highly complex and highly boring. If we were to assign our own rankings to PC operating systems in terms of how tough they are to break into, we'd come up with a scale like Table 9-1.

Table 9-1	Weadock/Wilkins Security Rankings
Operating System	*Security Equivalence*
Windows NT	Bulletproof vest
Windows 95	Wooden barrel
Windows 3.*x*	Wool sweater
MS-DOS	Speedo swimsuit

A wooden barrel doesn't stop bullets, but it does stop rocks and tomatoes, and that's why we refer to Windows 95 security as *casual security*. You can't prevent a professional cracker from breaking into a Windows 95 system, but you can make messing things up fairly difficult for the average computer user.

This chapter is about building the wooden barrel, which Windows 95 calls the *system policy file*. After you create it, the system policy file becomes part of the Registry.

If you don't let anyone else use your PC and you don't give a hoot about restricting access to Windows 95, sail right around this chapter. On the other hand, if this subject interests you but you haven't read Chapters 4 and 6 covering the Registry structure, now is a good time to look 'em over.

Many people believe that system policies only work on a network. While you can usually find system policy files on network servers, you can also use a policy file on a stand-alone PC. You can also use the System Policy Editor program as a Registry editor to impose access restrictions and to customize the desktop, even without creating a policy file.

System policies don't represent the only security mechanism available if you use Windows 95 in a network environment. Industrial-strength client/server networks, including Windows NT Server and Novell IntranetWare, have their own extensive security systems to protect shared programs and data files. We don't consider server-based security in this book except as it applies to system policies, but if you're interested in the subject, check out *Small Business Networking For Dummies* (Weadock, IDG Books Worldwide, Inc.), *Networking with NetWare for Dummies* (Tittel, Connor, and Fields, IDG Books Worldwide), or *Windows NT Networking For Dummies* (Tittel, Madden, and Follis, IDG Books Worldwide).

Finally, system policies can get fairly involved. If you're a network administrator who needs to use system policies for sophisticated access control, we suggest you read this chapter through once or twice to get the lay of the land; then hire a Windows 95 consultant with experience on your particular network to help you through the process.

"Policies" and Procedures

This section introduces the System Policy Editor, POLEDIT. POLEDIT is strong medicine. Before you start experimenting with it, make sure you have a current backup of your Registry and a current Windows 95 startup diskette (Chapter 2).

Installing the System Policy Editor

The Windows 95 setup program doesn't install the System Policy Editor, so you have to do so separately (but don't install it on every PC in a network, it's a dangerous utility!). You need the Windows 95 CD-ROM to install POLEDIT (or access to a hard drive or network directory that contains all the Windows 95 CD-ROM files). In the following procedure, we assume you're using the CD-ROM and that it's on drive D. Here's how to install POLEDIT:

1. **Pop the Windows 95 CD-ROM into the drive. If a Windows 95 installation screen appears, close it by clicking the close box.**

2. **Click Start⇨Settings⇨Control Panel and double-click the Add/Remove Programs icon.**

3. **Click the Windows Setup tab and then click the Have Disk button.**

4. **In the Copy Manufacturer's Files From text box, type**

   ```
   D:\ADMIN\APPTOOLS\POLEDIT
   ```

   Substitute your CD-ROM drive letter for D: in the above entry if you use something different.

5. **Click OK.**

   The dialog box in Figure 9-1 appears.

6. **Click the check box for the System Policy Editor; then click the Install button.**

   You see a fleeting message about shortcuts being updated, and then the Add/Remove Programs Properties dialog box reappears.

7. **Click OK in the Add/Remove Programs Properties dialog box.**

You're done! Piece o' cake. The System Policy Editor now appears when you click Start⇨Programs⇨Accessories⇨System Tools⇨System Policy Editor.

The Microsoft Office 97 Resource Kit comes with a more recent version of the System Policy Editor, which you should use if it's available to you. See the Office 97 Resource Kit documentation for installation instructions.

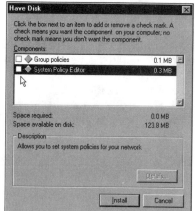

The two faces of POLEDIT

The System Policy Editor has two modes of operation:

- ✔ As a *Registry editor,* in which case you're directly editing the Registry of a local or remote computer — just as if you were using REGEDIT, although POLEDIT has a friendlier face. You don't create a policy file, but you do modify USER.DAT and SYSTEM.DAT. Your changes take effect after you exit POLEDIT.

- ✔ As a *policy file editor,* in which case you're creating or modifying a file with the suffix .POL. The POL file becomes part of the Registry after Windows 95 applies the file to USER.DAT and SYSTEM.DAT at the next startup, but nothing changes until then.

In order to use POLEDIT as a Registry editor, simply run the program and choose File⇨Open Registry. You can then double-click the Local User or Local Computer icon, make whatever changes you like, exit POLEDIT, and restart your computer.

Before you use POLEDIT as a Registry editor, read the rest of this chapter, especially the section titled "Gotchas."

In order to use POLEDIT as a policy file editor, run the program and choose either File⇨New File to build a new POL file, or File⇨Open File to read a POL file created earlier. You can then double-click the Default User or Default Computer icon (note the name changes), make whatever changes you like, and choose File⇨Save to store the modified POL file.

In policy file mode, the check boxes that appear when you set about making changes are normally grayed out, as shown in Figure 9-2. (They're either clear or checked when you use POLEDIT as a Registry editor.) The grayed-out check box simply means that the POL file that you're creating or editing doesn't change that Registry setting from its usual status. You only want the POL file to contain information about stuff you want to change, not stuff you want to leave alone (the file is much smaller and faster that way).

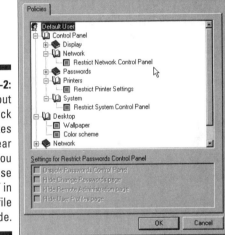

Figure 9-2:
Grayed-out
check
boxes
appear
when you
use
POLEDIT in
policy file
mode.

Okay, which POLEDIT mode should you use?

✔ On a network, where you probably want to make a bunch of settings that apply to every user (or at least to every user in a particular network group), you should use POLEDIT as a policy file editor. This way, you can do the work of defining your policy settings one time and then put that POL file up on a server where the file can apply to every user who logs onto the network.

✔ If you're working with several non-networked (stand-alone) PCs, use POLEDIT in its policy file mode. You can create a POL file that you can then copy to other PCs. All you have to do on the other PCs is place the POL file in the C:\WINDOWS directory (or wherever you like) and tell the Registry to look for it there, as described later in this chapter under the section "Single-user policies."

✔ If you're working with a single stand-alone PC, using POLEDIT as a Registry editor is probably more convenient because you're only concerned with one computer and you don't save yourself any effort by creating a POL file. If that single PC is set up for multiple users, how-ever, use POLEDIT in its policy file mode for the ability to specify different policies for each user.

A flock of user policies

As you can tell from the two icons that appear when you use POLEDIT in either Registry editing mode or policy file mode, two kinds of policies exist: user and computer. User policies apply to the USER.DAT file on disk, which is the *HKey_Users* branch in the Registry database. Figure 9-3 shows some of the user policies that you can set with POLEDIT.

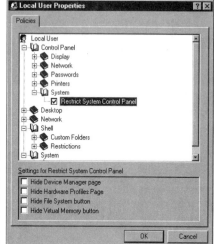

Figure 9-3:
Changing
user-
related
policies
with
POLEDIT.

In order to use system policies to control user settings, whether on a networked or non-networked PC, you must activate *user profiles*. Chapter 10 discusses user profiles in detail, so we won't duplicate the material here.

We don't have space to discuss each of the several dozen policies here. Most are self-explanatory, and the best way to get familiar with these policies is to experiment with them, anyway. As you click check boxes in the upper part of the System Policy Editor window, you may see more detailed settings in the lower part of the window. Here are the user policies that we recommend you look especially closely at:

- Restrict Network Control Panel
- Restrict Printer Settings
- Restrict System Control Panel
- Custom Folders
- Remove "Run" command

    ✔ No "Entire Network" in Network Neighborhood

    ✔ Disable Registry Editing Tools

    ✔ Only Run Allowed Windows Applications (don't use this one until
       you've read Chapter 14's section, "I Can't Reverse Restrictive Policies")

    ✔ Disable MS-DOS Prompt

A gaggle of computer policies

Computer policies apply to the SYSTEM.DAT file on disk, which is the
HKey_Local_Machine branch in the Registry database. Figure 9-4 shows
some of the computer policies that you can set with POLEDIT.

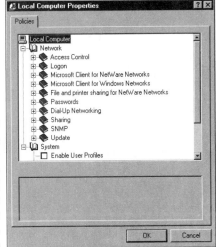

Figure 9-4:
Changing
computer-
related
policies
with
POLEDIT.

Here are some computer policies worth a gander:

    ✔ Require Validation by Network for Windows Access

    ✔ Require Alphanumeric Windows Password

    ✔ Minimum Windows Password Length

    ✔ Disable File Sharing

    ✔ Disable Print Sharing

    ✔ Enable User Profiles

A school of templates

The user and computer policies in the previous two sections all derive from the default policy *template file,* ADMIN.ADM, which you can find in the C:\WINDOWS\INF directory. However, you can use other template files to specify other policies, too. A template file is nothing more than a list of policies that you can set; the template provides the choices and knows which Registry keys to change as a result. For example, Microsoft supplies templates for Office 97 programs in its Office 97 Resource Kit (OFF97W95.ADM, ACCESS97.ADM, and so on).

Change the active template file within System Policy Editor by choosing Options⇨Template. Only one template can be active for editing at a time; however, you can use as many different templates as you want to create a single policy file. You can even write your own policy template files, but that's beyond the scope of this book; check out Chapter 15 of the *Microsoft Windows 95 Resource Kit* (Microsoft Press) for details.

Applying Policies to Networks, Groups, and Individuals

System policies can apply to everyone on a network, members of particular network groups, or individual users on networked or non-networked PCs.

System-wide policies

If you want a single policy file to apply to all users on a client/server network, Windows 95 makes life easy for you. Use the System Policy Editor to create a POL file with the settings you want and save the file with the name CONFIG.POL. (This special name is mandatory.) Where you copy the CONFIG.POL file depends on what sort of network you have:

- ✔ On a Novell network, place CONFIG.POL on the server in the SYS:PUBLIC directory.
- ✔ On a Windows NT Server network, place CONFIG.POL on the server in the NETLOGON share.

When any user logs onto the network, Windows 95 looks for the CONFIG.POL file in the predetermined standard location on the server. If Windows 95 finds the file, it automatically downloads a copy and applies the file to the user's Registry. Slick!

Group policies

If your network supports groups of users, you can assign policies on a group basis. To do so, you must install extra software on each user machine. Follow the instructions in "Installing the System Policy Editor" earlier in this chapter, but in Step 6, choose Group Policies instead of System Policy Editor. You can now choose Edit⇨Add Group in POLEDIT and specify an existing network group.

If you create policies for multiple groups, prioritize the groups by choosing Options⇨Group Priority. The highest priority group gets processed last by Windows 95 and therefore overrides other, lower-priority group policies. Prioritization tells Windows 95 what to do when certain users belong to multiple groups that have potentially conflicting policy settings.

Single-user policies

How about assigning system policies to individual users? No problem. If a user or two on the network needs a different set of policies than those contained in the simple CONFIG.POL, you can use POLEDIT to create special user policies just for them. For example, you may want to create a less restrictive set of policies for people who perform administrative duties on the network. Here's the procedure:

1. **Start the System Policy Editor and open the CONFIG.POL file.**
2. **Choose Edit⇨Add User.**
3. **Type the user's network logon name into the Add User dialog box and click OK.**

   A new user icon appears in the Policy Editor window.
4. **Double-click the new user icon and make whatever settings you want for that user by checking the relevant boxes.**
5. **Save the CONFIG.POL file and exit System Policy Editor.**
6. **Copy CONFIG.POL to the network server.**

You can use the same basic trick to set up different SYSTEM.DAT restrictions. Just change Step 2 in the preceding list to Edit⇨Add Computer. The name you give the new computer policy must match the computer name that appears on the Identification tab of the user's Network control panel. Figure 9-5 shows a sample CONFIG.POL as viewed by the System Policy Editor.

When Mark logs onto the network, his user name appears separately in CONFIG.POL, so Windows 95 applies the "Mark" user policy instead of the Default User policy. If a user logs on from a PC with the *computer* name "Accounting1," similarly, Windows 95 uses that specific computer policy instead of the Default Computer policy. Windows 95 assigns the Default User and Default Computer policies to users whose names or computer names don't show up separately in CONFIG.POL.

Now, what if you have a bunch of non-networked PCs and you still want to create a POL file that you can copy to their hard drives, in order to impose the same restrictions on every user? Here's the little-known technique:

Figure 9-5:
The CONFIG.POL file can contain exceptions for specific users and computers.

1. **On your PC, create the POL file in the System Policy Editor. Give it a name (say, ALL.POL) and copy it to diskette.**

2. **Go to the computer you want to restrict and copy ALL.POL from diskette to the hard drive (we recommend the C:\WINDOWS directory).**

3. **Run the System Policy Editor.**

    Install the System Policy Editor if it isn't present, using the steps this chapter presents earlier under "Installing the System Policy Editor."

4. **Choose File⇨Open Registry and double-click the Local Computer icon.**

5. **Expand the Network branch and the Update branch; then click Remote Update.**

6. **Under Settings for Remote Update, select Manual (use specific path) in the Update Mode field and type in the file location (for example, C:\WINDOWS\ALL.POL) of the POL file in the Path for Manual Update field.**

7. **Click OK, close the System Policy Editor, and click Yes to save the changes to the current Registry.**

8. **Deinstall POLEDIT from the PC by using the Control Panel's Add/ Remove Programs wizard (so that the user can't override your settings).**

Repeat Steps 2 through 8 for each computer.

Gotchas

System policies have their weaknesses. For example:

✔ Some Windows 95 help files (*.HLP, usually in the C:\WINDOWS\HELP directory) include shortcut buttons to run specific programs. You may have used POLEDIT to restrict those programs, but users may still be able to run them from the help files.

✔ You can use system policies to disable Registry editing tools, but a user with Norton Utilities can run Norton Registry Editor without a problem. Also, if you leave the System Policy Editor on a user's PC, the user can run POLEDIT and reverse the REGEDIT restriction. (The way around this is to set the user policy *Only run allowed Windows applications* by clicking the Policy Editor checkbox of the same name, and make sure that no Registry editing programs are on the list.)

✔ You can press F8 when rebooting Windows 95 and choose Safe Mode, and Windows 95 bypasses system policies. You can then run REGEDIT to remove policy settings already present, and run the System Policy Editor to change the restrictions that are reset at boot time by the policy file. (One way around this problem is to add the line `BootKeys=0` to MSDOS.SYS, which disables the F8 key.)

✔ Unless you're using network-based POL files that have been restricted by using your network's built-in access control features, a user may be able to locate the POL file and delete it, bypassing system policy restrictions if the user also has access to REGEDIT and can disable the policies already set in the Registry.

If you need bulletproof security, you should be using Windows NT Workstation rather than Windows 95. Nevertheless, the policy component of the Windows 95 Registry can be made watertight enough to withstand fairly rugged seas.

Chapter 10

Customizing User Profiles So Bob Always Sees Bob's Icons

. . . .

In This Chapter

▶ Finding out when to set up user profiles

▶ Discovering what user profiles do to your Registry and your PC

▶ Setting up user profiles

▶ Removing user profiles

. . . .

*O*ne of the big problems with Windows 3.*x* is that it isn't network-friendly (or really even network-aware). Windows 95 helps correct the problem by providing a built-in mechanism for splitting up the Registry so that some files go with the user, not with the PC. This chapter tells you all you ever need to know about *user profiles,* maybe even more than you ever *want* to know — including some fairly significant *gotchas* that can send you to the aspirin bottle if you don't know about them ahead of time.

When to Use Profiles

One of the great things about the Registry is the way it splits out user-specific settings from machine-specific settings. This need to split is the whole idea behind creating the Registry with two core files, USER.DAT and SYSTEM.DAT. These two files don't have to come from the same location — unlike the situation with Windows 3.*x,* where all your core INI files have to exist in the same directory on your disk. Furthermore, although a Windows 95 PC starts its life with a single USER.DAT file, no rule exists against having a whole bunch of 'em (although you can't have more than one SYSTEM.DAT file per PC).

Roamin' your network

Nowadays, most PCs in business environments connect in networks. One of the great benefits of networking is that you can (theoretically, at least) sit down at any PC, wherever you happen to be at the time, and work as efficiently as though you were at your regular PC.

That's handy for technical support people who have to hoof it around the office working on different users' computers. You can also find networking handy when your usual computer is a slacker of a 486, but the woman in the neighboring cubicle has a zippy Pentium II machine and she's off on vacation for a week. (Just don't leave doughnut crumbs all over her workspace.) Finally, if you work in a company that frequently reorganizes people and teams, you'll be happy that you don't have to lug your PC to your new workplace in order to get working again.

Bringing the theory of roaming users into the real world takes a bit of doing, however. Bob may go to some lengths to get his Windows 95 desktop the way he wants it:

- Bob's vision isn't great, so he likes larger than normal icon titles.

- Bob digs Alfa Romeos, and he puts a picture of one onto his system as wallpaper.

- Bob uses five or six programs on a regular basis, so he customizes his Start menu and his desktop shortcut icons so he can get to those programs fast.

- Bob works with a dozen or so data files routinely, too, so they get convenient desktop icons as well.

After all, PCs aren't called *personal* computers for nothing. Now, when Bob moves over to Janet's fast Pentium II machine, he doesn't want to have to live with small icon titles, a sleep-inducing rustic landscape for wallpaper, and a different set of desktop icons and Start menu options that don't pertain to what Bob does for a living. He darned sure doesn't want to muck around with Janet's PC so that it looks the way he wants, only to have her jump down his throat when she comes back from Bermuda two days early. Bob's situation is a job for . . . *user profiles*.

Thanks for sharing

User profiles make it possible for different users to share the same computer and for each to keep their own settings. Perhaps in the ideal world (in the view of some computer industry executives), there's a chicken in every pot and everyone who wants a PC has one. In reality, although PCs are less expensive than ever, a lot of companies still don't buy every employee a computer.

Have you ever seen a residential real estate office that has a single community PC for the agents to use when the need arises? In a situation like this, Broker A doesn't want to log on to the PC and deal with all the rearranging that Broker B did while using the PC previously.

Consider also the home front, where many families share the same PC. Many grownups like having free Internet access and may even enjoy occasionally visiting certain dimly lit alleyways off the information superhighway that would make their parents blush in embarrassment, yet they don't want their kids to be able to see that stuff. Or the adults in the house may want to access to the household finances but don't want their teenagers copping their credit card numbers and ordering up designer snowboard equipment by mail.

If you use a notebook PC, you may even want to set up different software configurations for when you're using your notebook at work and at home. You can log on as BobWork and see all the serious stuff; log on as BobPlay and see your fun programs and icons.

For both desktop users who must all share the same computer and road warriors who use the same computer in different settings, user profiles can come to the rescue. The Registry can handle the different needs of multiple users — although you need to be careful how you set up user profiles, and you do pay a price for using this feature.

Setting Up User Profiles

Activating user profiles is deceptively easy. Here's the procedure:

1. **Click Start⇨Settings⇨Control Panel and double-click the Passwords icon.**

   The Passwords Properties dialog box appears.

2. **Click the User Profiles tab (see Figure 10-1).**

3. **Click the radio button that reads** Users can customize their preferences and desktop settings. Windows switches to your personal settings whenever you log in.

4. **In the User Profile Settings area, check the box that reads** Include desktop icons and Network Neighborhood contents in user settings.

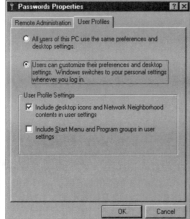

Figure 10-1:
Setting up
user
profiles
in the
Passwords
control
panel.

You see another check box in this area, which is labeled Include Start Menu and Program groups in user settings. This option sounds attractive, but watch out! If you choose this option and then want to install a new program on a PC, you may have to run the installation program multiple times to get the new program to appear on each user's Start menu. That is, you have to log on as user A, install the software, log on as user B, install the software, and so forth. (Quicker alternatives may exist for some programs, but reinstallation is the only procedure we know that works for *every* program.)

5. **Click OK and restart Windows 95.**

6. **Log on with a new user name. Click Yes when you see the dialog box in Figure 10-2, and confirm your new password.**

7. **Repeat Steps 5 and 6 for as many users (that is, user profiles) as you want to create.**

Figure 10-2:
Confirming
that you
want to
create a
new user
profile.

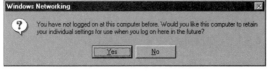

What Profiles Do to the Registry

Here's a brief list of the settings that the Windows 95 user profiles allow different users to set separately:

- ✔ User interface settings, such as color schemes, desktop icons, icon spacing and titles, wallpaper, sounds, and so on

- ✔ Most control panel settings, including the display size and color depth

- ✔ Printer settings

- ✔ Application-specific settings (as long as the applications support user profiles, and most 32-bit programs do), such as menu layouts and window customization

- ✔ Network Neighborhood contents and network-related information such as preferred logon server, shared resources, and so on

- ✔ Recent documents list (Start⇨Documents)

- ✔ Start menu settings (this one's optional)

Naturally, all this information is in the Registry! You can look at the effect of user profiles on the Registry from two angles: the files (physical structure) and the keys (logical structure).

File cloning: The physical changes

User-specific settings live in the USER.DAT Registry file. When you activate user profiles, you tell Windows 95 that it needs to look elsewhere for USER.DAT than the usual C:\WINDOWS directory. Exactly *where* Windows 95 looks depends on whether you're in a multiple-user-per-PC situation or a roaming-user situation. That is, a stand-alone or networked environment.

Stand-alone PC

In the first case, on a non-networked PC, Windows 95 doesn't bother checking a network server because one doesn't exist. Windows 95 activates the USER.DAT file in C:\WINDOWS, but as soon as you log on with a user name, Windows 95 then proceeds directly to a new, user-specific USER.DAT file in a special location. That location is under the master profile directory C:\WINDOWS\PROFILES, in a subdirectory that's the same as your user name (see Figure 10-3). The USER.DAT in C:\WINDOWS\PROFILES\username overrides the settings for the USER.DAT in C:\WINDOWS, which Windows 95 loaded just moments earlier.

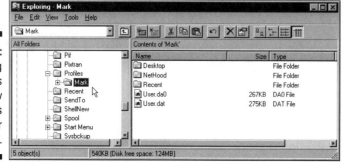

Figure 10-3:
Activating
user profiles
creates new
directories
under
C:\WINDOWS.

Every time a user logs on to Windows 95 with a new user name, Windows 95 creates a new subdirectory under C:\WINDOWS\PROFILES and puts a new USER.DAT in that subdirectory, based on the default user information in C:\WINDOWS\USER.DAT. Windows 95 also creates subdirectories underneath C:\WINDOWS\PROFILES\username, typically *Desktop, Nethood* (for Network Neighborhood), and *Recent* (for the recent document list), and optionally *Start Menu.*

If PCs have a limit to the number of user profiles that you can define on a single machine, we haven't bumped into it yet.

Networked PC

On a networked PC, Windows 95 also maintains a user-specific copy of USER.DAT under C:\WINDOWS\PROFILES\username, but Windows 95 keeps a copy on the network, too. That is, as long as your network is of the client/server variety, and you use a 32-bit network client that Windows 95 supports — such as the built-in network software for Windows NT Server or Novell IntranetWare.

Here's what happens on the network. When you log on, Windows 95 checks for a USER.DAT on your local hard drive in C:\WINDOWS\PROFILES, *and* for a USER.DAT in the user's directory on the server. (The user's server directory where USER.DAT resides is the *mail directory* in NetWare 3.*x* and the *home directory* in NetWare 4.*x* and Windows NT Server.) If either copy of USER.DAT is newer than the other, Windows 95 updates the older version, and then starts up.

If you use NetWare or IntranetWare file servers and you want to activate user profiles, you must install support for long filenames on the server. See your network documentation for details, under the subject "OS/2 name space" or "Windows 95 name space."

How USER.DAT is Like a Ping-Pong Ball

Windows 95 compares the versions of USER.DAT on the server and on your local hard drive. Stop and think for a minute about why this is necessary. You may have logged onto Windows 95 at your last work session without also logging on to the network, in which case the USER.DAT in C:\WINDOWS\ PROFILES\username is newer than the USER.DAT in your network directory. On the other hand, if you're roaming, then Windows 95 must use the USER.DAT in your network directory because your USER.DAT file may not exist under C:\WINDOWS\PROFILES on a particular PC's hard drive. Even if you've used a PC before, your USER.DAT file on that PC is bound to be stale.

Okay, say you put in some hours on the machine and before long, it's five o'clock, time to turn off the boss and tell the lights goodnight.

If you change settings during a work session, Windows 95 copies your local USER.DAT up to the network at shutdown, to keep everything in synch (that's one reason why shutting down a networked PC can take longer than a stand-alone PC). Remember, you may log on to a different PC later, in which case Windows 95 needs your updated USER.DAT from your directory on the network.

We realize that all this information is a little confusing, so read this sidebar again a couple of times until you get the idea. If you think about it, this system is the only way network-based user profiles *could* work. And the design feature that makes this system possible is the ability to sling USER.DAT files around the network and onto different directories on the PC's hard drive, while leaving SYSTEM.DAT serenely nestled in C:\WINDOWS.

Backups

What about backups? When you start Windows 95 initially, after a successful load, Windows 95 copies C:\WINDOWS\USER.DAT to C:\WINDOWS\USER.DA0, as usual. Later, when you log on to Windows 95 and activate a user profile, Windows 95 backs up that specific USER.DAT file to a USER.DA0 file in the same subdirectory (C:\WINDOWS\PROFILES\username).

A spare set of keys: The logical changes

The view from REGEDIT changes when you activate user profiles, but things are a bit simpler from the standpoint of the Registry's logical structure. Without user profiles, the *HKU* branch contains only one subkey, *.Default.* With user profiles, *HKU* contains two subkeys: *.Default,* plus a new subkey named after the current user (see Figure 10-4).

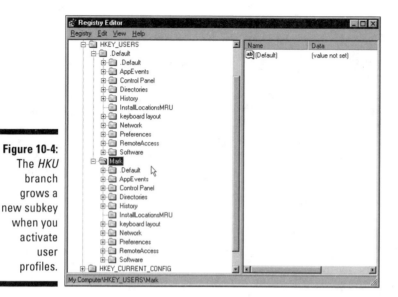

Figure 10-4:
The *HKU*
branch
grows a
new subkey
when you
activate
user
profiles.

When a user logs onto Windows 95 with a new name, Windows 95 uses the
contents of *HKU\.Default* (corresponding to the default USER.DAT file in
C:\WINDOWS) to create a new subkey with the user's name (corresponding
to the new USER.DAT file under C:\WINDOWS\PROFILES\username). As the
new user makes changes to the system, the new subkey (that is, the active
profile) changes, but *HKU\.Default* (that is, C:\WINDOWS\USER.DAT)
doesn't change.

Even if many different users have logged on to a given Windows 95 PC and have
created a new USER.DAT file and a new C:\WINDOWS\PROFILES\username
directory each time, only two users show up in *HKU* at any one time: .Default
and the currently logged-on user. Any Registry changes that affect user
settings get logged to the subkey for the current user and don't affect the
.Default subkey.

What if you've enabled user profiles, but you *want* to modify *HKU\.Default*?
For example, you may want to modify the default user profile before creating
other user profiles that base themselves on that default profile. Doing so is
easy: Just don't log on. You can click Cancel or press Esc at the logon dialog
box. Now, any changes you make to user settings will apply in the future to
anyone else who starts Windows 95 on that PC without logging on. (Note
that this tip doesn't work if you use system policies (see Chapter 9) to
require a user to log on to the network in order to see the Windows 95
desktop.)

Profile Downsides

We mention early on in this chapter that you pay a price for the convenience of user profiles. Well, actually, *two* prices. Just think of them as luxury taxes.

Luxury tax #1: Performance

We've never seen this information published in Microsoft or non-Microsoft publications, but we know it to be true from experience: User profiles slow your system down. In fact, user profiles slow your system down a lot more than we think they should. After Windows 95 locates the proper USER.DAT file, things shouldn't take any longer than if you use the default USER.DAT in C:\WINDOWS, but they do. We freely admit that we're not expert enough to know why user profiles slow down a PC's performance, and if anyone else does, they're not talking so far.

The amount of this "performance tax" varies, but we've run benchmark tests on a few PCs to try and quantify the answer. Based on our tests, you can plan on about a 10 percent performance hit for disk activity with profiles turned on. (Graphics activity doesn't seem to be affected in the least.) That may not seem like a huge tax, but think of it as a dime out of every dollar, and you begin to feel it.

Luxury tax #2: Convenience

The second tax is on convenience. Managing your PC gets more complicated when user profiles are on. For one thing, backing up the Registry gets more involved because you have to worry about those individual USER.DAT profiles under C:\WINDOWS\PROFILES, not just the one in C:\WINDOWS. If you don't back 'em all up when you back up your Registry and if you're unlucky enough to encounter a hard drive problem bad enough to affect several files, you may be up the creek. Even if you do back up the individual USER.DAT profiles, you have to make sure you restore them to the right places.

None of the Microsoft-supplied tools for backing up the Registry — not Configuration Backup, not the Emergency Recovery Utility — can back up user profile information stored in C:\WINDOWS\PROFILES.

The complexity of user profiles also carries a convenience cost when you perform nifty user-oriented Registry edits such as some of the ones that we discuss in this book. If you make a Registry modification that affects USER.DAT (or, in the logical structure, the *HKCU* branch), that modification doesn't apply to all users on the PC — just the one currently logged on. So you find yourself logging on as different users and making your Registry modifications multiple times. You can ease the inconvenience by using a REG file, as Chapter 12 explores, but the process is still drudgery.

Finally, in a company setting, employee turnover is a fact of life. More than one administrator has cursed the user profiles feature while cleaning out hard drives filled with ex-employees' files.

Mandatory User Profiles

On a client/server network, you can replace the USER.DAT file that resides in the user's network directory with a USER.DAT file that you want to make mandatory and unchangeable. Name the file USER.MAN, and you've created a mandatory user profile. (You have to make this change for every user individually.)

In the case of USER.MAN, Windows 95 never copies a USER.DAT on the user's PC hard drive back to the network location, as it may do with regular user profiles. Instead, Windows 95 always uses the USER.MAN file.

Not too many companies in our experience use mandatory user profiles, because mandatory user profiles don't provide any control over the settings in SYSTEM.DAT. Yes, you may be able to use system policies (see Chapter 9) in combination with mandatory user profiles, but doing so creates a security environment that is so complex that not many organizations would want to manage it. Organizations can choose either mandatory user profiles or system policies to impose restrictions on users — probably nine out of ten go with the latter. However, mandatory user profiles do one thing that system policies don't: They can freeze user settings for application programs.

Exorcising User Profiles

So, you turn user profiles on, and you find that a month or a year later, you don't need them anymore. Perhaps your personal computer becomes more personal and you're the exclusive user, or you find that your network doesn't have any users who need to roam from machine to machine. Mindful of our gentle cautions regarding the performance and convenience penalties that user profiles impose, you decide to exorcise them from your PC. You hunt around the various control panels for a one-button command that says "Remove User Profiles." You can't find that button, because it doesn't exist.

The lack of a convenient way to remove user profiles is a problem Microsoft probably figured users wouldn't discover until Microsoft had sold 50 million copies or so, and they were probably right on that score. We wish Microsoft had provided an automated solution for the problem by now, but it hasn't. Fortunately, the procedure you must follow isn't terribly complex, and we're here to show it to you.

If you're not already familiar with the Registry Editor, please read through Chapter 4 before performing the following procedure. We also suggest you make a Registry backup (see Chapter 2 for all the grisly details).

Here's how to remove all user profiles from your system:

1. **Restart Windows 95 but don't log on. Click Cancel at the Windows logon dialog box.**

   You may have to first disable system policies if they're active (see Chapter 9 for details).

2. **Click Start⇨Settings⇨Control Panel and double-click the Passwords icon.**

   The Passwords Properties dialog box appears.

3. **Click the User Profiles tab.**

4. **Click the radio button that reads** All users of this PC use the same preferences and desktop settings, **then click OK and restart.**

5. **Run the Registry Editor, for example by clicking Start⇨Run, typing REGEDIT in the Open field, and clicking OK.**

6. **Delete the key** *HKLM\SOFTWARE\Microsoft\Windows\CurrentVersion\ProfileList*, **for example by selecting the key and pressing Del.**

7. **Close the Registry Editor.**

8. **Run Windows Explorer, highlight the directory C:\WINDOWS\PROFILES, and press Del to delete it.**

   The user subdirectories go away when you delete the main directory.

When you restart Windows 95, every user setting goes back to the value in the *HKU\.Default* key (that is, C:\WINDOWS\USER.DAT). You may have some customizing to do if you've been using a particular user name to make most of your Windows 95 settings and preferences.

Chapter 11

Customizing the Desktop for Speed, Form, and Function

● ●

In This Chapter

▶ Using the Registry to wring more speed out of your PC

▶ Changing icons and icon names with REGEDIT

▶ Filling the Windows 95 security holes with a nifty INF file

▶ Taming the beast that is Object Linking and Embedding

● ●

*T*he Windows 95 desktop is highly customizable right out of the box, but you can customize it in even more ways than the manuals tell you if you don't mind performing a little Registry surgery.

For many of you, this is the chapter you've been looking for. You may have no interest in future installations of Windows 95 (see Chapter 8), slapping access restrictions on PC users (see Chapter 9), or setting up a multi-user Windows 95 environment (see Chapter 10). However, almost everyone has an interest in tuning up the Windows desktop so it's faster, prettier, and more useful — the subject of this final chapter in Part III.

We spend almost no time here telling you how to do things with the Registry Editor that you can do other, safer ways. If you want to customize the desktop in ways that the System Policy Editor makes easier and safer, use the System Policy Editor. If you want to make settings that a standard control panel can make, use the control panel instead of REGEDIT. And if you want to set up your computer with animated wallpaper that shows Bill Gates mud wrestling Janet Reno, go right ahead. (If you figure out how, let us know — that would really be cool.)

This chapter assumes that you already know your way around the Registry and the Registry Editor. If not, please take a look at Chapters 4 and 6 before cruising these waters.

For Customizers and Custom Misers

Although we give you tips for using REGEDIT to customize your desktop, you can use the Do-It-Yourself methods we provide, or you can perform some of the tweaks by using freeware or shareware programs. Both approaches have advantages: Using a freeware or shareware program is probably safer, but using REGEDIT is always free. Using REGEDIT also makes it easier for you to create REG files that you can then distribute for others to use (see Chapter 12) because you know exactly which keys and values to export.

The following section covers two shareware programs that you can use for customizing your desktop.

PowerToys

The Microsoft PowerToys utility, TweakUI, is actually a control panel (see Figure 11-1) and one of several goodies that you can download for free from `www.microsoft.com/windows95/info/powertoys.htm`. The Web page contains complete installation instructions. Be sure to spend some time especially with the General, Desktop, and Paranoia tabs.

The PowerToys package contains a lot of other nifty utilities, such as the CAB file viewer that enables you to peek inside those annoying *.CAB files (Microsoft's *cabinet* archiving format used to store Windows 95 and application files) to see what they contain — and to extract the file you need. Highly recommended. Make sure that you get the most recent version.

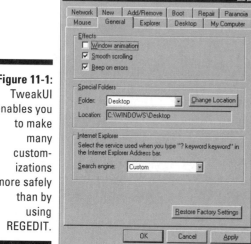

Figure 11-1:
TweakUI enables you to make many customizations more safely than by using REGEDIT.

WinHacker

Wedge Software's WinHacker 95 is one of the more popular Windows 95 downloads on the Internet, offering even more customization options than TweakUI. You can add and remove shell icons, rename the Start button, hide drives, customize startup options, and so on. You do have to fork over $17.95 US for this shareware package, and some of the features overlap with the free TweakUI. WinHacker also does not completely remove its keys from the Registry when you uninstall it. (Then again, these days, what programs do?)

Customizing for Speed

If you've ever gone sailing in a 14-foot boat, you know that it feels faster than if you travel at the same number of knots in a 40-foot boat. The perception of speed can be separate from the objective measurement of speed. And while Windows 95 may be running on a high-speed Pentium II system, it can still "feel" sluggish because of several Registry settings that Microsoft didn't set for speed.

Sluggish performance has two causes: *system settings* that don't let Windows 95 respond as quickly as it's capable of responding, and *common activities* that Windows 95 normally requires you to perform with too many keystrokes and mouse movements. The following tips address both areas.

System settings

Here are a few system settings that you can tweak with the Registry to make Windows 95 more responsive to the tiller.

Animated windows

You've probably noticed that when you minimize or maximize a window, Windows 95 displays a zoom effect, or "visual whoosh." Any window shrinks down toward the taskbar when you minimize it and expands up from the taskbar when you maximize or restore it. The animated visual whoosh does take a little time and makes Windows feel slower than it has to. We like to turn the visual whoosh off on every PC that we get our hands on.

Microsoft claims that this zooming business helps new users understand where windows go when minimized — namely, the taskbar. We think all this whooshing is an example of Microsoft imitating the Macintosh a little too thoroughly.

All you have to do to turn off the zoom effect is run REGEDIT, add the string value *MinAnimate* to the key *HKCU\Control Panel\Desktop\WindowMetrics,* and set it to "0." (If the value already exists, all you have to do is change it from "1" to "0" — the computer programmer's way of turning things on and off.) The change takes effect at the next system restart. The speed with which windows now snap up or down is very satisfying.

Cascading menus

You may not be a Type A personality who gets somewhat frustrated at relatively minor delays. However, if you've ever wished in the back of your mind that those cascading menus that branch off the Start button would pop up just a little faster than the default half-second, here's a tip for you.

Run REGEDIT and change *HKCU\Control Panel\desktop\MenuShowDelay* to the number of milliseconds (thousandths of a second) delay you prefer. The default is 500. We like to change this setting to zero for maximum speed, although you do have to get out of the habit of leisurely moving the mouse diagonally across cascading menus if you eliminate the delay.

Hot-rodding the keyboard

The keyboard control panel's Speed tab enables you to modify the delay period before a key begins repeating, as well as the repeat rate (the speed with which a key repeats after it starts repeating). Experienced typists appreciate the responsiveness that Windows 95 suddenly gains when they set the delay period as short as possible and the repeat rate as fast as possible. For one thing, scrolling around a document with the arrow keys becomes much faster.

The relevant Registry keys are *HKCU\Control Panel\Keyboard\ KeyboardDelay,* which ranges from 0 (short) to 3 (long), and (in the same key) *KeyboardSpeed,* which ranges from 0 (slow) to 31 (fast). We don't normally mention settings that you can change via control panels, but in this case, we find that changing the keyboard settings at Windows 95 installation by modifying the Registry settings in MSBATCH.INF (see Chapter 8), or with a REG file, is handy. Many users, especially Windows 95 novices, don't venture into the control panels for months, if ever.

Turbocharging dial-up Internet links

If you don't use TCP/IP for dial-up Internet access, sail right past this section.

One Windows 95 problem that has received surprisingly little press is the issue of *TCP/IP packet size* over dial-up connections. *TCP/IP,* or Transmission Control Protocol/Internet Protocol, is the network communication language of the Internet and (increasingly) of internal company networks. A *packet* is a unit of data transmission over a network.

The problem, in a nutshell, is that Windows 95 sets the maximum packet size at a fairly large value (1500 bytes). This size is fine for a company network but not so great for a dial-up Internet connection. Many Internet traffic devices can't handle a 1500-byte packet, so they chop it up into smaller pieces and then reassemble it at the destination. That can slow down a dial-up link's performance by 50 percent or even more.

The relevant Registry entry for changing TCP-IP packet size is *HKLM\System\CurrentControlSet\Services\Class\NetTrans\000n\MaxMTU* where *000n* is the number of the dial-up network adapter's TCP/IP link. Change this value to 576 (add the value if it doesn't exist) to reduce the likelihood of packets getting chopped up in transit.

To figure out what 000n should be in the Registry entry from the previous paragraph, first go to *HKLM\Enum\Root\Net\0000* and look for the *DeviceDesc* value, which may say something like "AOL Adapter" if, for example, your Internet dial-up link uses America Online. If you don't see such a description, look in *HKLM\Enum\Root\Net\0001,* and so on. After you find the right key, look at the *Bindings* subkey, which will say something like *MSTCP\0002.* Assuming that's the case for this example, jump to *HKLM\Enum\Network\MSTCP\0002* and look for the value named "Driver." This points you to *NetTrans\000n,* which is the number you need. Yes, this is horribly convoluted, but you can let a shareware program run down the right number for you (see the "On the CD" icon two paragraphs down).

Other Registry entries have an effect on dial-up TCP/IP performance, too, but the subject gets very complicated very fast. Fortunately, some cool tools exist to handle the Registry modifications for you.

Rob Vonk's EasyMTU, Mike Sutherland's MTUSpeed, and Patterson Software Design's TweakDUN are all handy freeware or shareware utilities for modifying the TCP/IP packet settings. Our favorite is EasyMTU (see Figure 11-2) because it clearly shows you which of the possibly several TCP/IP connections that your PC uses are dial-up connections, and which are local network connections (which you don't want to change). You can find the latest version of all these programs on the Internet at www.download.com.

Common activities

One of the best ways to make Windows 95 faster in your day-to-day work is to put some of the common activities that are usually buried under a series of keystrokes and mouse clicks up onto the Start menu, where you can get to them posthaste. Examples may include the word processor you use daily, your favorite Internet connection, and so on.

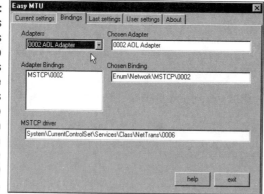

Figure 11-2:
EasyMTU's
Bindings
tab
indicates
that the
program is
about to
modify an
America
Online
(AOL)
connection.

Adding the URL History folder to the Start menu

If you spend a fair amount of time on the Internet, you may find adding the Uniform Resource Locator (URL) History list to your Start menu a convenient customization. By doing so, you can quickly return to a site you visited recently without having to run Internet Explorer as a separate step. Here's the procedure:

1. **Right-click the Start button and choose Explore.**

   You see an Explorer window that displays the structure of the Start menu.

2. **Right-click any empty space in the right pane and choose New⟹Folder.**

3. **With the new folder name highlighted, type in the following:**

   ```
   URL History folder.{FF393560-C2A7-11CF-BFF4-
        444553540000}
   ```

   If you want to make sure that you avoid a typing error, you can use REGEDIT to pluck the URL history folder CLSID out of the Registry by searching for "URL history folder" in the value Data fields. After you locate the URL history folder, right-click the CLSID key, choose Rename, and press Ctrl+C to copy the CLSID key to the Clipboard. Press Ctrl+V to paste the key into the Explorer window, after typing the **URL History folder.** prefix (don't forget the trailing period). Press Esc to get out of the Rename operation, then close REGEDIT.

4. **Close the Explorer window and try out your new Start menu option.**

Adding Dial-Up Networking to the Start menu

The procedure for adding Dial-Up Networking to the Start menu is almost identical to the procedure in the previous section. Just replace the folder name in Step 3 with the following:

```
Dial Up Net.{992CFFA0-F557-101A-88EC-00DD010CCC48}
```

You can add the Control Panel to the Start menu, too; Chapter 3 gives the procedure.

Customizing for Form

This section is about cosmetics — changing the icons and icon titles that programs and data files and Windows 95 itself use. This section is short because we don't care very much about this stuff. In fact, you can skip it and sail right over to the "Customizing for Function" section, unless you have a burning curiosity about how to change desktop icons — in which case, we suggest that you read the next few paragraphs and then see a specialist.

Changing icons

Applications that register a particular file type have the option to define a special icon for that file type, too. The relevant Registry key is *HKCR\ filetype\DefaultIcon,* where *filetype* is a file type entry in the bottom half of the *HKCR* branch. Figure 11-3 shows an example for Adobe Photoshop. The value data "C:\program files\Photoshp\photoshp.exe,1" indicates that the icon is the second one (0 being the first) stored within the main Photoshop program, PHOTOSHP.EXE. (Yep, EXE files can store icons!)

Figure 11-3:
Where the Registry stores the default Photoshop icon information.

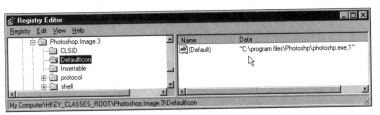

The easiest way to change an icon for a particular file type is not to use the Registry Editor at all because REGEDIT doesn't give you any visual feedback about the alternative icons available. Instead, follow this procedure:

1. **Start Windows Explorer the fast way, by right clicking the My Computer icon and choosing Explore.**

2. **Click View⇨Options to display the Options dialog box.**

3. **Click the File Types tab to display the File Types dialog box (see Figure 11-4).**

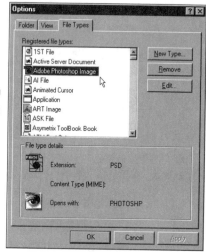

Figure 11-4:
The File
Types
dialog box
is an easy
place to
change
data file
icons.

4. **Choose the file type you want to change and click the Edit button.**

5. **Click Change Icon, type in a File name, and make a selection for the Current icon in the scrolling window.**

   The currently displayed filename may have multiple choices; if you want different ones, specify a filename of C:\WINDOWS\MORICONS.DLL, C:\WINDOWS\SYSTEM\SHELL32.DLL, or (if you have the Plus! add-on product) C:\WINDOWS\SYSTEM\COOL.DLL. It turns out that DLL files aren't just for programs, after all!

6. **Click OK, Close, Close, and then close Windows Explorer (for example, by clicking the close box in the upper-right corner).**

The above technique is much safer and easier than using the Registry Editor. You'll find that you still can't change a few icons with this procedure, but not many. If you want to go icon hunting in REGEDIT, look in *HKCR* and *HKCR\CLSID* for keys named *DefaultIcon*. Windows 95 stores its own icon settings in *HKLM\SOFTWARE\Microsoft\Windows\CurrentVersion\Explorer\ Shell Icons* if you have the Plus! package installed.

Renaming desktop icons

Many Windows 95 desktop icons have names that you seemingly can't change. The usual method for renaming an icon, clicking its name once and then changing it, doesn't work. Here's an example — the Recycle Bin — for how you can change such icon titles. Just remember that if you do so, you may confuse other users who work with your PC.

1. **Run REGEDIT (for example, by choosing Start⇨Run and typing** REGEDIT**).**

2. **Press Ctrl+F to open the Find dialog box.**

3. **Enter** Recycle Bin **in the Find What field and clear all check boxes other than Data.**

   The name *Recycle Bin* appears as the data field in a value under *HKCR\CLSID,* so you can speed up your search by only looking for data field items.

4. **Click Find Next to initiate the search.**

5. **After the key under HKCR\CLSID appears, double-click the (Default) value in the value pane and change the name from Recycle Bin to whatever you prefer.**

6. **Close REGEDIT. Your change takes effect at the next restart (see Figure 11-5).**

You can use the preceding steps to rename just about any desktop icon in Windows 95.

Figure 11-5:
The
Recycle Bin
has a new
name.

Customizing for Function

Manipulating the Registry can become a powerful tool for enhancing Windows 95's behavior in ways that don't pertain to speed or cosmetics. The two areas we look at here are improving Windows 95's security and making the file association system work the way you want it to.

Filling security holes

Windows 95 maintains several different records of your activities, mainly for your convenience if you want to work later with documents or programs that you recently used. However, these *history lists* do create several security holes. Anyone can easily see what documents you've been working on (say, RESUME.DOC, or perhaps LIST OF SECRET DOCUMENTS TO SELL TO MAJOR COMPETITOR.DOC) by examining the history lists.

Unfortunately, Windows 95 offers no method for turning these history lists off. Fortunately, your Registry knowledge (and a little guidance from us) is all you need.

We read through four different published explanations of how to pull off this little trick and found mistakes in every single one. We've gone through the following steps ourselves twice to verify that they work.

First, we need to identify the various lists. Here they are:

- **The recent documents list** (Start⇨Documents). Supposedly contains the most recent 15 documents that you've opened, although it doesn't list documents that you open in 16-bit Windows programs or DOS sessions.

- **The Run MRU list** (MRU = Most Recently Used). This list appears after you choose Start⇨Run and click the list display arrow; you see a history of program command lines that you've typed via Start⇨Run.

- **The Find MRU list**. When you use the Windows 95 Find facility (Start⇨Find⇨Files or Folders), you can see this list by clicking the arrow next to the Named field.

- **The Find Computer MRU list**. You can view this list from Start⇨Find⇨Computer.

The recent documents list is not stored entirely in the Registry; it's also in C:\WINDOWS\RECENT. The other three lists exist entirely in the Registry. You can create an INF file that deletes the Registry entries. (REG files don't delete existing entries, so the REG technique doesn't work here.)

Chapter 12 covers INF files, if you want to understand the following file completely. If you don't, trust us, the file works properly.

Here's the text:

```
[version]
signature=$Chicago$
[DefaultInstall]
DelReg=Security
[Security]
HKCU,Software\Microsoft\Windows\CurrentVersion\Explorer\RecentDocs,
HKCU,Software\Microsoft\Windows\CurrentVersion\Explorer\
  RunMRU,
HKCU,"Software\Microsoft\Windows\CurrentVersion\Explorer\Doc
  Find Spec MRU",
HKCU,Software\Microsoft\Windows\CurrentVersion\Explorer\
  FindComputerMRU,
```

Save the INF file as SECURE.INF in C:\WINDOWS\INF. Windows 95 rebuilds the keys automatically the next time you perform an action that normally creates an entry in the MRU list. Notice that you *must* put double quotes around the entry for *Doc Find Spec MRU* because the key name contains spaces. If you get into the habit of always putting key names in quotation marks, then you're smarter than the average bear.

Now, create a batch file in Notepad (call it SECURE.BAT if you like) that activates the INF file and deletes the shortcuts in C:\WINDOWS\RECENT to clear the Documents list:

```
@ECHO OFF
C:\WINDOWS\RUNDLL.EXE SETUPX.DLL,INSTALLHINFSECTION
    DEFAULTINSTALL 132 C:\WINDOWS\INF\SECURE.INF
ECHO Y | DEL C:\WINDOWS\RECENT\*.*
```

That second line is one long one, although we had to break it for the page.

All you have to do now is create a desktop icon to run SECURE.BAT (for example, by dragging and dropping the file to the desktop). Double-click the icon and restart Windows 95 whenever you want to clear all the various history lists. The Documents, Find MRU, and Find Computer MRU lists clear immediately, but the Run MRU list doesn't clear until you restart. If that doesn't bother you, skip the restart in the knowledge that your batch file clears three out of four lists right away.

If you use the TweakUI control panel as described in the earlier section "PowerToys," the Paranoia tab lets you do what SECURE.INF and SECURE.BAT do. You still may want to create your own security files if you work for a company that forbids installing unsupported software like TweakUI.

File associations and OLE

One of the more powerful aspects of Windows 95 is something called *Object Linking and Embedding (OLE),* although the trendier term *ActiveX* is becoming more accepted these days. A big part of OLE and ActiveX has to do with file type associations. The little three-letter suffix after the period in a filename unlocks a whole set of OLE instructions that help Windows 95 understand how to deal with that kind of file. Those instructions all live in the Registry — specifically, the *HKCR* branch, and even more specifically, the lower half of that branch. This section presents two OLE-related tips, one that involves REGEDIT and one that doesn't.

Opening unknown file types

We've all seen files named READ.ME, README.NOW, README.1ST, and so on. These files are almost certainly plain old text files that Notepad or Wordpad can open with ease, but double-clicking such files presents the Open With dialog box — requiring some tedious mousing around and even presenting the risk of inadvertently associating the .ME or .NOW file type with Notepad for evermore.

Here's a better way to open unknown file types that involves a little Registry wizardry. (You can't perform this trick with the File Types dialog box we discuss in the next section.) You can set up the Registry so that if you double-click a file with an unknown file extension, Windows 95 automatically runs Notepad (or Wordpad or whatever other text editor you like). Here's the procedure:

1. **Run REGEDIT (for example, by selecting Start⇨Run⇨REGEDIT).**

2. **Scroll to *HKCR\Unknown* and expand the subkeys.**

    HKCR\Unknown is in the bottom half of the HKCR structure; that is, it's a file type, not a file extension. (See Chapter 6 for more on the organization of the HKCR branch.) The subkey expands out to *HKCR\Unknown\ shell\openas\command,* where you see the code that displays the usual Open With context menu option.

3. **Add the new key *HKCR\Unknown\shell\open\command* containing the (Default) string value**

    ```
    C:\WINDOWS\NOTEPAD.EXE "%1"
    ```

    You can substitute the path name for any preferred text editor.

    The *%1* is a stand-in for the actual filename that you want to open. You can often get by without specifying *%1* when defining open commands, but we include it here as a matter of good practice. Figure 11-6 shows the old key and the one you just added.

4. **Close REGEDIT and try out your new command.**

Figure 11-6:
Adding a
program to
handle
opening
unknown
file types.

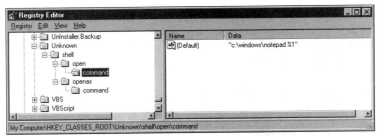

Now, when you double-click a file with an undefined extension, Windows 95 opens the file in Notepad. Obviously, if you try this trick with a binary file that isn't a simple text file, nothing productive happens; but no harm's done either.

Modifying the context menu

In Chapter 1, we allude to the fact that you can add programs to the right-click menu (that is, the *context menu*) of a data file that you may not always want to open with the same program. Here's a step-by-step example of how you add a context menu option for TXT files to open them in Microsoft Wordpad for Windows.

1. **Start Windows Explorer the fast way, by right-clicking the My Computer icon and choosing Explore.**

2. **Click View⇨Options to display the Options dialog box.**

3. **Click the File Types tab to display the File Types dialog box (see Figure 11-4).**

4. **Scroll down to Text Document, click it, and click the Edit button to display the Edit File Type dialog box (see Figure 11-7).**

5. **Click the New button to display the New Action dialog box.**

6. **In the Action list, type "Open in Wordpad" and in the Application Used to Perform Action, type**

   ```
   C:\Progra~1\Access~1\WORDPAD.EXE "%1"
   ```

   (We assume that you installed Wordpad in the usual location.) Notice the use of the DOS-equivalent short filenames here. Also, the *%1* just refers to the data file itself; you may be able to omit it with some programs, but including it is good practice.

7. **Click OK, Close, Close, and then close Explorer (for example, by clicking the close box in the upper-right corner).**

Figure 11-7:
The Actions
list in the
Edit File
Type dialog
box defines
right-click
behavior.

Now, when you right-click a file with the suffix TXT, you see `Open in Wordpad` as a new option. Having this option may be handy if you know you're opening a large text file that's too big for Notepad. You can apply the preceding technique to any data file that you may want to use multiple applications with: BMP with Windows Paint and Adobe Photoshop, HTM with Internet Explorer and Netscape Navigator, and so on.

To see the effect that the preceding steps have on the Registry, look up *HKCR\txtfile\shell* and notice the new subkeys, shown in Figure 11-8.

If you want to get a bit fancy, you can change the default action that occurs when you double-click a file. Just click the desired action in the Actions list (see Figure 11-7) and click the Set Default button. The double-click action always appears in boldface.

Figure 11-8:
The
Registry
reflects
a new
context
menu
command.

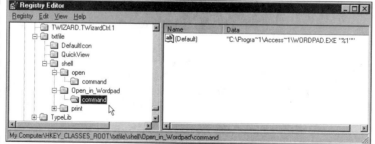

Part IV
The America's Cup: Registry Mastery

The 5th Wave   By Rich Tennant

"IT STARTED OUT AS A KIT, AND WHILE I WAS WAITING FOR PARTS, THEY MERGED WITH A VACUUM CLEANER COMPANY."

In this part . . .

This part is for those among you who are bored with lake sailing and want to venture out into the ocean. Here, we explain how to track what happens to the Registry when you install or remove software or hardware, change a Control Panel setting, or do just about anything else affecting your system's configuration. After you use your newfound monitoring skills to unearth great new tips, we show you how you can share Registry changes with others, in the form of INF and REG files.

Finally, this part offers tips on trimming Registry fat to reduce disk and memory waste and improve speed, and even shows you how to compress the entire Registry so it's as lean and mean as possible.

Chapter 12

Tracking and Hacking

. . . .

In This Chapter

▶ Tracking Registry changes by using snapshots

▶ Tracking the Registry in real time with REGMON

▶ Building your own INF and REG files to share Registry hacks with others

▶ Distributing your cool Registry-editing files four different ways

. . . .

*W*atching what happens to the Registry after you change a control panel setting or even install a new program is a great way to explore how the Registry works and to discover new Registry tricks. Being able to share your tricks with other users is even more rewarding. This chapter shows you how to do both.

You've heard the saying that if you give a man a fish, you feed him for a day, but if you teach a man to fish, you pretty much guarantee that his wife will one day gut him with his own cleaning knife because he'll never stay home on weekends anymore to help around the house.

This chapter is inspired by that time-honored cliché. Sure, we could give you a few dozen more pages on specific ways you can customize the Registry. But true Registry mastery means discovering your *own* Registry tricks and distributing them to other PC users (thereby increasing the public store of knowledge for the good of all and sundry). Fortunately, some handy tools and techniques can ease your pioneering journey as you track and hack the Registry in search of the Next Great Registry Tip.

Tracking the Wild Registry

How can you find out exactly what happens to the Registry after you change a control panel setting, install a new program, or install an INF file? You have several options, including snapshotting and using REGMON.

Snapshotting

One method to track Registry changes is to take a snapshot of the Registry before you do something that you think will alter the Registry, take another snapshot afterwards, and compare the "before" and "after" pictures to see what changed. You can make this comparison without any fancy special-purpose software; just create an export REG file by using REGEDIT's Registry⇨Export Registry File command. Name your "before" snapshot BEFORE.REG and your "after" snapshot AFTER.REG.

If you have a pretty good idea of which key an action is likely to affect, export that key only. Comparing very long files, such as an entire export of *HKLM,* can take several minutes even on a fast PC.

Okay, now you need some way to compare the differences.

- **Use any top-of-the-line word processor.** For example, in Word 97, load the first file by choosing File⇨Open. Then load the second file by choosing Tools⇨Track Changes⇨Compare Documents. Whatever the "after" snapshot includes that's missing from the "before" snapshot shows up as strikethrough text in a different color. Whatever entries were deleted show up as underlined text.

- **Use a special file comparison utility.** Microsoft offers a freebie called *WinDiff,* which comes with programming toolkits like Visual C++. Norton Utilities comes with Norton File Compare, which works in similar fashion to the word processor comparison method mentioned in the previous bullet (see Figure 12-1).

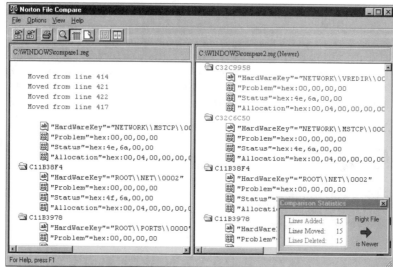

Figure 12-1: Norton File Compare can highlight REG file differences.

✔ **Use a specialized utility.** Programs such as First Aid 98 from CyberMedia or Norton Registry Tracker from Symantec (part of Norton Utilities, see Figure 12-2) are specially designed for taking and comparing Registry snapshots.

Figure 12-2:
Norton
Registry
Tracker
marks
deletions,
made here
by an
uninstall
program,
with a −
sign.
(Additions
appear with
a + sign.)

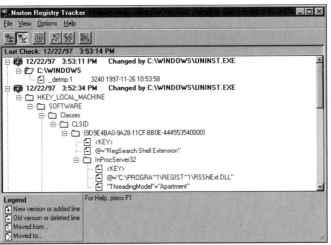

Watching in real time: REGMON

Snapshotting isn't the only way to track Registry changes. One of our favorite Registry utilities and one we include on the enclosed CD-ROM is a freebie: REGMON from Mark Russinovich and Bryce Cogswell (see Figure 12-3). REGMON tracks Registry accesses in *real time,* or as they occur. The data can be overwhelming, but you get a complete picture of every Registry access — reads as well as writes and edits. You'll be amazed by how many Registry accesses even a seemingly simple act like opening Network Neighborhood generates.

Hack Packing (Not through Europe)

After a bit of practice, you master the arts of snapshotting and real-time Registry monitoring. You discover some nifty Registry hacks by tracking what happens when you perform different Windows 95 tasks. Now, you want to share those hacks with other people — at the office, in your local computer users group, or even on the public Internet. Or, maybe you're a

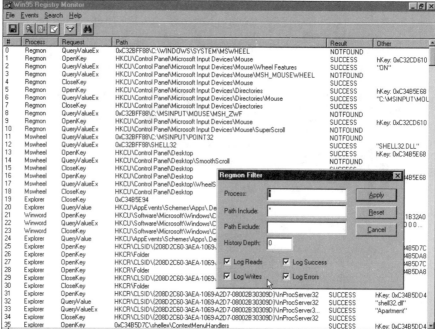

Figure 12-3: REGMON gives you a complete picture of Registry activity.

network manager, and you see the convenience of grouping a bunch of control panel settings together into a single file that you can run on each PC in one fell swoop. Whatever the situation, a Registry master must know about the different ways available to distribute Registry modifications safely and effectively.

Shooting yourself in the foot with a Registry error is one thing, but walking down the hall and shooting 10 or 20 other people in the foot with a Registry error that you propagate is something else entirely. REG, INF, and BAT files are powerful tools. Be very careful with their design and test them yourself before distributing them to others.

REG and INF files: Registry road maps

The two types of files that you can use to distribute your Registry hacks to others are REG (for REGistry file) and INF (for INstallation File). The two file formats have several similarities:

✔ Both are plain text files that you can edit with Notepad.

✔ You can run both file types from a batch file (*.BAT), although with different commands.

✔ Both can add new Registry entries and modify existing ones.

✔ Both can mess up someone's PC in a big hurry if they're buggy.

Here's a quick summary of the differences between REG and INF files:

✔ REG files are simpler.

✔ REG files can only change existing Registry entries or add new ones. INF files, however, can delete existing Registry entries.

✔ INF files can do lots of things in addition to modifying the Registry, including file copying, renaming, and deleting, as well as modifying INI file settings. Because of the flexibility of INF files, hardware vendors use them to install device drivers via the Add New Hardware control panel wizard.

✔ Accidentally installing changes in a REG file is easier because double-clicking a REG file updates the Registry, while you have to right-click an INF file and choose Install to update the Registry.

Rules and REGs

REG files are easy if you don't have to create them yourself from scratch. Just run the Registry Editor, highlight the key in the key pane that you want to export, and choose Registry⇨Export Registry File. Give the thing a name and that's it!

You do need to guard against exporting Registry values that don't pertain to the change you want to distribute to others. Accidentally exporting too many values or keys is easy to do. You can always trim the REG file in Notepad after you create it, if you find that you exported a tad bit too much.

If you want to create your own REG file from scratch — and we can't think of too many cases where you'd prefer doing so versus just modifying the current Registry and performing an export — then you must pay close attention to the rules of REG file construction. Here they are, in brief:

✔ Begin your REG file with a single line that reads `REGEDIT4` in all capital letters.

✔ For every key in which you want to add or change a value, create a new REG file section with the key name in square brackets.

✔ To enter a Default value, use the format `@=valuedata` where valuedata is in double quotes.

✔ If a backslash appears in a Registry value, it appears as a double backslash in the REG file.

The best way to get familiar with these rules is to export a good-sized REG file from the current Registry and then open the REG file with Notepad or a word processor. Compare the lines in the REG file that identify specific keys and values with how the keys and values appear in REGEDIT.

Instructions for INFs

You can't automatically create an INF file like you can create a REG file, so the following section is a crash course in writing your own INF files for modifying the Registry. (We don't take the time to tell you how to copy, delete, or rename files from within an INF file; that's a skill that hardware manufacturers must master, not Registry editors. If you need that sort of information, check out the "Microsoft Windows 95 Resource Kit," Appendix C.)

The header

An INF file for Registry editing should begin with the following lines:

```
[Version]
Signature="$Chicago$"
```

Chicago was the code name for Windows 95 during its development. (The dollar signs are self-explanatory.)

The main section

After the header, add the following lines:

```
[DefaultInstall]
AddReg=Add.Entries
DelReg=Del.Entries
```

You can make *Add.Entries* and *Del.Entries* whatever you want, but you must leave *DefaultInstall*, *AddReg*, and *DelReg* as shown. The values to the right of the = signs tell the INF file to be on the lookout for later sections called [Add.Entries] and [Del.Entries] that contain information to add to or remove from the Registry, respectively.

If you're only adding information to the Registry, you can omit the DelReg line, and vice versa.

Add entries

The part of the INF file that adds keys or values to the Registry looks something like this:

```
[Add.Entries]
HKLM,HARDWARE\Junk,JunkVal,,"INFTest"
```

Again, you can name the section something other than Add.Entries, but it needs to match the name on the AddReg line under [DefaultInstall]. The above example adds a new key, *HKLM\HARDWARE\Junk* and creates the new string value JunkVal with the value data "INFTest."

The generic format for a Registry entry in an INF file is as follows:

```
Branch, Key, ValueName, ValueDataType, ValueData
```

where Branch is the abbreviated main Registry branch (*HKLM, HKU, HKCU, HKCC,* or *HKCR*), and where ValueDataType is 0 for string (ValueData in quotes, like "INFTest"), 1 for binary (ValueData expressed as hexadecimal numbers separated by commas), 2 for string (but don't replace an existing value if one exists), and 3 for binary (but don't replace an existing value).

If you leave out the ValueDataType, as we do in the JunkVal example, then the value is assumed to be a string type, rather than binary. You do, however, have to leave in the same number of commas as when you specify the ValueDataType (note the two commas between JunkVal and "INFTest").

Delete entries

If you want to delete a key or value, your INF file lines look like this:

```
[Del.Entries]
HKLM,HARDWARE\Junk,JunkVal
```

This example removes the JunkVal value from *HKLM\HARDWARE\Junk,* but leaves the *Junk* key intact. Omit the value name JunkVal if you want to delete the entire *Junk* key.

Comments

You can put your own notes and comments in an INF file if you begin the line with a semicolon (;). Providing comments in your files is a good idea. Other people can understand your work more easily, and you can go back to a file that you created months earlier and understand it more quickly, too.

Chapter 8 offers a taste of what INF files can do by looking at the special case of MSBATCH.INF, the file that controls the Windows 95 installation process. You can also look at some sample INF files by checking out C:\WINDOWS\INF*.INF. Most of these files are for installing hardware device drivers, but many of them modify the Registry.

Distributing INF and REG files

Okay, you've put in some quality time creating safe, accurate, reliable INF or REG files. You've tested them once, and then tested them again. You're ready to share them with other Windows 95 aficionados.

Via e-mail

E-mail can be a convenient way to distribute Registry changes. You can send INF and REG files as e-mail *attachments*, which is far preferable to sending the files' text as part of an e-mail message's main body. The chance always exists that your recipient may not copy the text accurately in creating his or her own INF or REG file.

We recommend, however, that you compress your INF or REG files into a ZIP format, using a tool such as WinZip (provided on this book's enclosed CD-ROM). A recipient can easily and accidentally double-click a REG file attachment. You may even want to change the file suffixes to something like IN_ or RE_, and include instructions in your e-mail for renaming the files just before installing them.

Via batch files

You can use the old standby batch file (*.BAT) to install REG or INF file changes. True, users can easily install REG file changes by just double-clicking the REG file, but you can't just double-click an INF file to apply its changes. Further, in either case, you may want to make the process completely automatic — for example, by including your batch file in a network logon script. Or, you may want to offer a polite caution to users and give them the option to cancel the program if they don't have a current Registry backup.

The commands that you use vary depending on whether your Registry changes use the REG or INF file type. The following is a batch file for a REG file called NEW.REG that lives on drive F:, which may be a network drive or a removable cartridge drive. (You would replace NEW.REG and F: in the following example with the name and location of your REG file. Also, this example assumes Windows 95 lives in the usual C:\WINDOWS directory.)

```
@ECHO OFF
REM Sample Batch File to Install a REG File
CLS
ECHO This program modifies your Registry.
ECHO If you don't have a current backup of
ECHO your Registry, press Ctrl-C now.
PAUSE
START C:\WINDOWS\REGEDIT.EXE F:\NEW.REG
CLS
ECHO Registry update complete!
```

If you want to change the batch file to accommodate an INF file, you can do so, but it takes a bit of wizardry. Replace the third to last line (START and so on) with the following (which must be all one line):

```
C:\WINDOWS\RUNDLL.EXE SETUPX.DLL,INSTALLHINFSECTION
   DEFAULTINSTALL 132 F:\NEW.INF
```

For the curious, a bit of explanation: The RUNDLL.EXE program calls the SETUPX.DLL program library, which actually processes the INF file's [DefaultInstall] section. We're not entirely sure what the "132" does, but we know you need it.

A Microsoft tech note stating that your REG file must be in the same directory as your BAT file to avoid an error message seems to be flat-out incorrect. Just remember to specify the full path name of your REG file on the line that runs REGEDIT, and you should be fine.

Via network logon scripts

If you want to update user Registries automatically and your users are on a network, you can use the batch file technique from the previous section and call your batch file from a system-wide network logon script.

Unlike some other kinds of automatic upgrades, you don't have to worry about the Registry changes being applied repeatedly by people who log on multiple times during the period when the batch file is part of the logon script. It doesn't hurt anything to update a user's Registry with the same change several times.

We suggest that you at least consider placing an informative message in the logon script that the user's Registry is about to be modified and provide an "escape clause" if the user is nervous about proceeding. Check the documentation for your particular network regarding the details for creating or modifying logon scripts.

Via diskette

There's nothing wrong with using a diskette to distribute your new REG or INF file, but we suggest you place them in a subdirectory rather than at the diskette's root directory. (Bet you can guess why by this point! It's less likely that someone can accidentally activate a REG or INF file if you put it out of sight a bit.)

Chapter 13

Keeping the Registry Lean, Mean, and Efficient

· ·

In This Chapter

▶ Finding out why you should periodically clean up the Registry

▶ Speeding up the Registry by defragmenting your hard disk

▶ Using the Microsoft REGCLEAN utility

▶ Compressing the Registry

· ·

*T*he Registry is like the attic or basement in an old house: Over time, it collects all sorts of junk that you don't really need anymore. This chapter provides tips for cleaning and optimizing the Registry files for better performance — the tips appearing in order from the simplest to the most complex.

Why Trim the Sails?

We have yet to see the computer operating system that performs all house-keeping chores automatically. Macintosh users periodically have to rebuild the desktop and perform a chore known cryptically as "zapping the PRAM." DOS users have to run the SCANDISK hard drive utility from time to time. Windows 3.*x* users have to clean out their INI files and delete temporary files. Windows 95 users need to run SCANDISK, defragment their disks, and — ta-daa! — clean out and compress the Registry, the subject of this chapter.

Nowhere in the Microsoft-supplied documentation — not even the *Windows 95 Resource Kit* — do you see advice on how to keep your Registry lean, mean, and efficient. However, doing so is a very good idea, from several standpoints.

Disk Space

Much like the population of coat hangers in your clothes closet, the Registry's natural behavior is to grow over time, and never to shrink. But unlike the coat hanger population, the Registry doesn't even shrink if you remove entries from it. After a while, the Registry grows from its typical initial size of about 1MB to 2MB or even more.

That may not sound like much space, but a 2MB Registry can mean the difference between a Registry that fits on a diskette and one that doesn't. Also, on a network of 100 users, with all users backing up their Registries to a network drive, the size difference becomes magnified. (Those server disks tend to be expensive, too.)

RAM

The bigger the Registry, the more Random Access Memory (RAM) Windows 95 and programs like REGEDIT need in order to load its contents. On a machine with 32MB of RAM, the need for additional RAM isn't a big problem. On a machine with 16MB or less, it can affect performance.

Speed

Contrary to some comments that you may see in computer magazines, a smaller Registry doesn't usually help Windows 95 and other application programs access specific Registry entries faster. The Registry's tree-like structure means that programs can get to particular keys fairly quickly, even if the Registry database is large; that's one of the Registry's big advantages over the old INI file system in Windows 3.*x*.

However, a smaller Registry is certainly faster to back up and restore — especially if you use the Registry Editor's export and import feature to do so. Those REG files can take a *long* time to process. And if you ever need to print a large chunk of the Registry, keeping it lean and mean reduces print time, too.

Easier troubleshooting

Navigating the Registry and hunting down potential problems is worlds easier if you don't have to wade through a bunch of flotsam and jetsam left over from old software you don't use anymore.

Defragmenting the Registry

We remember, not that many years ago, when a 5MB hard drive cost $3,000. (It was the Apple Profile, and it was about the size of a small briefcase.) Some older computer pros can remember when hard drives cost upwards of $20,000 per megabyte. In those days, operating system designers had to put a very high premium on squeezing the most possible space out of those expensive disks. So, these designers of yesteryear built in the ability to *fragment* files — chop 'em up into little pieces — just in case a hard drive only had a few separate pockets of free space left. The operating system could then break the file down into pieces and store those pieces in the pockets of free space.

What does that have to do with Windows 95? Everything. Much of Windows 95 traces its roots back to MS-DOS, CP/M (Control Program for Microprocessors), and older operating systems. Windows 95 still fragments files in the course of its daily activities. This fragmentation occurs behind the scenes, and it slows down your computer. The hard disk read/write head has to bounce around all over the disk in order to read a fragmented file.

Windows 95 includes provisions to protect its *swap file* from fragmentation (the swap file is the disk file that Windows 95 uses as a slow substitute for RAM memory when RAM is in short supply). You can just set a minimum swap file size in the System control panel and guarantee that at least that part of the swap file remains *contiguous* (defragmented). However, Windows 95 has no such provision for protecting the Registry files USER.DAT and SYSTEM.DAT from becoming fragmented. When these files are fragmented, they slow down. It's not a huge problem, but it is noticeable, and a Certified Registry Expert Par Excellence won't stand for it.

Windows 95 provides a command to defragment a hard drive. Just right-click a drive icon in My Computer or Explorer, choose Properties, click the Tools tab, and click the Defragment Now button. Defragment your hard drive once a month, and your system will work faster. If the C drive is more than 75 percent full, you should defragment it more often, say weekly.

The problem with the Microsoft-provided defragment command is that it skips hidden files. Guess what! The Registry files are hidden. So, although using the built-in defragment command does make your system faster, it doesn't do squat for the Registry, which is the most frequently accessed set of files on the computer.

You need a more competent utility to defragment the Registry; the most popular one being the Speed Disk program that comes with Symantec Norton Utilities. You can even tell Speed Disk to put the Registry files at the very end of your disk, where they become fragmented less quickly (see Figure 13-1).

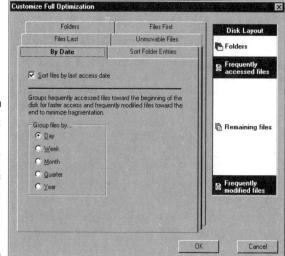

Figure 13-1:
Norton
Speed Disk
offers a
variety of
options to
fine-tune
disk defrag-
menting.

Symantec provides the Norton Scheduler with the Norton Antivirus program. If you have Norton Antivirus and if you leave your PC on overnight, you can automatically schedule Speed Disk to run daily at, say, 2:00 a.m. You can then start computing each morning with a freshly defragmented hard drive, Registry files and all.

If you don't have Norton Antivirus, you can also use the System Agent program to automatically schedule disk defragmentation. System Agent doesn't come with the base Windows 95 product, but it does come with the Plus! add-on package, which most PC vendors throw in with a new system (it may even come on the same CD-ROM as Windows 95). You can install System Agent with the supplied Plus! installation program. System Agent wants you to use the Microsoft-supplied defragmenter, but you can force it to run Speed Disk instead. The System Agent help files supply all the details you need.

Defragmenters typically can't defragment open files, so close all other programs before running the defragment command.

Nuking Old File Types

Now we move into the subject of ridding the Registry of stuff you don't need anymore. A good example of this kind of junk is old *file type associations*, which reside in the Registry.

Most application programs have their own file types — DOC for a word processor, HTM for a Web browser, and so on. When you uninstall a program by using the Control Panel's Add/Remove Programs wizard, the uninstallation procedure is supposed to delete these old file type associations, but in our experience, the deletion doesn't always happen. Also, many programs aren't considerate enough to put themselves on the list of uninstallable programs in the Add/Remove Programs screen, leaving you with no convenient way to even *try* removing old file type associations. Finally, you may have created some file type associations of your own, using the suggestions in Chapter 11, and you may now want to remove them.

Whatever your situation, you can manually strip out some junk from the Registry's *HKey_Classes_Root* (HKCR) branch by deleting old file type associations. Here's the procedure:

1. **Start Windows Explorer by right-clicking the My Computer icon and choosing <u>E</u>xplore.**

2. **Click <u>V</u>iew⇨<u>O</u>ptions to display the Options dialog box.**

3. **Click the File Types tab to display the list of registered file types.**

   The list looks something like Figure 13-2.

4. **Scroll through the list, deleting file types that you know you no longer need by selecting the file types to be deleted and then clicking the <u>R</u>emove button.**

   The Opens With line in the File Type Details area helps you by identifying the program that the Registry associates with each type, as you highlight a type by clicking it in the Registered File Types list.

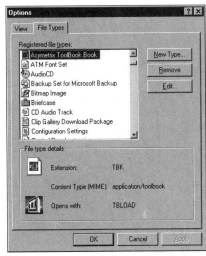

Figure 13-2:
Delete old
file type
associations
using
Explorer,
without
running
REGEDIT.

You can verify the Registry cleanup if you like, by running the Registry Editor and looking through *HKCR* at the list of file type extensions. The Registry doesn't become physically smaller, but the structure becomes simpler, and the list of file types becomes more manageable.

Removing a program's file type association doesn't necessarily remove all Registry entries relating to that program. Commercial utilities such as CyberMedia Uninstaller and Quarterdeck CleanSweep can do a more thorough job.

REGCLEAN: Free, Unsupported, and Mysterious

REGCLEAN is a little utility that can be a handy aid for stripping the cholesterol out of your Registry's arteries. Microsoft supplies REGCLEAN free on its Internet Web site. (The location of the program varies from month to month, but you can go to Microsoft's home page, www.microsoft.com, and use the Search option to locate references to REGCLEAN. Microsoft has been known to take the program out of circulation periodically and fix bugs and enhance the program, so if you don't find it today, look again in a week or two.) You can also find REGCLEAN on the Office 97 Resource Kit's Tools and Utilities CD-ROM, and you may get a copy of the utility with a Visual BASIC program supplied by a software developer. The Visual BASIC license that software developers enter into with Microsoft includes the right to redistribute REGCLEAN with their programs.

Installing REGCLEAN is simply a matter of copying the file REGCLEAN.EXE to your hard drive; no fancy setup program exists. We suggest that you use Explorer or My Computer to create the directory C:\PROGRAM FILES\ REGCLEAN and copy the file there.

REGCLEAN 4.1, the current version as we write, requires you to update some of the system files on your hard disk before REGCLEAN works reliably. At this time, the update file is named OADIST.EXE, and you can download it over the Internet from www.microsoft.com/kb/articles/q164/5/29.htm or from ftp://ftp.microsoft.com/Softlib/MSLFILES/oadist.exe. After you have OADIST.EXE on your PC, just double-click it to update the necessary files automatically. (Specifically, you need the updated files in order to avoid the error messages REGCLEAN.EXE is linked to missing export OLEAUT32.DLL:421 and A device attached to the system is not correctly functioning.)

REGCLEAN doesn't fix messed-up Registries. Only run REGCLEAN on a Registry that seems to be working correctly. Don't run any version of REGCLEAN earlier than 4.1; earlier versions can create problems by removing an important key (*HKCR\Interface\{00020400-0000-0000-C000-000000000046}*, if you're interested, and we hope you're not). Finally, as always, you're smart to back up your Registry before running REGCLEAN or any utility that modifies the Registry.

What REGCLEAN does

Microsoft hasn't documented REGCLEAN well, but here's what we've been able to determine by working with the program. REGCLEAN looks for Registry keys that are common to all Windows 95 and NT PCs and that pertain to Microsoft Office programs; the program then scans those keys for errors. Specifically, REGCLEAN looks for references to files on disk that no longer exist or that no longer exist at the location specified in the Registry. (If you have Symantec Norton Utilities, you may prefer its Registry cleanup features to REGCLEAN's; see "Distinguishing Good Orphans from Bad" later in this chapter.)

Most, if not all, of REGCLEAN's activity seems to focus on the keys *HKLM\SOFTWARE\Classes* and *HKLM\SOFTWARE\Classes\TypeLib*.

What REGCLEAN doesn't do

As is often the case with freebie software, REGCLEAN 4.1 has a number of limitations. Specifically, REGCLEAN doesn't

- Advise you when it finds no problems in your Registry. REGCLEAN behaves the same way whether it finds problems or not.

- Try to fix Registry references to files that don't exist where the Registry says they exist; REGCLEAN merely deletes the Registry references. If you move a Microsoft Office program to a different directory without rerunning that program's setup utility, REGCLEAN doesn't scan your hard drive to figure out where you've moved the program.

- Do a complete job on the first run-through. Microsoft advises that you shouldn't have to run it more than four times in a row, though (!).

- Come with a help file to explain what sort of surgery it performs on your Registry.

- Try to remove Registry entries that pertain to software other than the base Windows 95 product and Microsoft Office.

Running REGCLEAN

Fortunately, running REGCLEAN is easier than describing it. Here's the process:

1. **Double-click the REGCLEAN.EXE icon in the folder where you installed the program.**

   REGCLEAN loads a copy of the part of the Registry it knows about and scans for errors (see Figure 13-3). Microsoft advises that the scanning process can take from 2 to 30 minutes, depending on your Registry's size and your computer's speed, so don't give up if the program seems stalled.

2. **After the progress bars disappear, click the F̲ix Errors button to make the corrections REGCLEAN suggests, or click Cancel if you've had an attack of nerves.**

   No actual changes to your Registry have been made up to this point, but after you click the Fix Errors button, REGCLEAN makes the changes and creates an undo file (see "Recovering from a bad cleanup" later in this section).

3. **In My Computer or Explorer, right-click the most recent undo file created by REGCLEAN (located in the same directory as REGCLEAN.EXE) and choose E̲dit. If the undo file contains what appear to be Registry entries, repeat Steps 1 and 2. If it doesn't (see Figure 13-4), you're done.**

If you notice that some of your Microsoft Office icons have changed, simply running the affected program or programs from the Start menu is usually enough to fix the icons.

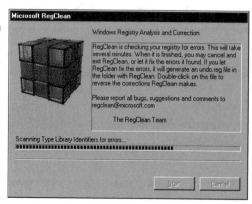

Figure 13-3:
The
Microsoft
REGCLEAN
utility
displays
progress
bars while
scanning
for errors.

After running REGCLEAN and restarting your PC, double-click one example of each different data file type (word processing, spreadsheet, and so on) you use on a regular basis to make sure REGCLEAN hasn't fouled something up for you.

Recovering from a bad cleanup

Although generally reliable, REGCLEAN can create certain kinds of problems as it fixes others. Most noticeably, REGCLEAN causes problems to users of the Microsoft Network online service.

The best feature of REGCLEAN from a safety standpoint is that you can easily undo the changes the program makes. After you run REGCLEAN and choose to save the changes it makes, REGCLEAN creates a file (in the same directory where REGCLEAN.EXE resides) with a name like *Undo MOOSE 19971203 120031.REG*. (The general format is *Undo **computername date time**.REG*.)

You can undo REGCLEAN's changes three ways:

- ✔ Double-click the undo file (assuming that you haven't changed the REG file association).
- ✔ Right-click the undo file, and choose Merge.
- ✔ Run REGEDIT, choose Registry⇨Import Registry File, and choose the undo file.

Note that REGCLEAN 4.1 always produces an undo file, even if the program finds no errors in the Registry. Figure 13-4 shows what such an undo file looks like.

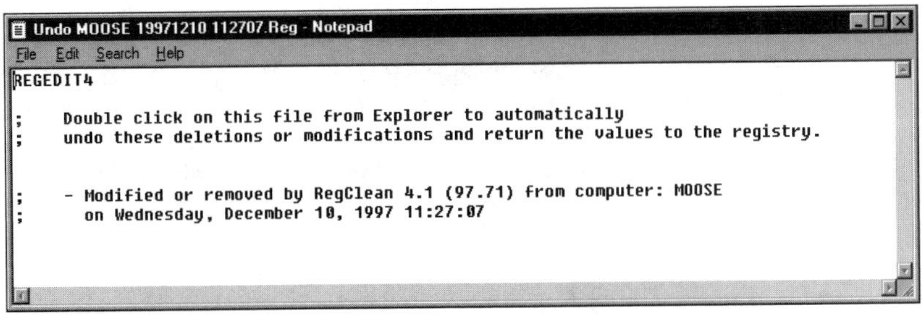

Figure 13-4:
If you see a file like this, you know that further REGCLEAN repetitions aren't necessary.

```
Undo MOOSE 19971210 112707.Reg - Notepad
File  Edit  Search  Help
REGEDIT4

;     Double click on this file from Explorer to automatically
;     undo these deletions or modifications and return the values to the registry.

;     - Modified or removed by RegClean 4.1 (97.71) from computer: MOOSE
;       on Wednesday, December 10, 1997 11:27:07
```

Distinguishing Good Orphans from Bad

A Registry *orphan* is an entry that points to a file or another Registry entry that doesn't exist. The most common reason for your Registry to have orphans is that an application program doesn't remove itself completely from the Registry when you run its uninstall program or when you uninstall the application manually by deleting directories and files in My Computer or Explorer.

Microsoft is a prime violator of the rule that a program should remove its unique Registry entries when you uninstall the program. The list of Registry keys and values that Microsoft Office leaves in your Registry after you remove Office contains dozens of entries. The tech notes that Microsoft publishes on this subject merely state that "This behavior is by design." We suspect that this statement is a euphemism for "This product ships tomorrow and tidying up the Registry is task number 366 on our to-do list." When a user reinstalls a Microsoft Office program, the setup utility re-creates any Registry entries that are missing and required, so no good reason exists to leave the entries behind after an uninstall.

Most orphans don't do any harm other than cluttering up the attic. They're just Registry entries that don't do anything. However, you can improve your operating speed, conserve RAM, and simplify your Registry by removing orphans that point to files on your hard drive that don't exist anymore.

Some orphans are actually *good* to leave in the Registry. Specifically, string values that point to directories on a CD-ROM drive may be useful when you rerun a particular program's setup utility. If you delete these kinds of orphans, the setup program may no longer know where to look for the files it needs. You may have to tell the program where to find the files, which can be a bit of a pain, especially if the files lie several directories deep on the CD-ROM.

Other entries that you may as well leave in place are those that appear in keys having the name *Recent file list* or something similar. Many programs maintain a list of files that you've recently opened (you may see the acronym *MRU,* for *Most Recently Used*). Deleting such orphans doesn't free up any Registry space because these programs just rebuild the recent file list when you open more data files.

Finding orphans

REGCLEAN removes orphans that pertain to certain Windows 95, Windows NT, and Microsoft Office keys (see the previous section in this chapter, "REGCLEAN: Free, Unsupported, and Mysterious"), but it doesn't remove orphans that pertain to other software. So how do you go looking for these orphans?

REGEDIT doesn't include an orphan-hunting option, but Norton Registry Editor (NRE) does in Symantec Norton Utilities for Windows 95 Version 2.0 — which is a good thing because finding orphans manually would take you days and wouldn't be worth the effort. Here's the procedure:

1. **Run Norton Registry Editor, usually by clicking Start⇨Programs⇨ Norton Utilities⇨Norton Registry Editor.**

2. **Choose Edit⇨Find to display the Find dialog box.**

3. **Click the Orphans radio button and click the Find Now button.**

   NRE begins its search. It may consult CD-ROM drives, diskette drives, and network drives in its hunt for files that the Registry points to. The status bar at the bottom of the NRE window gives you a progress report and says "Done searching" after it's done searching. The process usually takes no more than a couple of minutes, and the results appear in the Find Results window in the bottom third of the NRE window.

Version 3.0 of Norton Utilities takes the orphan search out of the Norton Registry Editor and makes it part of the new WinDoctor utility (see Figure 13-5). The procedure is as follows:

1. **Choose Start⇨Programs⇨Norton Utilities⇨WinDoctor.**

2. **In the Norton WinDoctor Wizard dialog box, select Perform All Norton WinDoctor Tests (Recommended), and click Next.**

3. **When you see the** Finished Scanning **message, click Next, read the message, and click Finish to see the list of Problems Found.**

4. **Double-click each problem category to repair the listed problems.**

Deleting orphans

After you've identified orphans by using Norton Registry Editor or WinDoctor (see the preceding section), you're ready to do away with the little idlers. Remember, however, that you only want to get rid of the bad orphans (the ones that point to your hard drive); leave the good orphans (the ones that point to your CD-ROM drive) and the ones that just keep running back to the Registry (the recent file list orphans).

As you scroll through the list of orphans that NRE or WinDoctor found, you're likely to see a large number that point to your CD-ROM drive or network drives. You can detect these orphans by the drive letter that appears in the Data column of the Find Results window. If the drive letter is something other than C:, chances are that the value is pointing to a CD-ROM or network location. (Some PCs may have additional drive letters that point to the hard drive; when in doubt, open the My Computer window and look at the icons that correspond to the different drive letters.)

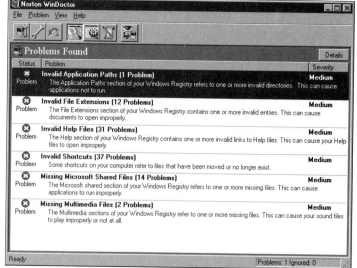

Figure 13-5:
The Norton
WinDoctor
program in
Norton
Utilities
Version 3.0
finds and
categorizes
Registry
orphans.

The entries that point to your hard drive are probably orphans that you can safely delete. Allow some time for this chore, as NRE or WinDoctor may find hundreds of such orphans.

Before you delete orphan values, back up your Registry, just in case! Chapter 2 provides all the gory details.

The procedure for deleting orphan values in NRE is simple. Just double-click the line under the Root column in the Find Results window pane, and NRE resets its top two window panes to display that entry. Take a look at the entry, and if you can tell that the entry pertains to a program you don't use anymore, delete it. Continue down through the list in the Find Results window pane until you reach the end (the procedure can take a while!). Restart your computer and enjoy your streamlined Registry. Test the programs you use to be sure that everything is copacetic, and you're done. If something has gone haywire, restore the Registry from the backup that you made prior to your orphan-deleting session.

Compressing the Entire Registry

Okay, here's where things get really fun. In this section, you're going to slim down your Registry so it's as skinny as it can possibly be. The way to make your Registry super-lean — in fact, the *only* way to do it — is to export the Registry's contents, create a brand-new Registry database, and reload the contents.

We tried the procedure on the machine that we're using to write this book. This procedure, using a Registry that had never been compressed, produces the results in Table 13-1.

Table 13-1	Registry Compression Results		
	Before Compression	*After Compression*	*Percent Reduction*
Size of SYSTEM.DAT	2517K	2084K	17%
Size of USER.DAT	357K	281K	21%

The Registry compression procedure is one of the riskier ones in the book, if you don't follow our instructions to the letter. Depending on which version of Windows 95 you have, compression can also be a rather messy process that requires a certain amount of cleanup after the fact. If you don't have an hour or so to go through the process or if you're not a patient person by nature, don't try to compress your Registry. And please, don't take any shortcuts in the steps that follow!

OSR2 method

Compressing the Registry is easier if you have the OSR2 version of Windows 95 because you don't have to work around a limitation of REGEDIT. Check the System control panel's General tab and look at the Windows 95 version number. If you see 4.00.950B, you have OSR2.0 or 2.1; if you see 4.00.95C, you have OSR2.5.

Do *not* try the method in this section if you have version 4.00.950 or version 4.00.950a. It probably won't work, and then you'll be in a pickle. We don't want you to be in a pickle. Yuck.

Here's the procedure:

1. **Back up the Registry by using your favorite method (see Chapter 2).**

   We suggest you also make a backup copy of SYSTEM.INI, WIN.INI, and ShellIconCache (these files are all in the C:\WINDOWS directory).

2. **Run REGCLEAN if you have it.**

   See previous section "REGCLEAN: Free, Unsupported, and Mysterious" in this chapter.

3. **Defragment your hard drive.**

   See the previous section "Defragmenting the Registry" in this chapter. This optional step makes everything go a little faster.

4. Reboot your computer and press F8 at startup.

5. Choose the Command Prompt Only option.

6. After the command prompt appears, type the command:

```
REGEDIT /E TOTAL.TXT
```

This command exports your entire Registry to a text file.

7. After the command prompt returns, type the command:

```
REGEDIT /C TOTAL.TXT
```

This command recreates your Registry, compressing it in the process.

8. Restart Windows 95 with the three-finger salute, Ctrl+Alt+Del. Let Windows 95 start normally.

You should notice a significant reduction in the sizes of SYSTEM.DAT and USER.DAT. The percentage reduction varies depending on how long you've been using your PC and how many programs you've installed on it. If you run into any problems while using your normal software, you can restore the original Registry from the backup that you made in Step 1.

OSR1 method

If you have one of the original versions of Windows 95, you have an older REGEDIT program that has a limitation that you must dance around. Check the System control panel's General tab and look at the Windows 95 version number. If you see 4.00.950 or 4.00.950a, you have OSR1.

The limitation is that your version of REGEDIT sometimes fails when attempting to import long keys, such as the keys under *HKU\.Default\ Software,* from a command prompt. REGEDIT can import these long keys with no problem when it's running in the Windows 95 graphical mode. So what you're going to do is create a minimal Registry in the command prompt mode, then boot Windows 95 into a safe graphical mode and finish the reconstruction process.

If the list of steps that follows seems long and involved, please let us reassure you that the procedure is no more difficult than designing your own communications satellite. (Seriously, take it one step at a time, and it's not all that hard.)

1. Back up the Registry by using your favorite method (see Chapter 2).

We suggest you also make a backup copy of SYSTEM.INI, WIN.INI, and ShellIconCache (these files are all in the C:\WINDOWS directory).

2. Run REGCLEAN if you have it.

See previous section "REGCLEAN: Free, Unsupported, and Mysterious" in this chapter.

3. Defragment your hard drive.

See the previous section "Defragmenting the Registry" in this chapter. This optional step makes everything go a little faster.

4. Run REGEDIT and click Registry➪Export Registry File.

The Export Registry File dialog box appears.

5. In the Export Registry File dialog box, make sure that the All radio button is checked in the Export Range area and that the C:\WINDOWS directory is highlighted in the Save In field. Type TOTAL in the File Name field.

6. Click the Save button.

REGEDIT creates the file TOTAL.REG in the C:\WINDOWS directory.

7. Expand the HKEY_USERS branch to display whatever subkeys exist under it.

You see one named .*Default,* and possibly one other.

8. Expand the first subkey under HKEY_USERS and expand the subkey named Software.

You see a bunch of subkeys with the names of software companies whose programs you've installed.

9. Delete every subkey *under* the Software key, leaving the Software key itself.

What you're doing here is getting rid of the keys that the real-mode version of REGEDIT will likely find troublesome.

10. Repeat Steps 8 and 9 for the other subkey immediately under HKEY_USERS, if one exists.

11. Click the HKEY_USERS key in the Registry Editor's key pane to highlight it.

12. Click Registry➪Export Registry File.

13. In the Export Registry File dialog box, make sure that the Selected Branch radio button is checked in the Export Range area and shows the key HKEY_USERS. **Also make sure that the C:\WINDOWS directory is highlighted in the Save In field. Type SMALL in the File Name field.**

14. Click the Save button.

REGEDIT creates the file SMALL.REG in the C:\WINDOWS directory. SMALL.REG is the file you use to create the miniature fresh Registry database at the command prompt.

15. Reboot your computer and press F8 at startup.

16. Choose the Command Prompt Only option.

17. After the command prompt appears, type the command:

```
REGEDIT /C SMALL.REG
```

This command re-creates a new Registry, but without the troublesome software keys.

18. Reboot your computer and press F8 at startup.

19. Choose the Safe Mode option.

Windows 95 starts in Safe Mode, making an awful hard drive racket and messing up your desktop icons and taskbar in the process. Don't worry about the desktop, you'll clean it up later. Don't worry about the hard drive noise, either; Windows 95 doesn't read the disk efficiently in Safe Mode. You should see the Safe Mode indicators in the four corners of your screen.

20. Click Start⇨Run and type C:\WINDOWS\REGEDIT TOTAL.REG **in the Open field. Click OK.**

Windows 95 runs REGEDIT and imports the contents of your full Registry export that you created in Step 6, including those software keys you deleted to make SMALL.REG. Because you're running the graphical mode of REGEDIT, the program can handle those software keys without a problem. Windows 95 may appear as if it isn't doing anything for a few minutes, but if you glance at your PC's hard drive light, it should be flickering.

21. Wait patiently (maybe five minutes, tops) until you see the message, Information in TOTAL.REG has been successfully entered into the Registry. **Then click OK.**

22. Restart Windows 95 normally.

23. Fix the icons on your desktop so they're back the way you want them and resize and reposition the taskbar if necessary.

That should do it. You should notice a significant reduction in the sizes of SYSTEM.DAT and USER.DAT. The percentage reduction varies depending on how long you've been using your PC and how many programs you've installed on it. You may well find that your Registry is now small enough to back up onto a single diskette. In any case, it will be simpler, take less RAM, and maybe run a little faster, too.

If you run into any problems while using your normal software, you can restore the original Registry from the backup that you made in Step 1.

Part V
Computer Overboard! Registry Troubleshooting

"The image is getting clearer now... I can almost see it... Yes! There it is – the glitch is in the HKey_Classes_Root\Drive key."

In this part . . .

*E*ven the most expert sailors occasionally find themselves out at sea when a thunderstorm hits. Part V is your guide to getting safely to port when you find yourself suddenly faced with Registry trouble.

From solutions for the most common Registry problems to methods of recovering your Registry from a backup, this part prepares you for most of the unpleasant surprises that the Windows 95 Registry can send your way.

Chapter 14

A Dirty Dozen Registry Problems (And Solutions!)

. . . .

In This Chapter

▶ Fixing problems at Windows 95 startup

▶ Discovering what to do when double-clicking and right-clicking don't work correctly

▶ Solving REG file problems

. . . .

*P*roblems are inevitable if you spend very much time working with PCs. This chapter presents some of the more common Registry-related problems and ways to get around them.

Windows 95 Displays a Registry Error at Startup

When starting Windows 95, you may see one of the following error messages:

```
There is not enough memory to load the Registry.
```

```
Windows has encountered an error accessing the system
        registry. You should restore the registry now
        and restart the computer.
```

```
Registry file was not found. Registry services may be
        inoperative for this session.
```

```
SDMErr(80000003): Registry access failed.
```

In some cases, Windows 95 then kicks you out to a command prompt, leaving you staring at C:> and wondering where all your windows went.

Non-Registry causes

Even though Windows 95 tells you that something's wrong with the Registry, it ain't necessarily so. For example, something may be wrong with the startup file C:\MSDOS.SYS. The file may be missing, in which case you can restore the startup file by using the Emergency Recovery Utility's ERD program (see Chapters 2 and 15). Or, the file may be damaged, in which case you can also restore it with ERD.

1. **At the command prompt, type the command**

```
ATTRIB -R -H MSDOS.SYS
```

This command clears the startup file's Read-only attribute.

2. **Run the DOS text editor with the command**

```
EDIT C:\MSDOS.SYS
```

3. **Change the first few lines so that they read as follows:**

```
[Paths]
WinDir=C:\WINDOWS
WinBootDir=C:\WINDOWS
HostWinBootDrv=C
```

4. **Save MSDOS.SYS, set the attributes back to read-only and hidden (same command as in Step 1 but use + instead of – both places), and restart.**

If the Registry error message goes away, you must be living right!

Registry causes

If MSDOS.SYS is Okay, then you may truly have Registry problems. If you have the newer version of REGEDIT that comes with Windows 95 version 4.00.950B (the so-called OEM Service Release 2), which you can check by glancing at the General tab on the System control panel, then life is grand. You can rebuild the Registry at the command prompt with the following three commands, in sequence:

```
CD C:\WINDOWS
REGEDIT /E TOTAL.REG
REGEDIT /C TOTAL.REG
```

The second command (/E) exports the Registry to the file TOTAL.REG, and the third command (/C) rebuilds the Registry by importing TOTAL.REG. If you're not at the command prompt, get there by restarting Windows 95, pressing F8 at the Starting Windows 95 message, and choosing *Safe mode command prompt only*.

If you don't have the newer version of Windows 95 (that is, if your version number is 4.00.950 or 4.00.950a), refer to Chapter 15 for techniques to restore the Registry from a previous backup. See especially "Restoring from DA0 files."

REGEDIT Displays Error Messages

Here are a few of the more common error messages that the Registry Editor may display:

- **The specified file is not a registry script.** The only way REGEDIT can tell whether a file is a registry script or not is by looking at the very beginning of the file for the line REGEDIT4. If this line is missing, you get this error.

- **Unable to delete all specified values.** REGEDIT doesn't let you delete the (Default) value in the value pane (right window). If you want to get rid of a key, delete it in REGEDIT's key pane (left window).

- **Unable to rename (key name). The specified key name contains illegal characters.** You see this message if you try to use the backslash character in a key name; it's *verboten.*

- **The specified key name already exists.** Key names have to be unique, at least within a particular group.

I Can't Boot to Safe Mode

Several times in this book, we advise you to restart Windows 95 in its so-called "safe mode," which enables you to make changes to the Registry — such as a total restore — that you otherwise can't safely make. Working in safe mode is also a way of sidestepping problems with certain hardware device drivers that don't want to start properly in a normal boot.

The usual procedure for getting to safe mode is to restart the operating system, press F8 after you see the Starting Windows 95 message, and choose *Safe mode command prompt only* from the menu that appears. (You can use a graphical version that's just called *Safe mode,* which you may need in order to run the Registry Editor without errors — see the section later in this chapter titled "Importing Fails with Real-Mode REGEDIT.")

What if you can't get the F8 key to display the menu of choices after you restart the operating system? One possibility is that someone's tinkered with the MSDOS.SYS text file, either to reduce the boot delay period during which you can press the F8 key or to disable it altogether. Here's how to fix this problem:

1. **In Explorer, right-click C:\MSDOS.SYS and choose P̲roperties.**

2. **Clear the Read-only and Hidden check boxes and click OK.**

3. **Shift+right-click MSDOS.SYS and choose Op̲en With.**

4. **Clear the check box (if it's checked) that reads Always U̲se This Program to Open This Type of File, and select Notepad from the list of programs.**

5. **If you see the line** BootKeys=0 **in the [Options] section, change the line to read** BootKeys=1 **so that the F8 key works at startup.**

   If you want to give yourself more time to hit the F8 key, under the [Options] section, add or modify the line BootDelay=n where n is the number of seconds you want.

   If you don't want to worry about hitting F8 at all, and want the system to always present the boot menu choices, under the [Options] section, add the line BootMenu=1.

6. **After you're finished, close Notepad, and reverse the changes you made in Steps 1 and 2.**

For a detailed discussion of safe mode, please see Chapter 15, specifically the section "There's no mode like safe mode."

I Can't Reverse Restrictive Policies

The System Policy Editor, POLEDIT, allows you to set a policy for the current Registry that disables the Registry Editor (expand *Local User – System – Restrictions;* and select the Disable Registry Editing Tools check box). Later, you can use POLEDIT to reverse this setting if you want to run REGEDIT.

However, you may not be able to run POLEDIT if you've also added restrictions to what programs Windows 95 is allowed to run (expand *Local User – System – Restrictions;* select the Only Run Allowed Windows Applications check box). Figure 14-1 shows POLEDIT after the user has selected the Disable Registry Editing Tools and Only Run Allowed Windows Applications check boxes. If POLEDIT isn't on the list of allowed Windows applications, then you can't run the program to remove the restrictions on itself and on REGEDIT. Oh no! A vicious circle!

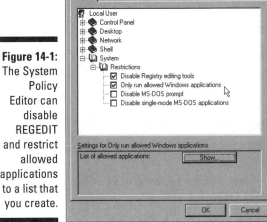

Figure 14-1:
The System
Policy
Editor can
disable
REGEDIT
and restrict
allowed
applications
to a list that
you create.

Well, you're not really trapped. Microsoft's *Windows 95 Resource Kit* hints that you may have to reinstall Windows 95 in this scenario, but that's baloney. What you need to do is create a REG file that looks like the following:

```
REGEDIT4

[HKEY_CURRENT_USER\Software\Microsoft\Windows\CurrentVersion\Policies\Explorer]
"RestrictRun"=dword:00000000
```

You can even create this text file on another computer and bring the file over on diskette, if you find that you can't run any programs at all. This REG file — call it UNLOCK.REG or something similar — resets the RestrictRun value to zero, effectively switching off the policy that restricts you to only running certain applications.

You can't run REGEDIT directly in order to import this REG file because you've disabled Registry editing tools with the Policy Editor. However, this situation is no sweat for those in the know. Use Windows Explorer to locate the REG file, right-click it, choose Merge, and presto chango — the program restrictions disappear. You can now run the Policy Editor and fine-tune the restrictions until they're the way you *really* want them.

After reading this section, you may think that setting restrictions by selecting the Disable Registry Editing Tools check box isn't very secure because you can still modify the Registry by simply right-clicking a REG file. Hey, this restriction is even less secure than that! You can also right-click an INF file and choose Install, which enables you to not only modify and add to Registry values but also to outright delete them. Remember, Windows 95's security is West Coast casual.

The Wrong Program Runs When I Double-Click a File

When you double-click a data file and run an unexpected program, the usual culprit is a messed-up file type association list. Fortunately, you can probably fix the problem without using the Registry Editor, although you do modify the Registry (specifically the *HKCR* branch).

1. **Open My Computer or Explorer and choose View⇨Options.**

2. **Click the File Types tab, then scroll down to the file type that's acting up and click it.**

3. **Click Edit and modify the Open action in the Edit File Type dialog box to specify the program that you want.**

   ("Open" is the same as "double-click" in Windows 95.)

The Properties Option Crashes Windows 95

If you can't see the property sheet for data files and desktop icons when you right-click them and choose the Properties option, you have to run REGEDIT to correct the problem (or, at least, to identify the problem). Many variations of this problem exist, but we offer up one example from our own experience to illustrate the troubleshooting technique. The example borrows several tricks and techniques from different chapters. If you can read through it once or twice and understand more than half of it, you're ready to graduate from Registry U with honors!

Recently, after Glenn removed the Novell NetWare Client32 software from his Network control panel, he found that accessing the property sheet for just about any kind of Windows 95 object — shortcut, data file, program, you name it — crashed the system with the error message shown in Figure 14-2.

Because the problem seems to be nearly universal and affects almost all file types, we suspect the asterisk key (*) in the Registry's *HKCR* branch. Anything in the (*) key applies more or less universally to Windows 95 icons and files. Opening *HKCR*\shellex\PropertySheetHandlers* reveals the keys in Figure 14-3, which are unique tags — Class Identifiers (CLSIDs) — pointing to the programs that manage property sheets.

Figure 14-2:
Property
sheets
have gone
haywire on
Glenn's PC,
offering
only this
error
message.

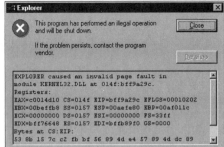

Figure 14-3:
REGEDIT
shows the
class IDs
for property
sheet
programs.

Those CLSIDs don't mean diddly to us. We know, however, that the Registry contains more information about each CLSID under *HKCR\CLSID*. (Chapter 6 explains this key in more detail.) We just have to find the right CLSID among the hundreds of CLSIDs on Glenn's PC. Fortunately, REGEDIT has a Find command.

Being essentially lazy and not wanting to retype the whole long CLSID, we highlight the CLSID key in the screen shown by Figure 14-4, right-click it, choose Rename, then hit Ctrl+C to copy the long ID to the Windows Clipboard. (A quick Esc deselects the key name, which we don't really want to change.) We then hit Ctrl+F to bring up the Find dialog box and press Ctrl+V to paste the suspicious CLSID into the Find What field. Our find operation brings up the entry that we need (see Figure 14-4).

Figure 14-4:
The
HKCR\CLSID
key holds
more clues.

Expanding the key, we see that a subkey called *InProcServer32* resides below it. This subkey indicates the program or program library that Windows 95 associates with the CLSID. Clicking *InProcServer32* reveals the file: NWSHELLX.DLL. Sure enough, a quick check using Windows Explorer shows NWSHELLX.DLL sitting innocently with most of the other program libraries in C:\WINDOWS\SYSTEM.

The "NW" at the start of the file name suggests that NWSHELLX.DLL is a NetWare related file. We can't check its property sheet (remember, the property sheets are broken), but it's a good working hypothesis. So, we go back to *HKCR*\shellex\PropertySheetHandlers* and delete the key that we've just discovered points to a NetWare file. We removed NetWare from the PC earlier, so we're not too worried that this key is something that we still need. Nevertheless, we export the key to a small REG file before deleting it, just in case we're wrong, so we can import it later. (See Chapter 4 for details on importing and exporting REG files.)

After closing REGEDIT, right-clicking NWSHELLX.DLL, and choosing Properties, the property sheet now appears — success! — and we see in the Novell Inc. copyright notice that this file is, in fact, a leftover from the NetWare Client32 software. The leftover file doesn't work right anymore because Glenn deactivated the Client32 software by using the Network control panel. Why is this file still hanging around and why does its property sheet handler still exist in the Registry? We may never know for sure, but a less-than-tidy deinstallation script seems a probable cause. The main thing is that the property sheets work again. We didn't have to reinstall Windows 95, and knowing about the Registry made the troubleshooting process a quick one.

Importing Fails with Real-Mode REGEDIT

You try to run REGEDIT in real mode (command prompt only, or safe mode command prompt only), for example, to import a tiny little REG file. Alas, every time you make the attempt, you see the following error message:

```
Unable to open Registry (14) - SYSTEM.DAT
```

Or, perhaps you're importing a rather large REG file, and you see the message:

```
Error accessing the registry: The file may not be complete.
```

Both of these errors stem from the same problem: REGEDIT's inability to deal with a large Registry, or a large REG file, in its command prompt mode of operation. Microsoft fixed the problem with Windows 95 version 4.00.950B ("OSR2"), but this fact doesn't help you if you have an earlier version of Windows (because you can't upgrade to OSR2).

The best solution is to boot Windows 95 normally, if possible, and use REGEDIT in its graphical, protected mode — where it has access to more memory. Chances are that your import operation now proceeds smoothly. If you can't boot Windows 95 normally, however, you have a few options, none of them especially convenient:

✔ See whether you can boot Windows 95 into safe mode (the graphical version, not *Safe mode command prompt only*). See the section earlier in this chapter, "I Can't Boot to Safe Mode," for details.

✔ Scrounge a copy of the new REGEDIT program from someone with an OSR2 machine and run it from diskette on your machine.

✔ Boot your PC from the emergency startup diskette and try running REGEDIT. Your PC should have a little more available memory this way.

✔ Chop your large REG file into two or more smaller pieces, using a text editor such as the DOS Edit program. (REG files list each key as a complete path, so where you perform your surgery doesn't matter much.)

Importing a REG File Misses Some Keys

You perform an import (or merge) of a REG file, maybe a REG file that you wrote yourself, but some or all the keys in the REG file don't appear in the actual Registry.

Windows 95 is very nitpicky about the punctuation in REG files. The most common problems are as follows:

✔ The file doesn't start with a separate line containing the word *REGEDIT4*. (This word must be all capital letters.) In this case, REGEDIT displays the message in Figure 14-5.

✔ The file includes keys or values that are missing a curly bracket ({ or }).

✔ The file includes string values that are missing the enclosing double quotes.

✔ The file includes path names that use single backslashes instead of the required double backslashes.

Figure 14-5:
If you
see this
message,
your REG
file doesn't
have the
correct
first line.

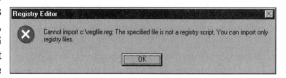

It's much easier to export a REG file of the key you want to modify and then change the REG file to your liking by using Notepad, rather than create the REG file from scratch.

We also need to mention that REGEDIT gives you absolutely no indication whether it finds invalid statements in a REG file after it finds the REGEDIT4 header at the beginning of the file. Because you don't see an error message, the only way you know your REG file works is to run REGEDIT and check the keys and values manually. To illustrate, take a look at Figure 14-6. We merged this utterly bogus REG file into the Registry (after making a backup first!), and the result was the cheery message that the information in JUNK.REG had been "successfully entered into the Registry." Yecch. (Incidentally, Windows 95 still ran perfectly normally.)

Figure 14-6:
This sham
REG file
imports
without
prompting
an error
message.

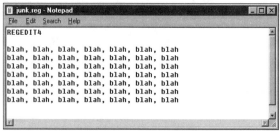

Importing a REG File Creates Unwanted Duplicates

This problem is a subtle variation on the preceding one. When Windows 95 processes a REG file, instead of changing the value of a particular key or value, REGEDIT seems to add a new key or value with the same name (see Figure 14-7).

Figure 14-7:
The strange
case of
duplicate
values,
which
supposedly
REGEDIT
doesn't
permit.

The most likely cause of this strange problem is a space at the end of the key name in your REG file. If such a *trailing space* exists, then REGEDIT interprets the key or value as new and different and adds it to the Registry, instead of changing the existing entry. Solution: If you write your REG files from scratch, make sure your key and value names have no trailing spaces.

After Restoring the Registry the Fonts Are Gone

You've restored your Registry to fix a particular problem, using any of the various methods we describe in Chapter 15. Your problem goes away as a result of your efforts, but now you have a new one: All the TrueType fonts seem to be absent from the font list in your application programs. When you go to the Fonts control panel, it's empty. When you try to add a font, Windows 95 gives you an error message stating that the font is already installed! It's a catch-22.

Most likely, the Registry key *HKLM\SOFTWARE\Microsoft\Windows\ CurrentVersion\Fonts* is either missing or damaged.

➤ If the key is missing, run C:\WINDOWS\FONTREG.EXE to create the key quickly; then go to the Fonts control panel and reinstall your fonts (they usually reside in C:\WINDOWS\FONTS) with the File⇨Install New Font command.

➤ If the key is present, it's probably damaged. Use Windows Explorer to move all the TTF files from C:\WINDOWS\FONTS to a different folder, run REGEDIT, delete the key mentioned previously, and re-add it. Go to the Fonts control panel and reinstall your fonts (they reside in the new directory you created) with the File⇨Install New Font command.

Changing a File System Profile Slows Windows Down

You read somewhere that Windows 95 has a secret method for speeding up machines with more than 16MB of RAM. Here's how:

1. **Run the System control panel.**

2. **Choose the Performance tab and click the File System button.**

   The File System Properties dialog box appears (see Figure 14-8).

3. **In the Typical Role of This Machine drop-down list, Select the Network Server option (rather than Desktop Computer).**

Figure 14-8: The trick to better speed — if not for a Registry bug.

However, unless you have the OSR2 release of Windows 95 (that is, the General tab on your System control panel says 4.00.950B), changing the file system profile actually slows your PC down. The reason is that someone at Microsoft got two numbers mismatched. (Actually, four numbers; the settings for Mobile or docking station are reversed, too.) Microsoft quietly fixed the bug in OSR2, so if you have this version, you don't have to hack the Registry. If you don't have OSR2, fire up REGEDIT and modify the keys under *HKLM\SOFTWARE\Microsoft\Windows\CurrentVersion\FS Templates* so that they appear as in Table 14-1.

Table 14-1	Correct File System Profile Settings	
Subkey Name	*NameCache*	*PathCache*
Server	a9 0a 00 00	40 00 00 00
Mobile	51 01 00 00	10 00 00 00

If you have other non-OSR2 PCs in your home or office, you can export the FS Templates key from the PC on which you've fixed the bug. Carry the REG file around on diskette and then double-click it on the desktops of those other PCs, as an easy way to distribute the fix.

System Policy Editor Doesn't Save a File

You're working with the System Policy Editor (POLEDIT.EXE), creating a policy file to restrict or customize Windows 95 along the lines we mention in Chapter 9, and you want to save the POL file. When you do, you see the message in Figure 14-9.

Figure 14-9:
A crotchety
POLEDIT
decides not
to save your
file if the
target
directory
uses a long
filename.

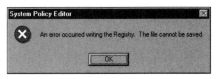

Why is the Policy Editor, as the error message states, trying to write the Registry? Maybe the message means that POLEDIT has encountered an error when "writing" to (saving) a file (your POL file) that will ultimately become part of the Registry. Or maybe the message is just screwy.

Fortunately, the correction is simple, but it's gonna make you mad. Turns out that POLEDIT can't handle directories with long filenames. (Wasn't that one of the reasons we all moved to Windows 95 in the first place? Grrr.) If you're trying to save TEST.POL in the directory C:\TEST DOCUMENTS, you have to type the short filename equivalent in the Save As dialog box's File Name field, like this:

```
C:\TESTDO~1\TEST.POL
```

Then POLEDIT saves your file properly. The short name equivalent is usually just the first six characters of the long directory name, followed by ~1. When in doubt, run Windows Explorer and check the directory's property sheet; the General tab shows the short name equivalent.

Oh, and by the way, you may see another error message (although different, for variety) if you browse to a file using the File⇨Open (by choosing File⇨Open, clicking the Browse button, navigating to the file and highlighting it, and clicking the Open button). Here again, if you type the complete path with the short filename equivalent in the File Name field of the Open Policy File dialog box, POLEDIT opens your file without a problem.

Avoid this problem completely by keeping all your POL files in directories with eight or fewer characters.

Chapter 15

Restore and Restart as a Last Resort

● ●

In This Chapter

▶ Understanding Windows 95 safe mode

▶ Finding out how to restore your Registry files from backups

▶ Using a secret file to avoid a complete Windows 95 reinstall

● ●

*I*n Chapter 2, we advise you to make Registry backups for a rainy day. This chapter explains the reverse procedure: restoring your Registry from those backups.

Just as a sailboat skipper hopes he'll never need to use his life preserver, we hope that you never need this chapter. However, if the troubleshooting tips in Chapter 14 don't cure your seasick PC, do not induce vomiting and do not despair. You can probably fix whatever is ailing your machine by restoring your Registry from an earlier backup.

Depending on how diligent you've been about making periodic backups, restoring the Registry may not turn out to be a big deal. (We had to do it a few times in the course of researching this book, and it never took more than ten minutes.) Even if you've been a delinquent backer-upper, we may at least be able to save you from having to wave the white flag and reinstall Windows 95 from scratch.

As Chapter 2 discussed, you can back up your Registry with several differ-ent tools and techniques. This chapter is a mirror image of Chapter 2 and provides the restore procedures that match up with the various backup procedures.

There's No Mode Like Safe Mode

You may need to start Windows 95 in *safe mode* to restore your Registry, so here's the least you need to know about this mode. Windows 95 can run in two modes. Its usual, graphical mode is called *protected mode* (or in some Microsoft documentation, *protect mode*). In this mode, Windows 95 is actively using the Registry. You can back up the Registry in protected mode, although you're better off doing so with no Windows programs running, as we advise in Chapter 2. Restoring the Registry, though, is a different matter.

If you only need to restore part of the Registry, you may be able to do so in protected mode. Importing a small REG file doesn't usually present a problem. However, if you need to restore the whole dadgum Registry, you generally don't want to be running in protected mode. Doing so is a little like changing a flat tire while your car's still moving. You need to restart Windows 95 in *real mode,* or what the Windows 95 startup menu calls *Safe mode command prompt only* (we abbreviate it SMCPO). This method brings up Windows 95 in a text-only command prompt screen that looks a lot like MS-DOS. (It also avoids Windows 95 overwriting the *.DA0 backup files, which occurs in a "regular" safe-mode startup.)

The procedure for starting Windows 95 in real mode is simple. Start the computer and as soon as you see the message `Starting Windows 95`, hit the F8 function key. The following menu appears (it may not be identical on your PC):

```
Microsoft Windows 95 Startup Menu
=================================
1. Normal
2. Logged (\BOOTLOG.TXT)
3. Safe mode
4. Safe mode with network support
5. Step-by-step confirmation
6. Command prompt only
7. Safe mode command prompt only
Enter a choice:
```

Choose the *Safe mode command prompt only* option, either by typing the corresponding number (7 in the above example) or by scrolling with the up and down arrow keys.

When it starts in SMCPO, Windows 95 skips processing the startup files — CONFIG.SYS, AUTOEXEC.BAT, SYSTEM.INI, and the Registry. Therefore, even if your Registry is badly damaged, Windows 95 can start in SMCPO without hiccuping because it doesn't so much as glance sideways at the Registry in this mode.

If you're on a network, when you restart and hit F8, notice the choice *Safe mode with network support* (it's option 4 in the example menu). This option doesn't work if your Registry is badly damaged because unlike SMCPO, *Safe mode with network support* processes the Registry.

We recommend that instead of running *Safe mode with network support,* you choose SMCPO and then run a batch file to connect to your network in real mode. Such a batch file would basically contain the network-related AUTOEXEC.BAT commands from a DOS or Windows 3.*x* PC. Or, if you're able to run Windows 95 in protected mode and connect to the network that way, you can copy whatever Registry backups you need from the network down to your local hard drive, and then restart in SMCPO to perform the restore.

Specific Restore Procedures

Here are the restore procedures that go with the backup procedures we talked about in Chapter 2. Read this stuff carefully, sloooowly, twice, before you actually do anything.

Restoring from DA0 files

As Chapter 2 explains, Windows 95 automatically backs up USER.DAT and SYSTEM.DAT to the hidden copies USER.DA0 and SYSTEM.DA0 every time the operating system starts without detecting any major problems.

If you think you've made a mistake during a Registry editing session, you haven't made your own Registry backup, and you want to go back to these *.DA0 files, *don't restart Windows 95 normally!* If Windows doesn't think that your mistake is any big deal, it views the restart as a successful one and overwrites the *.DA0 files with new ones — burning your bridge behind you.

Here's how to restore your Registry from the *.DA0 files:

1. **Restart Windows 95 in Safe mode command prompt only (see "There's No Mode Like Safe Mode" earlier in this chapter).**

   Windows 95 doesn't copy the *.DAT files to the *.DA0 files when it starts in Safe mode command prompt only.

2. At the command prompt, type the following lines:

```
CD C:\WINDOWS
ATTRIB -H -S *.DA0
ATTRIB -H -S -R USER.DAT
ATTRIB -H -S -R SYSTEM.DAT
COPY USER.DA0 USER.DAT /V /Y
COPY SYSTEM.DA0 SYSTEM.DAT /V /Y
ATTRIB +H +S +R USER.DAT
ATTRIB +H +S +R SYSTEM.DAT
ATTRIB +H +S USER.DA0
ATTRIB +H +S SYSTEM.DA0
```

The /V switch tells COPY to perform a quick verification check, and the /Y switch suppresses the normal warning of a file overwrite.

3. Restart Windows 95 normally.

You may want to use Notepad to make a little batch file containing the commands in Step 2. We like to call the file DA02DAT.BAT, but you can pick whatever name you like. Just don't give the file a long name; remember, you'll be running it from a command prompt.

For those of you who read Chapter 2 with an eagle eye and are wondering why we don't just use the XCOPY command to save a lot of typing in Step 2, here's the reason. XCOPY doesn't offer the /H, /K, and /R qualifiers when it runs in real mode (don't ask us why). (The /H switch copies system and hidden files, /K copies file attributes, and /R overwrites read-only files.) So we have to use ATTRIB to make the *.DA0 files visible to the COPY command and to make the *.DAT files overwriteable. The last four lines put all the file attributes back the way they were.

CFGBACK to the future

We don't discuss how to use the Microsoft Configuration Backup program to make backups in Chapter 2 because even Microsoft admits that this program is unreliable (although the company still distributes it). However, you may have to work with a PC on which someone else used CFGBACK to save the Registry. If so, here's the restore procedure:

1. Buy the person who ran CFGBACK a copy of this book and dog-ear Chapter 2, so the user doesn't depend on CFGBACK in the future.

2. Start Windows 95 normally, but don't load any programs.

CFGBACK doesn't run in safe mode, either the graphical version or the command prompt version. If the Registry is so traumatized that Windows 95 insists on starting in safe mode automatically, then you can't restore with CFGBACK. To make things worse, CFGBACK's backup files use a unique compressed format that no other program can read. (You can begin to see why we don't recommend this program.)

3. **If the backup file or files that you want to restore aren't in C:\WINDOWS, copy them there now, using Windows Explorer.**

   The filename has the form REGBACK*n*.RBK, where *n* is a number from 1 to 9. CFGBACK looks for previous backups in C:\WINDOWS only.

4. **Run CFGBACK.EXE by locating it in Windows Explorer and double-clicking it.**

5. **Click the Continue button three times to get past all the information screens.**

   You see the Configuration Backup dialog box in Figure 15-1.

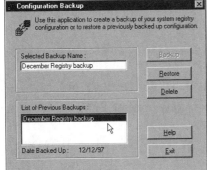

Figure 15-1: Restoring the Registry with CFGBACK.

6. **Click the backup that you want to restore in the List of Previous Backups window.**

7. **Click the Restore button.**

8. **Click Yes in the Warning dialog box to completely replace the current Registry with your backed-up version.**

9. **If you see yet another confirmation dialog box, click Yes again.**

   CFGBACK displays a message about separating system and user information (it combines SYSTEM.DAT and USER.DAT into a single file when it makes a backup). After a ridiculously long time (five minutes is typical), CFGBACK displays a success message.

10. **Restart the computer normally, cross your fingers, kneel in the direction of Redmond, Washington, and hope everything went well.**

A word about ERD

If you made a backup with the Emergency Recovery Utility (ERU) that ships with Windows 95, then restoring is a simple procedure. You use the ERD.EXE program that ERU created in your backup directory. (We'd like to think that ERD stands for End Registry Despair or Excellent Recovery, Dude, but it probably just stands for boring old Emergency Recovery Disk.) Here are the details:

1. **Restart Windows 95 in Safe mode command prompt only (see "There's No Mode Like Safe Mode" earlier in this chapter).**

   Unlike CFGBACK, ERD runs in safe mode, and safe mode only. If you try running ERD in a regular DOS window in Windows 95 protected mode, ERD fusses at you and refuses to run. Restoring in safe mode avoids problems with any Windows programs that may be writing to the Registry during a restore operation. Being able to restore the Registry is also nice if Windows 95 can *only* start in safe mode, as may be the case with a seriously trashed Registry.

2. **At the command prompt, change to the disk and directory where your backup files reside, with a command such as** CD C:\REGBACK.

3. **Type** ERD **and press Enter to run the recovery program.**

4. **Use the up and down arrow keys and the Enter key to pick the files that you want to restore.**

   Normally, you include both SYSTEM.DAT and USER.DAT.

5. **Arrow down to the Start Recovery option and hit Enter.**

   ERD goes about its business much more quickly than CFGBACK, and in a minute or less, you see a success message.

6. **Restart the computer and let Windows 95 boot normally.**

The export/import bank

If you've created a Registry backup by using the export technique, you can restore the Registry with the (you guessed it) import technique, described here. If you want to restore a partial Registry backup and you can boot to Windows 95 normally, follow these steps:

1. **Close all Windows programs and then run the Registry Editor, for example by clicking Start⇨Run⇨REGEDIT and OK.**

2. **Click Registry⇨Import Registry File to display the dialog box in Figure 15-2.**

Figure 15-2:
Importing,
or merging,
a REG file
into the
current
Registry
with
REGEDIT.

3. Specify the directory in the Look In field and name the file in the File Name field.

REGEDIT defaults to showing files with the suffix .REG.

4. Click the Open button to restore the data.

If you don't already have REGEDIT open and you know where your REG file is, you can save a few mouse clicks and import your REG file by right-clicking it in Explorer and choosing Merge. The results are identical.

Be aware that an import operation isn't a complete replacement of an existing Registry key. Importing can only change or add keys — it can't delete keys. If you feel that you need an exact image of the earlier backup, you must first delete the current key in REGEDIT (back it up first for safety) and then perform the import.

You can't restore a *full* Registry backup when Windows 95 is running in its graphical, protected mode, and be completely certain that the resulting Registry is identical to the one you backed up. To restore the entire Registry, follow these steps:

1. Restart Windows 95 in Safe mode command prompt only (see "There's No Mode Like Safe Mode" earlier in this chapter).

2. At the command prompt, change to the Windows directory with a command like CD C:\WINDOWS.

3. Create a new Registry from your backup file with the command

```
REGEDIT /C filename.REG
```

4. Restart the computer normally.

The REGEDIT /C command is *very dangerous!* It creates a whole new Registry based on the contents of *filename*.REG. If that REG file doesn't contain a full Registry backup, you're in a heap o' trouble. Make *very* sure that the REG file that you specify is the result of a complete Registry export operation.

Here's another *gotcha* if you're creating a new Registry in safe mode. If you have one of the original versions of Windows 95 (4.00.950 or 4.00.950a on the System control panel's General tab), your version of REGEDIT can't handle importing long keys, and a full restore may not work — REGEDIT gives you an error message. In this case, either try to lay your hands on the newer REGEDIT program that comes with the OEM Service Release 2 (OSR2) release of Windows 95 — it shows up as 4.00.950B — or restore using SYSTEM.1ST, using the procedure in the section later in this chapter, "SYSTEM.1ST is really SYSTEM.LAST." After you can boot Windows 95 into its graphical protected mode, run REGEDIT and import the file that way. The import problem doesn't affect REGEDIT when it's running in protected mode, just command prompt mode. The basic reason is that REGEDIT can use a bunch more memory in protected mode.

If you need to restore a single Registry key but Windows 95 won't start into its graphical protected mode, you can use the real mode REGEDIT program. Follow the numbered steps listed previously, but in Step 3, leave out the /C qualifier. Again, the newer REGEDIT that comes with Windows 95 OSR2 is more reliable. (Alas, Microsoft doesn't post OSR2's REGEDIT on its Internet site. Send Bill a postcard.)

Batching it

If you took our advice in Chapter 2 and used a batch file and DOS commands to back up your Registry, you're sitting in the catbird seat (that is, sitting pretty). If you haven't read James Thurber's short story, *The Catbird Seat,* check it out at the library and treat yourself; it's hilarious. But we digress. Here's the modus operandi for a full Registry restore:

1. **Restart Windows 95 in Safe mode command prompt only (see "There's No Mode Like Safe Mode" earlier in this chapter).**

2. **At the command prompt, type the following lines (replace** E:\REG **with the drive letter and directory where your backup files reside):**

```
CD C:\WINDOWS
ATTRIB -H -S -R USER.DAT
ATTRIB -H -S -R SYSTEM.DAT
RENAME USER.DAT USER.BAD
RENAME SYSTEM.DAT SYSTEM.BAD
COPY E:\REG\USER.DAT /V /Y
COPY E:\REG\SYSTEM.DAT /V /Y
ATTRIB +H +S +R C:\WINDOWS\USER.DAT
ATTRIB +H +S +R C:\WINDOWS\SYSTEM.DAT
```

3. **Add lines such as the following if you've enabled user profiles on the PC (repeat for each user):**

```
CD C:\WINDOWS\PROFILES\MARK
ATTRIB -H -S -R USER.DAT
RENAME USER.DAT USER.BAD
COPY E:\REG\PROFILES\MARK\USER.DAT /V /Y
ATTRIB +H +S +R USER.DAT
```

4. Restart Windows 95 normally.

Note that we rename the existing Registry files with the *.BAD suffix in the preceding procedure. You may find that these files are okay and that the problems that cause you to restore the Registry turn out to be non-Registry-related. If that happens, you can go back to the *.BAD files, which may be convenient if your most recent Registry backup — the one you restored — was a few weeks or months old.

Norton to the rescue (disk)

If you've used Norton Utilities version 2.0 or newer to make a set of rescue diskettes, restoring the Registry is a snap. Here's the drill:

1. **Pop the first of your rescue diskettes into the diskette drive (it's a boot diskette).**

2. **Restart the computer.**

3. **When you see the command prompt, type** A:\RESCUE **and press Enter.**

4. **Select the items you want to restore.**

5. **Press Alt+R to begin the restore process and follow the instructions on screen.**

   Here's what happens behind the scenes. Version 2.0 of Norton Rescue restores key files from diskette but restores the Registry from the file C:\WINDOWS\NUSYSTEM.REG. Version 3.0 of Norton Rescue restores the Registry from the file C:\WINDOWS\REGISTRY.RSC, unless you use the ZIP-plus-diskette combination and specified at the last backup that you wanted to copy the Registry files to the ZIP disk.

6. **When the rescue program is done, take the diskette out of the drive and hit** R **to reboot the PC to Windows 95.**

Restoring from general-purpose backup programs

If you've made a backup by using a general-purpose disk backup program, such as Cheyenne Backup, Seagate Backup Exec, or NovaBACKUP, then you can restore the Registry files from within your backup program. Each package works differently, but the general sequence is to run the backup software, insert your backup media (such as a tape cartridge), tell the program to read the catalog of files on the backup media, choose the files to restore, and then run the restore operation.

Booting to a diskette or in Safe mode command prompt only before running the restore program is a safer approach than restoring the Registry while running Windows 95 in its graphical protected mode.

SYSTEM. 1ST is really SYSTEM.LAST

When you first install Windows 95, the setup program creates a file in the root directory called SYSTEM.1ST. Windows 95 doesn't touch this file again, so it remains a snapshot of your initial PC setup. But the file isn't there merely for nostalgia.

When all else fails and you can't seem to get your Registry back to working condition, you may consider restoring this primordial version of SYSTEM.DAT. You have to reinstall all your application software and drivers for any hardware that you've added since your initial Windows 95 setup. However, this situation may be preferable to reinstalling Windows 95 itself from scratch.

The easy way to activate SYSTEM.1ST is to rename SYSTEM.DAT and SYSTEM.DA0 so that Windows 95 doesn't find them. Windows 95 then automatically uses SYSTEM.1ST. Here's the procedure:

1. **Restart Windows 95 in Safe mode command prompt only (see "There's No Mode Like Safe Mode" earlier in this chapter).**

2. **At the command prompt, type the following lines:**

```
CD C:\WINDOWS
ATTRIB -H -S -R SYSTEM.DAT
ATTRIB -H -S -R SYSTEM.DA0
RENAME SYSTEM.DAT SYSTEM.BAD
RENAME SYSTEM.DA0 SYSTEM0.BAD
```

3. **Restart Windows 95 normally.**

Windows 95 doesn't build a similar initial snapshot of USER.DAT, but maybe restoring the original SYSTEM.DAT is enough to get you out of the rough water. Reinstalling all your applications is easier than reinstalling Windows 95. Note that we rename the suspect files with the suffix *.BAD in Step 2 so that you can go back to them if you eventually discover that the problem lies elsewhere.

Part VI

Docking at the Pier:
The Part of Tens

In this part . . .

Every ...*For Dummies* book ends with a "Part of Tens." We thought about breaking tradition to create a "Part of Sixteens" in honor of the Registry's use of hexadecimal notation to express binary values, but we decided that that was just too nerdy.

First, we list ten Internet sites that contain Registry-related material. Visit these periodically to stay current with the most recent tips and tricks, especially as Windows 98 makes its way into the marketplace.

Especially useful are ten slick Registry tricks that we couldn't figure out where else to include, but that we felt you'd want to know about.

Finally, we wrap up our Registry odyssey on a humorous note by presenting ten Registries that have nothing in the world to do with Windows 95.

The Windows 98 Registry: A First Look

. . . .

In This Chapter

▶ Discovering what's new with Windows 98

▶ Finding out how the Windows 98 Registry differs from the Windows 95 Registry

▶ Looking at the Windows 98 Registry-editing tools

▶ Mastering a different Registry backup mechanism

▶ Getting acquainted with new, changed, and unchanged system utilities

▶ Discovering a few Windows 98 Registry-related bugs

. . . .

The next step in the evolution of the mainstream workstation Windows platform is Windows 98. Microsoft hasn't made any earth-shattering changes to how the Registry works in Windows 98, but several differences do exist, and they're worth knowing about ahead of time.

As this book is going to press, Windows 98 is in its third beta release (beta releases are early copies of not-ready-for-prime-time software) and scheduled for commercial shipment in a matter of months. In this preview section, we give you a brief look at the new features Windows 98 promises and then focus on changes that affect the Registry in particular. We plan to publish a book on the new Registry soon after Windows 98 is commercially available, for those of you who may need more information than we can provide here.

Caveat Reader!

We base the material in this special Windows 98 preview section on the Beta 3 release of Windows 98, specifically, Build 1650 dated December 12, 1997. While this release is certainly more complete than the Beta 1 or 2 releases, when Microsoft releases Windows 98 commercially, the Gold release may look and act differently in some ways than the Beta 3 release. Therefore, PLEASE regard everything in this section as an informational preview that is subject to change and not to be taken as gospel.

What's New with Windows 98?

Windows 98 brings a long list of improvements and enhancements (as you would expect from an operating system that requires from 110MB to 289MB of hard disk space), but it's very much an evolutionary step up from Windows 95 OSR2. The hop from Windows 95 to Windows 98 is much shorter than the leap from Windows 3.*x* to Windows 95, and much more like the hop from Windows 3.0 to Windows 3.1. If you're comfortable with Windows 95, give yourself a day or two to get settled in with Windows 98 — maybe a little more if you use the Web View for the desktop, as described shortly.

No doubt Windows 98 will find its way onto all new PCs shortly after its commercial release. We're guessing, though, that the number of users who pay extra dollars to purchase the Windows 98 upgrade will be much smaller than the number who bought the Windows 95 upgrade.

The new features in Windows 98 just aren't all that dramatic or compelling, from where we sit, to induce a large percentage of the 80 million or so Windows 95 users to open their wallets. (This is especially true when you consider that, for $5, you can buy Internet Explorer 4 and get many of the goodies that come with Windows 98 — and that as of January 1998, computer makers now have a new version of Windows 95 to sell, OSR 2.5, that comes with Internet Explorer 4.01.)

Having said that, Windows 98 seems able to run most Windows 95 software without modification — so the migration from Windows 95 to Windows 98 should be easier than from Windows 3.*x* to Windows 95. (Note that the reverse is not true; we've already seen programs written for Windows 98 that don't run under Windows 95.)

This section sets the stage with a quick look at the key new features of Windows 98. Afterwards, we zero in on changes that specifically affect the Registry.

The desktop as Web page

The big change in Windows 98, and the closest thing to a "killer" feature, is the integration of the Internet Explorer 4.0 user interface onto the desktop — what Microsoft calls the *Integrated Internet Shell*. Your first clue as to the Internet's importance as a Windows 98 design influence is the appearance of the Internet Explorer icon on the taskbar.

As a Windows 98 user, you can choose to browse your local PC in much the same manner you browse the Internet:

- Selectable objects appear underlined, as hyperlinks do on a Web page.
- Moving the cursor over an object (file, folder, and so on) highlights it and changes the cursor to a pointing hand.
- Single-clicking a highlighted object selects it (you may never double-click again!), a feature Microsoft calls *Hover Select*.

You can see what the Web-view desktop looks like in the Control Panel window of Figure 98-1.

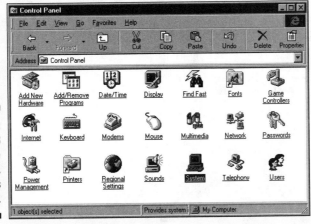

Figure 98-1: Windows 98 looks like the Web, underlines and all.

You can opt not to use the browser-like interface for navigating the desktop and instead choose the Windows 95 user interface, which Microsoft calls Classic Style (as opposed to Web Style) in the View⇨Options menu of My Computer or Explorer (see Figure 98-2). (Some people, including us, go crazy with all those underlines.) Alternatively, you can choose the Custom radio button and mix and match features of both styles, as in Figure 98-3.

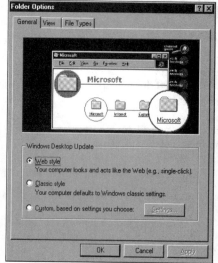

Figure 98-2:
Picking
a user
interface
for the
Windows 98
desktop.

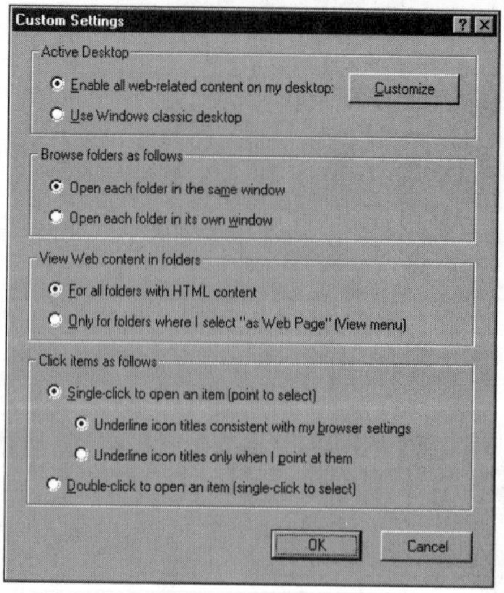

Figure 98-3:
Customizing
the
Windows 98
desktop
behavior.

The Windows 98 desktop becomes even more Web-like when you look at the My Computer command View⇨Customize this Folder, which displays the dialog box in Figure 98-4. You can create an HTML (HyperText Markup Language) page that defines the look of any folder on your PC. Or, less ambitiously, you can simply specify a background image that lives behind the folder's icons.

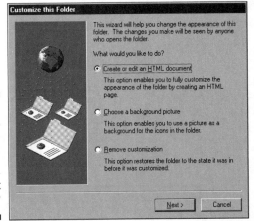

Figure 98-4:
Is it a folder
or is it a
Web page?
Floor wax,
or dessert
topping?

The *active desktop* enables you to collect and view a wide variety of Web components: HTML pages, Java applets, and even ActiveX controls right on your Windows 98 desktop along with the usual icons. The desktop is now a layered, three-dimensional affair; the background is an HTML layer, and the foreground is where the icons reside. The operating system manipulates the desired ActiveX and Java controls from the background layer.

Other aspects of the active desktop let you preview data files that you couldn't easily preview in Windows 95. Bitmap graphics, Excel spreadsheets, PowerPoint slideshows, and the like now appear with a thumbnail representation to help remind you of the file's contents — handy if you tend to use filenames like SLIDSHOW121497.PPT.

Speaking of the Windows 98 desktop, Microsoft has taken the "zooming windows" concept from Windows 95 to an even-more-annoying level in Windows 98's "zooming menus." (We can't believe anybody actually *asked* for this feature, which everyone we know finds highly distracting.) The Display control panel setting is Use menu animations, on the Effects tab (see Figure 98-5). If you want to make the change directly to the Registry, however, for example with a REG file, Microsoft has made it difficult.

Unlike some of the other display effects settings, the animated menus setting is not a separate value, but rather part of a composite binary value, *HKCU\Control Panel\Desktop\UserPreferencemask*. On our test machine, for example, turning menu animations off changed the UserPreferencemask value from AE 00 00 00 to AC 00 00 00 (see Figure 98-6). We don't yet know just what other settings affect the UserPreferencemask, so we can't advise you to simply set it to ac 00 00 00 — although you can try this approach and see if it works for you.

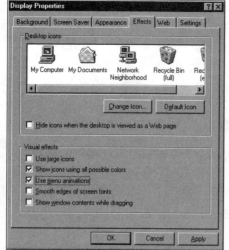

Figure 98-5:
Turn
zooming
menus off in
the Display
control
panel.

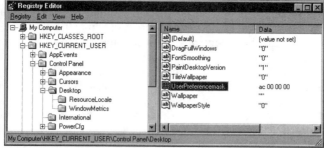

Figure 98-6:
Menu
zooming is
part of the
new
Registry
setting
UserPref-
erencemask.

You may also want to turn off the distracting little drop-down descriptions that appear when you click on desktop items. The setting from My Computer is View➪Folder Options➪View and clear the button that reads Show pop-up description for folder and desktop items. The Registry setting, which uses a DWORD value 0x00000001 for *on* and 0x00000000 for *off*, is *HKCU\ Software\Microsoft\Windows\CurrentVersion\Explorer\Advanced\ShowInfoTip*.

Other Internet-egration

Other ways that Windows 98 adds to its Internet capabilities include the following:

✔ **Push publishing:** The ability to select Internet "channels" that provide you with regularly updated content

✔ **The Internet Explorer 4 browser:** This browser supports a variety of new Web page styles (such as Dynamic HTML) and conferencing features in NetMeeting and NetShow

✔ **Outlook Express:** Formerly Internet Mail and News, a better Internet e-mail and newsgroup reader, although at this writing it can't handle e-mail sent via America Online, Compuserve, Microsoft Mail, Microsoft Exchange Server 4 or earlier, Microsoft Network (MSN), or cc:Mail

✔ **FrontPad:** An HTML editor, based on the editor in FrontPage 97

✔ **HTML Help:** The new Web-based standard for Windows 98 help files, using the same basic organization of Windows 95 help files but in browser-friendly form (see Figure 98-7)

✔ **The subscription folder:** A folder into which you can place Web addresses that you want to update whenever you go online

Figure 98-7: The Windows help engine gets a reworking in order to display its familiar features in a browser window.

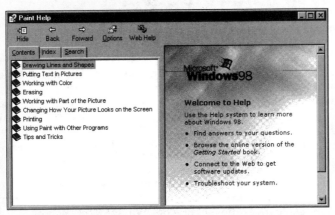

Of special interest to Registry aficionados is the new security model in the Windows 98 (and Internet Explorer 4) Java Virtual Machine. The Java Virtual Machine is the software that Internet Explorer uses to process Java programs on the Web. If you aren't already aware, one of the neat things about Java programs is that they can run on virtually any kind of computer, as long as the computer has a Java Virtual Machine to translate the program's commands into ones that the specific operating system can understand.

Java programs can now have three levels of security, and only the lowest (least secure) of the three permits Java programs to perform Registry operations. Software developers can preassign their Java programs with one of the three levels of security.

Migration support

Microsoft's original plan was to ship Windows 98 as a Windows 95 upgrade only, and to provide a version to upgrade Windows 3.*x* machines some months later. Computer makers howled, customers howled, and Microsoft rethought the situation. Now, Windows 98 includes provisions for upgrading both Windows 95 and Windows 3.*x* systems (including Windows 3.1, Windows for Workgroups 3.1, and Windows for Workgroups 3.11).

As of the Beta 3 release, Microsoft is not recommending that users try uninstalling Windows 98 after upgrading from Windows 3.*x*. Your best bet is to make a full system backup of your Windows 3.*x* machine, and use that to restore your system if you have problems with Windows 98.

Improved hardware support

Windows 98 gets up-to-date with better hardware support for existing and new devices:

✔ You can run Windows 98 across multiple monitors and video cards all connected to a single PC — a boon for graphics artists, computer slideshow presenters, and anyone who wants more screen real estate. The feature is limited, however, to display cards using a PCI or AGP port. (AGP, or Accelerated Graphics Port, is a relatively new display circuitry standard from Intel that is roughly twice the speed of a traditional PCI graphics card.)

✔ Windows 98 supports certain compatible TV tuner circuit cards with the optional *TV Viewer* application, so you can watch TV from an analog source (cable, over-the-air) on your Windows 98 desktop. Just think: *Wall Street Week* running right next to *My Computer*. You'll even be able to buy a remote control from your computer vendor.

✔ Windows 98 supports software optimized for Pentium MMX (MultiMedia eXtensions) processors.

✔ The infrared driver is newer (version 3.0).

✔ Windows 98 supports roughly 600 more printers than Windows 95 OSR2, which itself supports over 800 models. Windows 98 also supports some 300 new modems compared to Windows 95 OSR2, 175 new monitors, and 170 new network cards. All this means that Windows 98 supports a wider variety of hardware than any version of Windows to date.

✔ Color devices, such as color printers, take advantage of an updated version — 2.0 instead of 1.0 — of Microsoft's Integrated Color Matching (ICM) capabilities. Windows 98 now supports other color spaces than Red-Green-Blue (RGB) and makes a better platform for high-end color graphics work.

✔ The newer *PC Card32* or *Cardbus* standard is supported, as are PC Cards that work at 3.3 volts instead of 5 volts. Windows 98 can now independently configure each function of a single PC Card that offers multiple functions (network and modem, for example).

✔ The Universal Serial Bus (USB) promises to alleviate PC resource strain and make Plug and Play easier. USB supports up to 127 daisy-chained devices via a single connection (and interrupt) at the PC side. Currently, mice, keyboards, and scanners use USB.

✔ Firewire, or IEEE 1394, is another serial bus standard, oriented towards consumer audio and video products.

✔ Windows 98 now works with CD-ROM changers that can handle up to seven discs. Windows 98 depends on equipment manufacturers to provide software for CD-ROM devices sporting eight or more discs (*jukeboxes*).

✔ DVD (Digital Video Disc) is the next step in CD-ROM evolution, with the potential to combine multimedia and computer data on one high-capacity disc — if the industry can get its standards act together.

Many Windows 98 drivers adhere to a new standard called *Win32 Driver Model,* or *WDM.* Ultimately, you'll be able to use WDM drivers interchangeably between Windows 98 and Windows NT 5.0.

Windows 98 device drivers from Microsoft carry a *digital signature* to verify their authenticity. You can modify the Registry to tell Windows 98 to pay attention to these digital signatures (the default is to ignore them) when you try to install a new device driver. The relevant key is *HKLM\Software\Microsoft\Driver Signing,* and the options for the Policy Value entry are as follows:

✔ 00 00 00 00 turns signature checking off.

✔ 01 00 00 00 causes Windows 98 to display a message if the driver doesn't have a quality-assurance signature.

✔ 02 00 00 00 causes Windows 98 to prevent any driver from being installed if it lacks a signature.

Note that you can also run the new standalone utility, SIGVERIF.EXE, to view the certificates of files having a digital signature.

Dribbleware consolidation

Fred Langa of *Windows Magazine* coined the delightful term *dribbleware* to refer to Microsoft's habit of releasing bug fixes and new Windows 95 features piecemeal. Windows 98 takes many of the various dribbleware updates and rolls them into one package. (For example, all the updates available to Windows 95 Version 4.00.950 users in the form of the Service Pack 1 software distribution have been applied to Windows 98.)

Some of the goodies that have appeared piecemeal in the past include:

- The more efficient, if somewhat inconvenient and confusing, FAT32 file structure (introduced by Windows 95 OSR2), augmented with a FAT16 to FAT32 conversion utility. Microsoft claims that the Windows 98 implementation of FAT32 is substantially faster than the OSR2 implementation due to how the operating system places programs along memory segment boundaries

- Dial-up scripting to automate DUN (Dial-Up Networking) connections

- Multilink channel aggregation, a fancy way of saying that you can now use DUN with two or more serial communications lines that work like a single, faster line

- Point-to-Point Tunneling Protocol (PPTP) for more secure connections and virtual private networks over the Internet, using IP, IPX, or NetBEUI networking protocols

- The Dial-Up Server software formerly only included in the Plus! add-on package (not clear yet whether TCP/IP will be supported; the beta documentation specifies only IPX and NetBEUI)

- The light-duty Personal Web Server that enables Windows to host Web pages on a company intranet

- A program scheduler, similar to the one included in the Plus! add-on package as System Agent, called Scheduled Tasks (see Figure 98-8)

- Various other more or less useful Plus! features, such as full window drag and font smoothing

- The ActiveMovie video playback technology in Internet Explorer

- The client software for Novell NetWare and IntranetWare 4.*x* environments that use NetWare Directory Services

- The Data Link Control (DLC) network language for accessing IBM minicomputers and mainframes

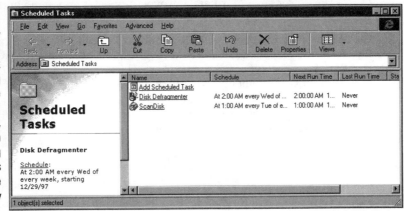

Figure 98-8:
You can
now
schedule
disk
defragmenting
without the
Plus!
add-on kit,
though
defragmenting
still seems
to skip the
Registry
files.

Mo' better utilities

Windows 98 brings several new utilities to the table, some of which have implications for the Registry. Here's a thumbnail sketch of the new or enhanced utilities, starting with the ones that don't directly impact the Registry:

- ✔ **The taskbar:** (We *guess* it's a utility; what else do you call it?) You can now build your own custom toolbars by simply right-clicking the taskbar and choosing New Toolbar. Drag-and-drop enables you to reconfigure the Start menu much more easily than in Windows 95.

- ✔ **Windows Update:** Updating Windows device drivers and programs has always been a big job. CyberMedia has done well with a product called *Oil Change,* which navigates the Internet and periodically updates Windows files automatically. In Windows 98 (and NT Workstation 5.0), Microsoft usurps this concept in the form of Windows Update, which links to www.microsoft.com/windowsupdate. Corporate sites, beware: The potential for *software fragmentation* (that is, different versions of system files on different PCs) has just increased dramatically. However, Windows Update does make it easier to obtain the latest device drivers, which should bring Plug and Play a step closer to reality.

- ✔ **Dr. Watson:** Dr. Watson is back from Windows 3.*x* after an unexplained absence in Windows 95. This utility catches system faults and creates a log file (*.WLG) documenting all the gory details of program and Windows crashes, including a list of which programs were running when the crash occurred.

- **FAT32 Converter:** This little utility lets you convert a regular FAT disk to the newer FAT32 format. However, it doesn't let you go in the reverse direction.

- **Windows Scripting Host:** After omitting Windows Recorder in Windows 95, Microsoft provides a new macro scripting tool with Windows 98 so you can "record" and "play back" a series of keystrokes and mouse movements. You still have to be familiar with a scripting language in order to make full use of this utility, however. The two languages that Microsoft supports "out of the box" include Visual BASIC Scripting Language and JavaScript.

And here are the utilities that relate to the Registry:

- **System File Checker:** You can now easily verify that specific files on disk (usually Windows 98 system files, such as *.DLL, *.VXD, *.DRV, *.INF, *.HLP, and so on) haven't been damaged since their initial installation. If you find by inspecting the Registry that a system problem traces its cause to a particular DLL file that you suspect is damaged, System File Checker makes restoring that file from the Windows 98 CD-ROM (or any other convenient location, such as a network server or Internet site) much easier.

  Run System File Checker by selecting Start⇨Programs⇨Accessories⇨ System Tools⇨System File Checker. This utility automatically creates a log file of its activities in SFCLOG.TXT, so you can examine the log file with any text editor to see exactly what System File Checker did after a particular work session.

- **System Troubleshooter:** TSHOOT.EXE makes modifying system configurations easier with yes-or-no check boxes that modify SYSTEM.INI, WIN.INI, CONFIG.SYS, AUTOEXEC.BAT, and selected parts of the Registry. System Troubleshooter purports to make checking for Registry corruption easier, although we haven't been able to see just how yet. It does certainly let you specify exactly which programs you want to start when Windows 98 boots.

- **System Information tool:** The Tools menu in MSINFO enables you to run the Registry Checker (see next section), as well as other utilities mentioned in this list.

- **Windows 98 Backup:** Windows 98 Backup (see Figure 98-9) is better. It now supports a wider variety of tape drives (including SCSI drives), as well as other devices such as removable cartridge drive and writable optical drives. As to the available methods for restoring a Windows 98 PC after a total hard disk failure, see the sidebar entitled "Restore this way — no, restore *that* way!") Remember to choose Options➪ Advanced➪Back up Windows Registry if you want to do a selective backup of the C:\WINDOWS directory and you want the Registry included in your backup.

✔ **PowerToys TweakUI.** It looks as though this control panel, which we mention in Chapter 11, will ship with the Windows 98 CD-ROM (or at least the Windows 98 Resource Kit). TweakUI provides a user-friendly way of modifying some of the Registry's user interface settings, such as the "visual swoosh" that Windows make when they minimize and maximize.

✔ **Configuration Backup.** CFGBACK.EXE appears as a new version, although it looks and acts just the same when you run it. CFGBACK still creates those unique .RBK files, and it still demands that those files be present in the C:\WINDOWS directory for restoring. We can't frankly see anything obviously different about the new version, but here's hoping that Microsoft fixed some of the bugs that led it to recommend against using this utility in its Windows 95 incarnation.

✔ **Emergency Recovery Utility (ERU).** This program retains the same version number as the original Windows 95 file and, according to our tests, behaves exactly the same way — with the exception that the Windows 98-supplied program uses a prettier font.

✔ **Registry Checker:** See the following section for an in-depth look.

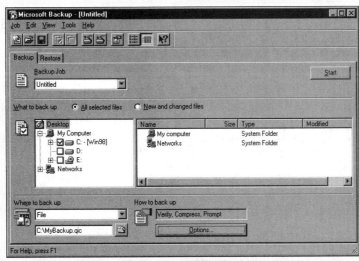

Figure 98-9: Windows 98 Backup is a scaled-down version of Seagate's Backup Exec.

Restore this way — no, restore *that* way!

We harp on the importance of good backups all through this book, so we fired up the Windows 98 Backup program with great interest. Our major beef about the older Windows 95 backup utility is that it requires Windows 95 in order to run, meaning that if your C: drive crashes and you replace it with a fresh disk, you have to reinstall Windows 95 before you can run Backup to restore all the files from your last full backup. And so it was with heavy heads that we read in a Microsoft Windows 98 tech note that "Before you can restore your files after a hard disk failure, you must first prepare your hard disk and reinstall Windows." It seemed like Windows 98's Backup program was still stuck in the Stone Age — yet another bundled Windows applet that's almost, but not quite, good enough to actually use.

However, you learn in this business not to take anything at face value, even if it comes straight from the horse's mouth. Another Microsoft Windows 98 tech note completely contradicts the one we saw first, stating that "Emergency Recovery enables you to rebuild the operating system and the latest full backup directly from media, without having to reinstall the operating system or the backup software." We were heartened, but confused. Further study was necessary. Fortunately, we can spare you that effort and tell you the situation as best we can figure it.

Emergency Recovery is certainly an option in the new Windows 98 Backup utility, and it can save you a lot of time over the older method that Windows 95 requires. You first create a Windows 98 startup diskette (we'll call it diskette #1) using the Add/Remove Programs control panel wizard. (The procedure is about the same as for Windows 95.) Then, start the Backup program and choose Tools⇨Recovery Diskettes. Select the backup device (for example, a tape drive) that you plan to contain your full disk backup. (The program needs this information so that it can prepare boot diskettes with the appropriate hardware device drivers.) Follow the on-screen instructions, and have a second diskette (#2) handy to pop in when requested.

Now, go about your business and make your full disk backups on whatever schedule you think best. If your C: drive suddenly craters, replace it, reboot your PC with the #1 diskette, run FDISK or FORMAT if your drive doesn't come preformatted, pop in the #2 diskette, and type RESTORE at the command prompt. Follow the instructions (have your tapes or other backup media at the ready) in order to complete the restore operation. Slick as a hound's tooth.

The "old" method of manually reinstalling Windows 98 onto your fresh drive using the SETUP program, and then running the Backup utility, still works, too. In fact, you *must* use this method if you use disk compression; if you have a dual boot PC that runs two or more operating systems; or if the Emergency Recovery method fails for some reason. Our advice is to make those two Emergency Recovery diskettes RIGHT NOW, and use the RESTORE command as your first choice. Keep the older method in reserve as a contingency plan.

Checking Out Registry Checker

After the brief Windows 98 overview in the preceding section, we need to roll up our sleeves and see just what's going on with the Windows 98 Registry. As you probably know, nearly all the new and changed features in Windows 98 affect the Registry in one way or another, but some more directly than others. One of the bigger bits of Registry news is the new Registry Checker utility, although it's not the industrial-strength, highly intelligent program that we would like to see.

Basics

The protected-mode file that runs from the graphical user interface is C:\WINDOWS\SCANREGW.EXE, and the real-mode file that runs from a command prompt is C:\WINDOWS\SCANREG.EXE. (Note that this program is *not* the same program as the SCANREG utility that comes with the Windows NT 4.0 Resource Kit and that we mention in Chapter 4.)

Windows 95 runs the Registry Checker at each restart, under control of the initialization file SCANREG.INI. When you run the Registry Checker in protected mode, it performs a Registry integrity check. If Registry Checker finds a problem with the active Registry files, it gives you the option to restore from the previous backup.

We're not completely clear yet on what sorts of problems Registry Checker is capable of fixing, but we know this much: Registry Checker doesn't look for *orphans* — that is, files referenced in the Registry that no longer appear on disk (see Chapter 13 for more on this subject). You still need extra software to find orphans. The Windows 98 version of Symantec Norton Utilities' WinDoctor should do the trick.

If you run Registry Checker manually (Start⇨Run⇨SCANREGW) and it doesn't find a problem with the currently active Registry files, it gives you the option to create another backup of the current files (see Figure 98-10). We look at the backup format more closely in the section "Call me a CAB: New automatic backups."

In command prompt mode (choose Restart in MS-DOS Mode from the Shut Down menu), Registry Checker offers the options shown in Figure 98-11, which may be handy if Windows 98 won't boot to the graphical user interface for some reason.

Figure 98-10:
Registry
Checker
offers to
create a
Registry
backup for
you if
you like.

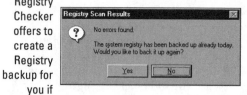

The commands for restoring the Registry to its state at the last successful startup, assuming you installed Windows 98 into the usual C:\WINDOWS directory, are simple:

```
CD C:\WINDOWS
SCANREG /RESTORE
```

You would then restart your PC with Ctrl+Alt+Del. Be careful, though; SCANREG may need more than 580K of conventional memory in order to conduct its repair operations, especially with larger Registries. Therefore, in order to run SCANREG, you may have to perform some memory management on your CONFIG.SYS file, such as removing Terminate and Stay Resident programs from AUTOEXEC.BAT and loading device drivers into high memory with the DEVICEHIGH command.

Figure 98-11:
The Registry
Checker in
real-mode
garb.

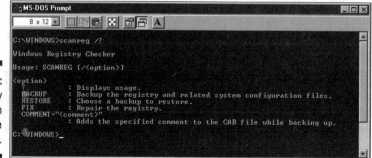

Speaking of command prompt mode, we should mention that Windows 98 doesn't present you with the Starting Windows. . . message at bootup, when (with Windows 95) you could press F4 or F8 to get a list of startup options. Now, you have to press and hold down the Ctrl key while the PC is going through its Power-On Self Test (POST), until you see the boot options screen. Why does Microsoft change this sort of thing as soon as we get used to the old method? In this case, the stated goal is to shave two seconds off the total startup time.

Beyond basics

Registry Checker seems like a fairly important animal, so it's worth taking a closer look.

Controlling Registry Checker

You can control the files that SCANREG backs up, the destination location, and how many backups Windows 98 makes before it starts dropping old ones off into oblivion.

The vehicle for controlling SCANREG's behavior is SCANREG.INI, a plain text file that you can edit with Notepad. Here's an actual SCANREG.INI file with comments to help you make your own customizations:

```
;Scanreg backup is skipped altogether if this is set to 0
Backup=1
ScanregVersion=0.0001
MaxBackupCopies=5
;Backup directory where the cabs are stored is
; <windir>\sysbckup by default. Value below overrides it.
; It must be a full path. ex. c:\tmp\backup
;
BackupDirectory=
; Additional system files to backup into cab as follows:
; Filenames are separated by ','
; dir code can be:
; 10 : windir (ex. c:\windows)
; 11 : system dir (ex. c:\windows\system)
; 30 : boot dir (ex. c:\)
; 31 : boot host dir (ex. c:\)
;
;Files=[dir code,]file1,file2,file3
;Files=[dir code,]file1,file2,file3
```

Note that Windows 98 still doesn't back up multiple USER.DAT files by default (how long must we wait for this important capability?), although you can customize the above INI file to add this feature.

Automatic compression

If the Registry contains over 500K in unused space, Registry Checker automatically compresses the Registry. We wish the number were more like 100K or 200K, but nevertheless, this feature is handy. It essentially removes the need to perform manual Registry compression such as described in Chapter 13. The benefits include lower memory requirements, quicker boot times, and faster Registry backups.

You can force Registry compression by rebooting Windows 98 to a command prompt and typing the command

```
SCANREG /OPT
```

where "OPT" is short for "optimize." If you want to get a little fancy, you can even write a batch file with this command and run it weekly or monthly with the Scheduled Tasks utility.

Automatic startup

Finally, we need to mention that SCANREG itself is activated by the Registry; check out the *HKLM\SOFTWARE\Microsoft\Windows\Current Version\Run* key, and you find the program listed.

Registry Checker is helpful if your Registry is damaged and you can still start Windows 98; however, you still need a startup disk if Windows 98 no longer boots from your hard drive. Your Windows 95 startup diskette *will not work* with Windows 98, so you need to make a new one. (Make two, just in case you spill coffee on one.) The new startup diskette, which Microsoft refers to as an EBD (Emergency Boot Diskette), now includes generic drivers for CD-ROM drives, both the IDE (Integrated Drive Electronics) and SCSI (Small Computer Systems Interface) varieties. These drivers mean that you may not even have to modify CONFIG.SYS and AUTOEXEC.BAT on the diskette in order to be able to "see" your CD-ROM drive after booting with the EBD.

A potential problem

When Registry Checker starts, either automatically or manually, it may display the following error message:

```
Windows found an error in your system files and was
        unable to fix the problem. You will need to
        install Windows to a new directory.
```

The error message, like many Windows error messages, tends to warn of dire consequences when the reality of the situation isn't nearly so alarming. The good news is that you may not need to install Windows to a new directory at all. You may simply not have enough free space on your hard drive for Registry Checker to create its backups.

You can use My Computer or Windows Explorer to see how much space is available. If the figure is less than 10MB or so, you should try to make some room, for example, by deleting or backing up data files, removing programs you don't need, emptying the Recycle Bin, or buying a bigger hard drive. Once you give your hard drive some extra headroom, restart Windows 98 or rerun Registry Checker manually. If the error message doesn't appear any more, you're out of hot water — at least until your hard drive fills up again.

Recognizing Registry Differences

Is the Windows 98 Registry different from the Windows 95 Registry? Yes and no. (Typical computer consultant answer!) The good news is that very little seems to have changed in the Windows 98 Registry in terms of the basic structure. However, many new entries exist for the new programs, features, and Class IDs that come with Windows 98. In fact, the Windows 98 Registry starts life at about 1.8MB before you even install any applications — that's nearly twice the typical initial size of the Windows 95 Registry. (We *told* you the Registry wasn't going away!)

New keys

The *HKCR* branch seems to have the most new keys, with more than 200 new entries covering file types relating to ActiveMovie for digital video, DirectX controls for video and animation, HTML controls handling browser functions, and a variety of new, shareable ActiveX objects. Figure 98-12 shows a small fraction of these new keys.

Now that you spend more time on the Internet, security issues become more of a concern. *HKLM\System\CurrentControlSet\Services\WinTrust\TrustProviders* sports new entries detailing the enhanced security providers for e-mail and Java.

Figure 98-12:
New file
extensions
and file
types adorn
HKCR.

Figure 98-13:
The Registry
reflects new
security
providers to
protect
Windows 98
from an
increasingly
connected
world.

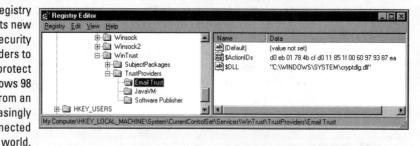

Windows 98 incorporates some push publishing features that automate the delivery of Internet content to the user. The default channel settings reside in *HKCU\Software\Policies\Microsoft\Internet Explorer\Infodelivery\ CompletedModifications*. You can also see new file types in *HKCR* under *ChannelFile* and *ChannelShortcut*.

The new System Troubleshooter utility stores a number of settings in the Registry under HKLM\SOFTWARE\TSHOOT, as you can see in Figure 98-14.

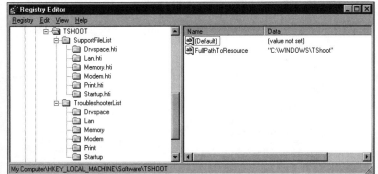

Figure 98-14:
HKLM hosts
new keys
for the
TSHOOT.EXE
program.

A new Control Panel key ties in with the more advanced power management features of Windows 98: *HKCU\Control Panel\PowerCfg* (see Figure 98-15). The key also appears in *HKU\.DEFAULT\Control Panel*. The acronym that you may see in this connection is ACPI, for Advanced Configuration and Power Interface. ACPI is a proposed standard that increases the ways that a PC can save energy during operation, for example, by spinning down hard drives that haven't been used for a set number of minutes.

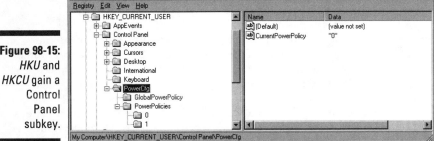

Figure 98-15:
HKU and
HKCU gain a
Control
Panel
subkey.

A new key, *HKU\Software,* appears to contain telephony information for voice modems (See Figure 98-16).

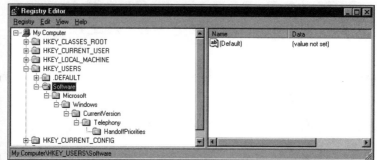

Figure 98-16:
A new key
exists in
HKU\Software.

Windows 98 also adds a new key to the Registry to control *Autonet address-ing,* a new feature for assigning IP addresses in a TCP/IP network. If a Windows 98 machine connects to a TCP/IP network and its Network control panel is set to "obtain an IP address automatically," Windows 98 first looks to see if a network server is set up to assign IP addresses using a method called DHCP (Dynamic Host Configuration Protocol). If not, Windows 98 uses the new Autonet addressing feature to assign the PC a unique IP address. The relevant value (are you ready for this one?) is *HKLM\System\ CurrentControlSet\Services\TCPIP\Parameters\Interfaces\Adapter\ IPAutoConfigurationEnabled,* where Adapter is the CLSID for the network card. It's a DWORD value; zero turns Autonet addressing off, any other value turns it on (the default is on).

Another networking key has to do with network management using the Desktop Management Interface (DMI) standard. DMI lets network adminis-trators perform certain support and management tasks remotely, over the network. (If you're familiar with SNMP, Simple Network Management Protocol, then DMI is a very similar technology.) If you install the DMI software that comes on the Windows 98 CD-ROM, using the Control Panel's Add/Remove Programs wizard (the software has the catchy name "Windows Management Infrastructure"), then a new Registry key appears: *HKLM\DesktopManagement.*

You get a new key for broadcast support, too: *HKLM\SOFTWARE\ Microsoft\TV Services.*

The Windows 98 Registry has many more new keys and values, but the ones we've listed here are some of the more obvious and important ones.

Greater use of CLSIDs

If you've read Chapter 6, you know about *Class IDs,* or *CLSIDs* for short:
unique, identifying numbers that the Registry uses to refer to every sort
of Windows 95 file type and object. The Windows 98 Registry makes
more extensive use of CLSIDs than the Windows 95 Registry. For example,
take a look at the key *HKLM\System\CurrentControlSet\Services\Class* (see
Figure 98-17). In Windows 95, this key contains no CLSIDs, but in
Windows 98, it's full of 'em.

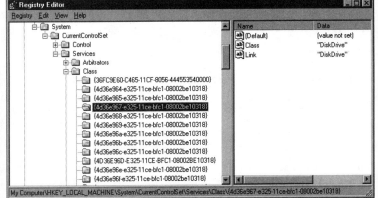

Figure 98-17:
Windows 98
uses CLSIDs
more
extensively
than
Windows 95.

The CLSIDs point to device types that appear later in the *Class* subkey (see
Figure 98-18), in much the same way that CLSIDs point to file types in *HKCR*.
The CLSIDs that you see in Figure 98-17 also refer to CLSIDs in *HKLM\Enum*,
where the Registry maintains information about every device ever installed
in the system.

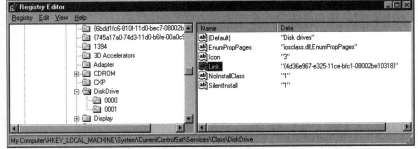

Figure 98-18:
Later entries
in the Class
subkey refer
back to the
device
CLSIDs.

You can more easily understand this new, expanded use of CLSIDs for hardware as well as software if you pick a CLSID in *HKLM\System\ CurrentControlSet\Services\Class* and then use the Registry Editor's Find command (Ctrl+F) to locate other references to the same CLSID. And don't be confused — Microsoft sometimes uses the acronym *ClassGUID* instead of CLSID, but both terms mean the same thing.

The advantage of assigning CLSIDs to hardware is that it unifies the method that programmers use to locate hardware objects as well as software objects. Joe and Jane End User won't see much direct benefit, but over the long run, software costs tend to drop as programmers' lives become easier.

New code

Microsoft claims to have improved the Registry-handling code in Windows 98 so the Registry is both faster and more reliable. These improvements are "behind the scenes" — that is, you can't see them if you use REGEDIT or even if you're a programmer and you use the Registry API (Application Program Interface) — but they should contribute to better overall speed with Windows 98 because Registry accesses are so frequent.

One improvement has to do with Registry disk write operations. In Windows 95, before saving a file to disk, the Registry examines the entire file — that is, every memory block — in order to compute a "checksum" that Windows uses to verify the file's accuracy. In Windows 98, the Registry only looks at the part of the file that's changed, saving considerable time (Microsoft claims a factor of ten).

Another code improvement has to do with the *key node table*. This is a database structure that lists every key in the Registry. Windows 98 stores the key node table more efficiently, using less memory space.

Call me a CAB: New automatic backups

Our old friends, the *.DA0 files, have departed Windows 98 in favor of another slightly more standardized format, the *.CAB file. The *CAB* (or *cabinet*) file debuted in 1994 as part of the new Microsoft Distribution Media Format (DMF) storage standard.

Rarely has any file format earned universal disdain as rapidly and as thoroughly as the CAB format. CAB files may have been convenient for Microsoft, but they weren't for users, who couldn't even peek inside a CAB file to view its contents without cranking up an archaic command prompt window. Anyone who's ever had to restore a particular file from a Windows 95 CD-ROM knows what we're talking about here. The command-line EXTRACT program isn't exactly a model of user-friendly design.

Thankfully, the PowerToys freebie package from Microsoft (see Chapter 11) includes a CAB file viewer tool, and Microsoft has incorporated that tool into Windows 98. You can now right-click a CAB file and choose View to see its contents. Doing so with the file RB000.CAB in the directory C:\WINDOWS\SYSBCKUP reveals a Registry backup that also includes WIN.INI and SYSTEM.INI (see Figure 98-19). (Yes, those INI files are still hanging around, even in Windows 98. Old habits die hard.)

Older versions of the PowerToys CAB file viewer tool don't seem to work well with the Windows 98 CD-ROM: Large CAB files show up empty, and extract operations on smaller files don't complete. We're guessing Microsoft has made some kind of change to the CAB file format. Until we figure this one out, use the new PowerToys utility that comes with Windows 98 and you should be fine.

Figure 98-19:
Same idea, different place (SYSBCKUP), different format (CAB): the Windows 98 automatic Registry backups.

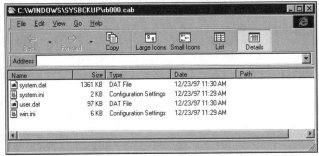

Please see the section "Beyond basics" earlier in this chapter for details on customizing the Registry Checker's CAB-format automatic backups.

Standing Pat: Registry-Editing Tools

If the Registry itself hasn't changed dramatically, neither have the Registry-editing tools: REGEDIT, POLEDIT, the Passwords control panel, or the File Types dialog box. This section details what's different and what's not.

REGEDIT

Our old friend, the Registry Editor, seems little changed from the version that ships with Windows 95 OEM Service Release 2 (OSR2, or Windows 95 version 4.00.950B). The file sizes are different and so are the version numbers — the OSR2 version is 4.00.1111, the Windows 98 version 4.10.1650 as of Beta 3 — but the program seems to function identically. The Windows 98 REGEDIT includes the Edit⇨Copy Key Name command from the OSR2 REGEDIT, as well as the real-mode command REGEDIT /D to delete a key.

As with Windows 95, REGEDIT is installed into C:\WINDOWS as part of a typical installation, but it doesn't appear on any Start menu lists. Microsoft didn't listen to the hundreds of network administrators who begged the company not to put REGEDIT on every user's hard disk during a typical Windows installation.

System Policy Editor

The System Policy Editor (POLEDIT) lives on in Windows 98; in fact, the files supplied on the Windows 98 CD-ROM are identical to those supplied on the Windows 95 CD-ROM. The list of user and computer policies that you can set seems to be unchanged, as do the group and individual user policies features. As far as we can tell, system policies work in Windows 98 exactly as they do in Windows 95 and as described in Chapter 9 — again, good news for this book's readers.

Good news, that is, except for the bug having to do with long filenames, which we discuss in Chapter 14 and which is still present after over two years (sigh). Stick with short (eight characters or less) file and folder names when using the Policy Editor, and you can avoid the bug. Maybe Microsoft will fix the problem with Windows 2001 (for which we're betting the code name will be "HAL").

User Profiles

Windows 98 seems to implement user profiles in much the same way as Windows 95, and you can activate user profiles via the Passwords control panel as before. However, Microsoft adds a new Users wizard to the control panel, which steps you through the process of enabling user profiles and creating the first user account (see Figure 98-20). (Windows 95 users who've installed Internet Explorer 4 can also see the new wizard.)

Figure 98-20:
A new
wizard for
kick-starting
user
profiles.

We're a little bit hard pressed to explain why Microsoft thought this new wizard was necessary, but maybe we'll come to understand the reason for it in the coming months.

File Types dialog box

The famous File Types tab, accessible by the View⇨Options command in My Computer or Explorer, seems completely unchanged in Windows 98. We still recommend that you use this tool rather than REGEDIT for modifying the Object Linking and Embedding (OLE) behavior of Windows 98 — that is, what happens when you double-click, right-click, or drag-and-drop different kinds of files.

Customizing the Initial Registry

The two utilities we mention in Chapter 8 for customizing the first Registry on your PC are NETSETUP.EXE and BATCH.EXE. One is still missing, the other is updated.

NETSETUP

Alas, NETSETUP has not returned since Microsoft stopped including the handy tool with OSR2. We can report, however, that we were able to copy the Windows 98 files to a network server by using the "brute force" method described in Chapter 8, and that we successfully installed Windows 98 onto a PC from the server directory.

Whether copying Windows 98 files to a distribution server constitutes a violation of the Microsoft license agreement depends on what that license agreement ultimately looks like. Make sure that you aren't running afoul of the legalese before you create your own LAN server directory for the purpose of installing Windows 98 onto your network's PCs.

BATCH

The BATCH.EXE tool gets an upgrade in Windows 98, and a new name ("Microsoft Batch 98"). The new version number is 3.00.0119. However, the new version works similarly to the Version 2 release discussed in Chapter 8. The main differences have to do with some user interface streamlining, better, more logical organization, and a few new setup options.

Nearly all of the settings from Version 2 made it into Version 3, but several are in different places. Here are some of the more significant changes:

- ✔ User and computer name information has moved from the main screen to General⇨User Information.
- ✔ Printer setup information has moved from the Installation Options area to General⇨Printers.
- ✔ Time zone information has moved from the Installation Options area to General⇨Regional Settings.
- ✔ User-level security information has moved from the Network Options area to Network⇨Access Control.
- ✔ The Optional component settings list has changed to reflect the current Windows 98 components and applets list.

Two new screens are the General options area's Desktop tab (Figure 98-21), which lets you specify which icons you want to appear on the desktop, and the Advanced options area (Figure 98-22), which lets you specify a Registry file (*.REG) to process, as well as whether you want manual or automatic system policies.

Microsoft has also published guidelines for which version of Batch Setup to use depending on which version of Windows you have:

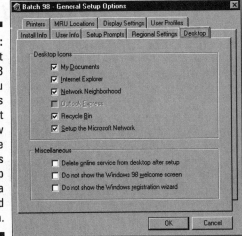

Figure 98-21:
Microsoft Batch 98 gives you choices as to what icons show up on the user's desktop after a standard installation.

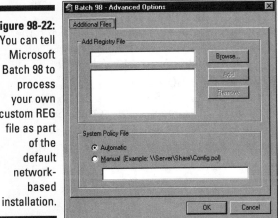

Figure 98-22:
You can tell Microsoft Batch 98 to process your own custom REG file as part of the default network-based installation.

✔ For Windows 95 OSR1 (version 4.00.950 or 4.00.950a — look at the System control panel's General tab), use Batch Setup Version 2.1.

✔ For Windows 95 OSR2 (version 4.00.950 or 4.00.950B), use Batch Setup Version 2.41.

✔ For Windows 95 OSR2.5 (version 4.00.950C), we don't know, but we're guessing that Microsoft would want us to use Version 2.41 here, too. It seems to work fine.

✔ For Windows 98, use Microsoft Batch 98 Version 3.

Known Windows 98 Registry Problems

As of the Beta 3 release, here are a few of the known problems that require Registry editing to fix or that somehow relate to the Registry. Please note that Microsoft may very well repair these problems by the time Windows 98 sees commercial release:

✔ Advanced power management may not give a modem enough time to arise from its sleep state. Use REGEDIT to add the DWORD value *ConfigDelay* to *HKLM\System\CurrentControlSet\Services\Class\ Modem\nnnn\root* (where *nnnn* is the number of the modem you want to use — there may only be one) and set the value to 3,000 or higher. This value is in milliseconds and sets how long Windows 98 waits after giving a modem the power-up command before Windows 98 tries to use the device. (3,000 milliseconds = 3 seconds)

✔ Another power-related problem has to do with Windows 98 not successfully "awakening" the monitor after a PC has gone into a sleep state. The recommended procedure is to reset the Registry's monitor keys and values by choosing a different monitor type in the Display control panel (Settings⇨Advanced⇨Monitor). Restart the PC and then change the monitor type back to what you had originally. (Yes, you *could* use REGEDIT, but the control panel procedure is faster.)

✔ Connecting to Unix/SAMBA servers requires unencrypted passwords, but Windows 98 defaults to sending encrypted passwords. Fix this problem by changing the value *HKLM\System\CurrentControlSet\ Services\VxD\VNETSTUP\EnablePlainTextPassword* from 0 to 1.

✔ When you're upgrading from Windows 95 to Windows 98, the setup program may fail with the message

```
Setup must be able to create short filenames with
        numeric tails for files with names longer than 8
        characters. Enable this option and try running
        Setup again.
```

The problem is that someone has modified the Windows 95 Registry to disable the "numeric tails" that appear on the short version of long file names (for example, the directory "Program Files" gets shortened to "Progra~1" in a DOS window, and the "~1" part is the numeric tail). We don't recommend disabling numeric tails for this exact reason; the practice can also wreak havoc on batch files that try to run programs in the "Progra~1" directory. However, we can tell you how to fix it: Use REGEDIT to delete the value *NameNumericTail* in the key *HKLM\System\ CurrentControlSet\Control\FileSystem*.

✔ Some DOS programs use a real-mode program called SHARE.EXE to handle file locking, which controls when a file can and can't be modified. Windows 95 includes a virtual device driver, specified in the Registry, that duplicates SHARE.EXE's functionality, but the operating system would still work with the real-mode SHARE.EXE. Windows 98, however, does not work with SHARE.EXE. If you need to run a DOS program that looks for SHARE.EXE under Windows 98, you have to create a dummy file with the name SHARE.EXE (you can use Notepad) and save it to the \WINDOWS\COMMAND directory.

✔ Internet Explorer offers security options via the SSL (Secure Sockets Layer) choices in the Security dialog box's Advanced tab. However, Internet Explorer doesn't properly update the Registry keys *HKLM\Software\Microsoft\Internet Explorer\AdvancedOptions\CRYPTO\ SSL2.0* and *SSL3.0*.

If you remember (from Chapter 14) the Registry bug that affects file system profiles in the original version of Windows 95 (OSR1), you may also remember that Microsoft quietly fixed it in the OSR2 release of Windows 95. We're pleased to report that it's still fixed in Windows 98. (Hey, you never take anything for granted in this business.)

Call for Comments

This brings us to the end of our first look at Windows 98. If some of you devoted readers discover slick new Registry tips or tricks that you think should appear in our Windows 98 Registry book, please let us know. Send your suggestions to IDG Books Worldwide at feedback/ dummies@idgbooks.com.

If we use your suggestion, we'll thank you in the Acknowledgments, and you can show your name in print to all your colleagues as proof of your Registry savoir-faire.

Chapter 16

Ten Registry-Related Internet Sites

In This Chapter

▶ Finding some of the Internet's best search services

▶ Discovering nine World Wide Web sites with Registry information

▶ Checking out one UseNet newsgroup

*I*n addition to its primary purpose of providing a seemingly endless variety of dirty jokes, the Internet offers several useful resources for Windows 95 users delving into the inner workings of the Registry. Here are ten locations to get you started.

Before running any program that you download from these or other Internet sites, scan the file or files with a good, up-to-date antivirus utility to make sure that you're not bringing a virus into your computer. Cheyenne, McAfee, and Symantec (among others) all make good antivirus programs (see Appendix B).

Internet *search services* are great for finding Registry-related information. You may want to use *Windows 95 Registry* as a search phrase; if you just use *Registry,* you're likely to pull up hundreds of references to Windows NT, too. Type in the name of the particular Registry branch you're interested in to narrow the search even further. Although most Internet documents use the standard Registry branch abbreviations that we use in this book (*HKLM, HKCR,* and so on), some use even shorter abbreviations (*HLM, HCR,* and so on). Here are some of the more popular search services:

- ✔ AltaVista (altavista.digital.com)
- ✔ Excite (www.excite.com)
- ✔ HotBot (www.hotbot.com)
- ✔ Lycos (www.lycos.com)
- ✔ Yahoo! (www.yahoo.com)

Unless you have a high-speed Internet connection, consider turning off Web graphics in your browser for faster surfing. In Internet Explorer 3.0, choose View➪Options➪General and uncheck the Show Pictures check box. In Netscape Navigator 3.0, choose Options➪Auto Load Images and then clear the check mark. Also take a look at the section "Turbocharging Internet dial-up links" in Chapter 10, if you connect to the Internet via modem.

www.imaginations.com

At this site, you can obtain the famous Windows 95 Registry FAQ (Frequently Asked Questions) document. Check this site occasionally for updates to the Registry FAQ.

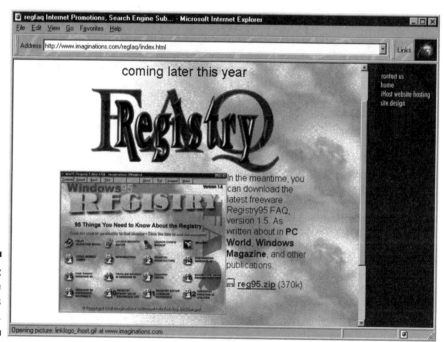

Figure 16-1:
The Imaginations Web site.

www.ntinternals.com

Mark Russinovich and Bryce Cogswell perform a great public service by posting useful Windows 95 and NT utilities on this site. In particular, REGMON and FILEMON are great to have (see Chapter 3).

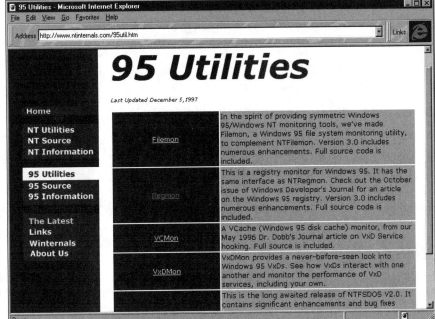

Figure 16-2:
Russinovich and Cogswell's NTInternals Web site.

www.winmag.com

Windows Magazine's online site is a wealth of information about the Registry. Just use the site search engine and type **Registry**. Most of the material that you find is helpful and technically accurate. You can find a ton of non-Registry Windows 95 stuff here, too.

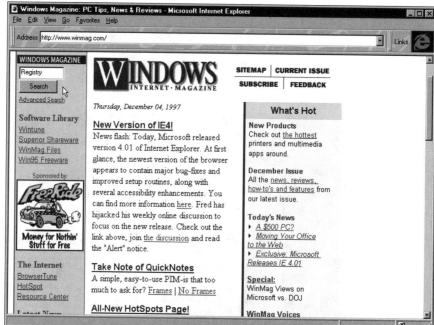

Figure 16-3:
The
Windows
Magazine
Web site.

www.zdnet.com

The Ziff-Davis Web site is a great place to keep up with the PC and Windows worlds; the home page is where we often go to see late-breaking news. This site is also your gateway to several online magazines, including

- ✔ PC Magazine (www.zdnet.com/pcmag)
- ✔ PC Computing (www.zdnet.com/pccomp)
- ✔ PC Week (www.pcweek.com)
- ✔ Windows Sources (www.zdnet.com/wsources)

Search the Ziff-Davis site by pointing your browser to www.zdnet.com/findit/search.html, as shown in Figure 16-4.

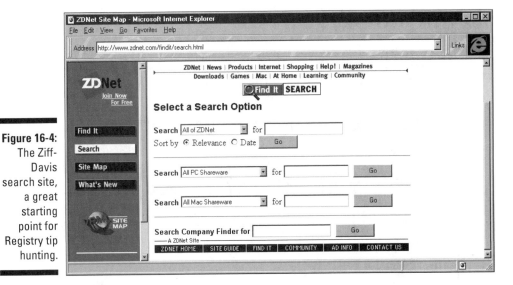

Figure 16-4:
The Ziff-
Davis
search site,
a great
starting
point for
Registry tip
hunting.

www.annoyances.org/win95

One of the more famous Windows 95 Web sites is the "Windows 95 Annoyances" site, created and maintained by Creative Element in San Francisco.
Here, you not only see what "bugs" other Windows 95 users (pardon the
pun), but you can also pick up workarounds and helpful tips.

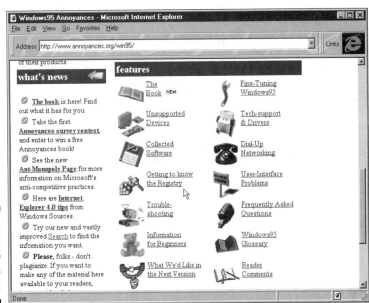

Figure 16-5:
The famous
Windows 95
Annoyances
Web site.

www.windows95.com

Steve Jenkins' Windows 95-dot-com is a good source for all kinds of tips, tricks, drivers, bug fixes, tutorials, and news. It's one of the better sites, especially if you couldn't care less about Windows NT.

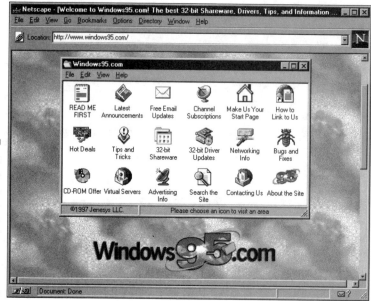

Figure 16-6:
The Windows95. com site, which deals exclusively with Windows 95.

support.microsoft.com/support

At Microsoft's Internet support site, you can gain access to the massive Microsoft knowledge base of common problems and solutions, as well as downloadable freebies.

www.microsoft.com/windows/windows95

Visit the main Microsoft Windows 95 site for news and product updates, straight from the horse's mouth.

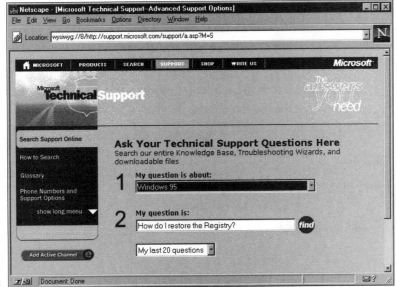

Figure 16-7:
Microsoft's
online tech
support
nerve
center.

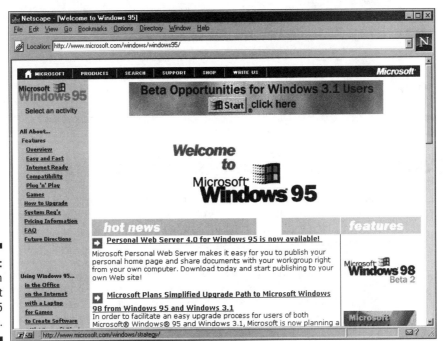

Figure 16-8:
The main
Microsoft
Windows 95
site.

www.download.com

This site, sponsored by CNET, is a great source of Windows 95 downloadable software. You can search the software library by using the keyword *Registry* to see only those freeware and shareware utilities that have to do with the Registry. We like to browse the top downloads occasionally, too.

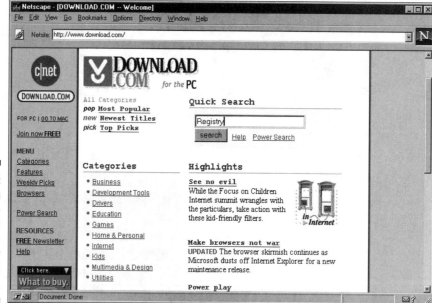

Figure 16-9:
CNET's compre-hensive and user-friendly download site.

comp.os.ms-windows.win95.misc

Not a Web site, but rather a *UseNet newsgroup* (a sort of Internet bulletin board) with lots of postings about the Windows 95 Registry, this location is a good place to post a question when you can't get an answer anywhere else or when you just want to read what other Windows 95 users are saying.

If you don't already have a newsreader, you need to get one in order to read postings from this newsgroup. Navigator users have a built-in newsreader, but Internet Explorer users can install the Microsoft Internet Mail and News software from the Internet Explorer setup program (included on this book's CD-ROM). If you use America Online to access the Internet, you also have a built-in newsreader. AOL users can just choose keyword *newsgroups,* click the Expert Add button, and type in the newsgroup name from this section's title.

Chapter 17

Ten Registry Tricks — Useful and Otherwise

· ·

· ·

*T*his little chapter contains ten miscellaneous Registry tricks. Nine are potentially very convenient and useful, and one (the last) is just for fun. Most of these tricks involve using the Registry Editor, so if you haven't looked over Chapter 4, you may want to do so. We assume in this chapter that you're familiar enough with REGEDIT to know how to add, delete, and change keys and values. Also, the standard caution applies here, as everywhere: back up your Registry before making any of the changes in this section.

Provide Your Own Startup Tips

You may have turned them off by now, but remember those startup tips that would appear whenever you started Windows 95? The Registry stores the text of those 48 tips — meaning that you can edit them to provide your own. You can make some Registry "flash cards" for yourself: "The HKEY_Classes_Root key is merely a pointer to a subkey of HKEY_Local_Machine." Or you can have a little fun and leave tips on your significant other's PC like "I'd like to meet you upstairs tonight and do what we did that night in Cancun."

Anyway, here's how to customize your startup tips. If you turned the startup tips off, turn them back on by editing *HKCU\Software\Microsoft\Windows\ CurrentVersion\Explorer\Tips* so that the binary value Show is 01 00 00 00.

Now, navigate to *HKLM\SOFTWARE\Microsoft\Windows\CurrentVersion\ explorer\Tips,* which is where the text of the tips resides (see Figure 17-1). Export the entire key to TIPS.REG. Edit this file with Notepad or your favorite word processor to contain your own customized tips, then save it as a text file with a new name, such as TIPSNEW.REG. Right-click TIPSNEW.REG and select Merge to update the Registry with your new tips (you can always go back to the original ones if you save TIPS.REG). Restart Windows 95, and check out your new startup tips!

Figure 17-1:
The famous
Windows 95
startup tips
actually live
in the
Registry.

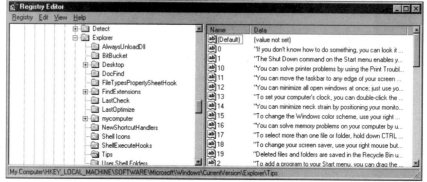

Recover a Lost Internet Explorer Password

Our modern heads are full of passwords, e-mail addresses, Personal Identification Numbers, clothing sizes, birthdays, and other codes that are hard to remember. As computer programs add more and more security capabilities, we're bound to forget a password at some point. If you forget the supervisor password for the content advisor ratings in Internet Explorer 3 or 4 (see Figure 17-2), which you may use to prevent little Jimmy from browsing www.playboy.com on your home PC, you're in luck: The Registry can help.

Run the Registry editor and sashay over to *HKLM\SOFTWARE\Microsoft\ Windows\CurrentVersion\Policies.* Delete the Ratings subkey, and the password restriction goes away. You can now go to Internet Explorer and create a new supervisor password.

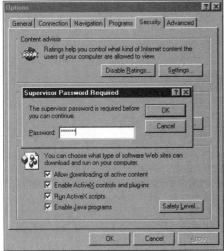

Figure 17-2:
Internet
Explorer's
content
advisor
requires a
supervisor
password
to make
changes.

Modify Your Screen Saver Timings

Screen savers aren't really needed anymore to protect today's monitors
from burn-in. However, they do offer the advantage of some light security
(you can password-protect them) and energy savings (you can set the
monitor to go into a low-power state or even shut off after a specific time
interval).

The Display control panel limits you in terms of the time intervals that you
can set to activate your screen saver, put your monitor into a low-power
mode, and turn it off after no user activity. Using the control panel, you can't
go less than one minute or greater than sixty, for any of these settings. While
the screen saver time-outs give an adequate range, we prefer to set the time-
outs for the low-power and shut-off options to a longer interval. You can do
it with REGEDIT, as shown in Figure 17-3.

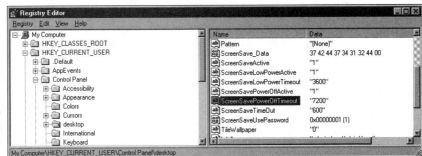

Figure 17-3:
The
Registry
enables you
to set
whatever
screen
saver
time-out
intervals
you want.

Fire up REGEDIT and navigate on over to *HKCU\Control Panel\Desktop*. The strings to change are ScreenSaveTimeOut, ScreenSaveLowPowerTimeout, and ScreenSavePowerOffTimeout. They're in seconds, and you can change 'em to whatever you want — say, 7,200 for a two-hour screen shutdown interval.

Restart the Registry Faster

Lots of changes that you make to the Registry don't take effect immediately — Windows 95 activates them the next time the operating system starts. Rebooting, however, can be a time-consuming process, especially on slower computers. Here's a great undocumented tip to force Windows 95 to rebuild the Registry (at least, all of it except *HKDD*, the Plug and Play branch) without actually rebooting your computer.

1. **Save any data files in open programs and then close all programs.**

   This step isn't strictly necessary, but we like to walk on the safe side of the street.

2. **Give your PC the three-finger salute (Ctrl+Alt+Del) to display the Close Program dialog box.**

3. **Click Explorer and End Task.**

   The "Explorer" in question is the Windows 95 desktop shell, not the Windows Explorer file manager. The Shut Down Windows dialog box appears because Windows 95 figures that if you want to shut down the desktop, then you want to shut down the computer. Not this time!

4. **Click No to tell Windows 95 that you don't want to shut down the computer in the normal way. (OSR2 systems don't show the No option, but that's okay, just count to five.)**

   After a few seconds, you see the Explorer message box. Windows 95 notices that you haven't shut down and wants to know whether it can kill the shell.

5. **Click the End Task button.**

   Explorer terminates, but then Windows 95 reloads it right away so you can continue using Windows 95. In the process, Windows 95 rebuilds the Registry and activates any settings that you made earlier. Slick! Just be aware that (for some bizarre reason) this method often erases the icons in the Taskbar's System Tray, even though the programs that normally appear there are still running.

Automatically Log On to the Desktop

Here's a tip to save you time at startup if security isn't a big concern for you. Just be aware that anybody can log on to Windows 95 (and your network, if you're on one) if you make the following change.

Run REGEDIT and hop on over to *HKLM\SOFTWARE\Microsoft\Windows\CurrentVersion\Winlogon*. Change the values DefaultUserName and DefaultPassword to match the ones you normally enter manually. If you don't see the entries, add them — they're string values. Also, add the string value AutoAdminLogon and key in "1" as the value data. The Winlogon key looks like Figure 17-4. That's it! Remove these keys later if you want to disable the automatic logon.

Figure 17-4:
Speedy
logons for
the non-
security-
conscious.

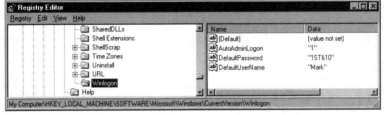

Remove Programs from the Install/Uninstall List

Sometimes, a user who isn't familiar with the Control Panel's Add/Remove Programs wizard tries to delete a program by simply running Explorer and deleting the program subdirectory. If that occurs, the program may still show up on the Install/Uninstall tab, even though the deinstall program doesn't work because the files aren't there anymore. If the deinstall program fails, the program doesn't remove itself from the list of installed programs.

Another possibility is that you update a program by installing a new version over an old one, but the deinstallation program for the old version is still hanging around on the Install/Uninstall tab. You can often avoid this problem by deinstalling the old version before installing the new version, but most programs don't require this step and you probably don't know which ones do. (Netscape Navigator comes to mind, but how could you possibly know that?!)

Fortunately, you can use the Registry Editor to remove those annoying holdovers from the Install/Uninstall list. Slide on over to *HKLM\SOFTWARE\Microsoft\Windows\CurrentVersion\Uninstall*. A screen like Figure 17-5 appears. Scroll around the list until you find the key corresponding to the program entry that you want to delete and delete the key. Voilà — the program no longer appears when you run the Add/Remove Programs wizard from the Control Panel.

Figure 17-5:
The
Registry
location of
the installed
programs
list.

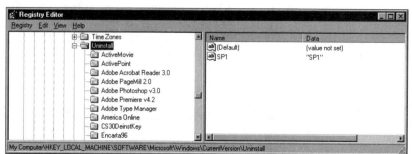

Change the Registered Organization and Owner Names

You decide that you no longer wish to be known as Mark Wilkins and legally change your name to Marcus Wilkinson. Or, your company reorganizes and changes its name from Acme Cognac to Bargain-Basement Spirits. However, Windows 95 maintains your old name and organization name internally and displays them on the System control panel's General tab. This bugs you. It can actually become slightly inconvenient, too: Often, when you install new software, the installation program consults these internal owner and organization names and pops them up by default.

Change these names with the Registry Editor by skipping over to *HKLM\SOFTWARE\Microsoft\Windows\CurrentVersion*. Here, you can modify the RegisteredOrganization and RegisteredOwner values (see Figure 17-6). To change either value as recorded by specific applications, use the Registry Editor's Edit⇨Find command. Just be aware that you may need to explain the change or changes when you call the vendor for technical support.

Figure 17-6:
The
Registry
location
of the
Windows
registered
organization
and owner
names.

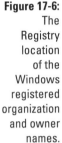

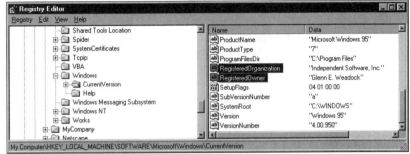

Change the Default Windows 95 Setup Directory

Often, when you buy a new computer, the default setup directory points to an area on the hard disk where the computer manufacturer has copied the Windows 95 installation files. These files can take up dozens of megabytes, however, and they duplicate the files on the Windows 95 installation CD-ROM. So you delete them, saving all sorts of disk space. However, the next time you do something that makes Windows 95 look for the original files — such as adding new software via the Network control panel — Windows looks for the original files in the original location (such as C:\WINDOWS\OPTIONS\CABS), doesn't find them, and asks you to locate them. Doing so isn't usually a big deal (the normal answer is X:\WIN95, where *X* is the drive letter that your computer assigns to the CD-ROM drive), but if you make a lot of changes to your system, retyping the correct location becomes a tad tedious. Fortunately, with the Registry Editor, you can tell Windows 95 to stop looking in the old location and automatically look in a new one.

Run REGEDIT and shuffle over to *HKLM\SOFTWARE\Microsoft\Windows\ CurrentVersion\Setup*. Modify the SourcePath string value to point to your CD-ROM drive (or a network drive or wherever the Windows 95 setup files reside).

Of course, if you have tons of hard disk space and you want to copy the files from the CD to a directory on your hard disk, you can do that, too, and use the same procedure to reset the location in the Registry. Putting the setup files on a hard disk makes a lot of sense for notebook computer users who don't have built-in CD-ROM drives.

Annotate the Registry

Documenting the changes that you make to your computer ranks right up there with cleaning the hall closet and flossing your teeth on the list of things you know you should do more often. (We know that we don't always record the changes that we make to our computers as often as we should.) You have two options open to you:

- ✔ Become more disciplined about documenting Registry changes in a word processing file somewhere on the computer.

- ✔ Find an easier method.

We, being essentially lazy, prefer the second option. Happily, it exists. Just make your own special Registry keys next to the ones that you've added or changed, or one level up from the ones you've deleted. Give the keys a consistent name, such as *TechTip*, and put a single string value in each key with a note about what you modified. Figure 17-7 shows an example. In this way, if you're ever surfing the Registry and you come across something that strikes you as odd, you can look for the relevant TechTip. Or, if you're troubleshooting a Registry problem, you can search for all the TechTips (hence the desirability of a consistent name) to see what Registry entries you've changed and that may be causing the problem. You don't have to hunt down a separate document — and because adding notes this way is so easy, you're more likely to do it.

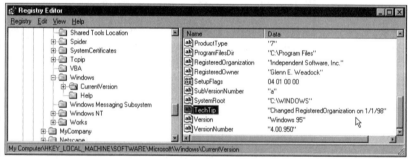

Figure 17-7:
Documenting your Registry changes in the Registry itself.

Create Application-Specific Sound Schemes

We end this chapter with a useless but fun tip. You probably already know that you can use the Windows 95 Sounds control panel to assign sounds to system events, such as the Windows 95 startup (Glenn likes the opening bars of Beethoven's Ninth) or a critical error message (Mark likes the sound of breaking glass).

Some application programs, such as CompuServe Information Manager, make Registry entries that enable you to assign sounds to those programs, too. However, most don't. If you want to assign sounds on a program-by-program basis to programs that don't already offer the capability in the Sounds control panel, you can do so with the Registry Editor and a little patience. Here's the procedure:

1. **Find out the name of the program.**

   The easy way to do this is to take a look at the property sheet for the shortcut on the desktop, or on the Start menu, that points to the program. What you want is the name of the main EXE file that the shortcut runs. You can also just use Windows Explorer to open the program's primary subdirectory and look for the EXE files, but sometimes you see more than one, so you have to double-click them until you get the right one. For example, the main EXE file for Ray Dream Designer is RDD.EXE, so the program name for our purpose here is RDD.

2. **Run the Registry Editor and navigate to** *HKCU\AppEvents\ Schemes\Apps.*

3. **Add a new key underneath the Apps key and give it the same name as the program to which you want to add sounds.**

   In our example, we name the new key RDD.

4. **Add keys underneath the key you added in Step 3 and name them according to the events that you'd like to associate with sounds.**

   The possibilities include Close, Open, RestoreUp, RestoreDown, Minimize, Maximize, MenuCommand, MenuPopup, SystemAsterisk, SystemExclamation, and SystemQuestion. Figure 17-8 shows the additions for our RDD example.

5. **Close REGEDIT and open the Sounds control panel.**

   Technically, we can continue using REGEDIT to finish the job, but we try to live by our rule to use control panels rather than REGEDIT wherever possible. Besides, the Sounds control panel enables you to browse for sound files and test them ahead of time.

6. **Scroll down the list until you see your newly added program, and assign sounds to events in the usual way.**

That's it! Your changes take effect immediately, so you can test them straightaway. You can find a bunch of fun sounds on the Windows 95 CD-ROM in the directory \FUNSTUFF\HOVER\SOUNDS. The Office95 and Office97 CD-ROMs have additional fun sounds under \SOUNDS and \VALUPACK. You may want to copy the sounds you like to the C:\WINDOWS\MEDIA directory, which is a semi-standard place to store system sounds. One last hint: Your PC may suspend other processing duties while playing a sound clip, so keep the clips on the brief side.

Figure 17-8:
Adding
sounds to
applications
that don't
normally let
you add
sounds to
them.

Chapter 18
Ten Non-Windows Registries

During our research for this book, we ran across several Internet sites featuring Registries that have nothing to do with Windows 95. Some are interesting, some useful, some weird, and some just tickled us. So, we end this book with the following reminders that there is life beyond Windows 95. *HKEY_Goodbye_HaveFun.*

International Scumbag Registry

www.biz-link.com/sc

If anyone has ever done you wrong and you've thought of wreaking revenge, here's a nonviolent outlet for your outrage: Sign that person up with the International Scumbag Registry. He or she will receive an official certificate proclaiming their induction as an Associate of the Scumbag Society (you figure out the acronym). You may designate the honored recipient as a Registered Dirtbag, Junior Bozo, Certified Shyster, or any one of a dozen other titles.

Yacht Club Registry

www.seafarers.com/yachts.htm

Admiralty Insurance Inc. presents this Web site for locating yacht clubs on the Internet and checking out upcoming events. We felt we should include this one just in case some of our readers really are seafarers, apropos of the book's running metaphor. If you sink your yacht, file it with the International Registry of Sunken Ships at www.cableregina.com/users/shipwreck.

Bloomingdale's Bridal Registry

www.bloomingdales.com/shoppingservices/bridal.html

Okay, we had to include a bridal registry, and Bloomies' site is the best-looking. We should also mention the Target bridal registry (www.targetstores.com/TargetWWW/ClubWedd) because of its clever name. The surreal bridal registry award goes to www.blackanddecker.com/bridal in case you'd rather have power tools than place settings.

duPont Registry

www.dupontregistry.com

Having trouble finding that Aston Martin Lagonda you've always wanted? No $5 million homes available in your immediate area? Just can't locate that executive yacht you truly need? Search no more. This is a fun place to visit even if your income is more on a par with a computer book author than a film star, and the fact that you don't have to listen to Robin Leach's annoying nasal voice is an added bonus.

Speedtrap Registry

www.speedtrap.com/speedtrap

Whether you've found your Aston Martin via the duPont Registry or just want to take that old Karmann Ghia out for some exercise, you may want to know how to avoid those strategically located speed traps designated to fill county coffers by ticketing you for going 2 mph over the limit. This Web site presents speed trap locations all over the world.

National Pet Registry

www.interlog.com/~pets/npr

This site combines commercialism and humanitarianism, which is better than pure commercialism alone, and it also happens to be nicely designed. It reports that over 12 million pets per year are lost in the U.S. and Canada.

Twenty-five bucks registers your pet and gets you a brass ID tag with an 800 number on it — just in case your pet wanders into the next county or is picked up by an unscrupulous petnapper and abandoned when the crook discovers he or she isn't house-trained.

Internet Social Registry

```
www2.aidg.com/isr
```

This service purports to match up people with common interests, and not just for the purpose of finding compatible dates (although the *Cupids Network* logo appears at the bottom of the site's home page). You fill out a questionnaire, and you get five matches per month for free (more and you have to pay something). If you're the type who isn't afraid to enter ads in the newspaper personals column, this site may be fun. If you find yourself out on a date with an ax murderer, don't blame us.

Official Registry of Persons Named Luke

```
users.uniserve.com/~lukec/luke.htm
```

Aside from the hilarious fact of this Web site's existence, we liked the Webmaster's sense of humor. ("I am interested in meeting other people named Luke. . . If you are a girl, then I'm interested in meeting you no matter what your name is.")

Registry of Educational Software Publishers

```
www.microweb.com/pepsite/Software/publishers.html
```

We thought this Web site, designed by Anne Bubnic and Warren Buckleitner for parents, educators, and publishers, was pretty cool. It includes a revue of children's software and links to hundreds of educational software vendors. Now that you've got your Windows 95 PC working properly with a little Registry knowledge, use it to teach your kids something other than how to rip an attacker's spinal cord out of his body.

Canadian Registry of Experts

`www.experts.ca`

We had to include this site because of the modest and unassuming name. We looked for a U.S. Registry of Experts, but apparently all the experts are in Canada. This site's major flaw is not listing your Canadian coauthor Mark — or your Canadian technical editor Gerry. Eh?

Part VII
Appendixes

The 5th Wave   By Rich Tennant

*Bill Gates dreams...

*Yes, he sleeps with his glasses on.

JUSTICE DEPT.

RICHTENNANT

"THAT'S RIGHT, MS. BINGAMAN, HE'S COLLECTING A ROYALTY FROM EVERYONE ON EARTH, AND THERE'S NOTHING WE CAN DO ABOUT IT."

In this part . . .

You've been blown by Aeolus to the final part of this book, the Appendixes. Here, you find four references dealing with issues from definitions, to sources for further study, to CD software, to the differences between the Windows 95 and Windows NT Registries. Beware, though, seafarer! If you venture beyond this part, you'll surely fall off the edge of the world!

Appendix A
Glossary

● ●

*T*his glossary defines most, if not all, of the technical terms in this book. We list definitions under acronyms rather than the expanded terms: If you look up the expanded term, the glossary points you to the acronym entry. Cross-referenced terms are in *bold italics.* You may see some cross-referenced terms that appear to be a single term but are really two adjacent single terms, such as *Registry branch.*

ActiveX. An evolution of the Object Linking and Embedding (OLE) technology in Windows, ActiveX enables programmers to create programs that run "inside" other programs and that share program modules across disks and even across networks. ActiveX also includes the file type associations in the Registry's *HKCR* branch.

Alias. A top-level *Registry* branch that points to a commonly used key somewhere else for more convenient access (that is, shorter key location paths) by programmers and users. For example, *HKey_Classes_Root* is an alias that points to *HKey_Local_Machine\SOFTWARE\Classes.*

Application program. Software that enables you to actually do stuff with your computer. Word processors and spreadsheets are examples of application programs. See also *data file.*

Association. See *file association.*

Attribute. See *file attribute.*

AUTOEXEC.BAT. A PC startup file, essential on *DOS* PCs, that stands for AUTOmatically EXECuting BATch file, and whose functions — loading startup programs and *device drivers* — the Windows 95 *Registry* mostly replaces. Some older devices may still require AUTOEXEC.BAT.

Back up. To create a copy of your computer files, either for long-term storage or to provide a way to recover from a failure, like one that may result from an incorrect or damaging *Registry* entry.

Backup. The tapes or disks created when a computer is backed up, also called a *backup set.*

Basic Input/Output System. See *BIOS.*

Batch file. A file with the suffix .BAT that contains a sequence of DOS commands that run one after the other. Batch files are handy for making Registry backups.

Batch Setup. A Microsoft program (BATCH.EXE) that enables you to create an *INF* file to control what happens when you install Windows 95 from a *network server,* including how you make various *Registry* settings.

Binary file. A *data file* that you can't read or modify without a particular software *application,* in contrast to a *text file.* If you open a binary file in a text editor like Notepad, all you see is gibberish. The *Registry* files are binary files.

Binary value. A *Registry* value whose *data field* consists of a sequence of two-digit *hexadecimal* numbers separated by single spaces. Modifying binary values is rarely necessary or advisable.

BIOS (Basic Input/Output System). Firmware (that is, software-on-a-chip) that loads before the *operating system* and handles low-level data transfer among disk drives, printers, keyboards, monitors and *memory.* The BIOS is an integral part of the *Plug and Play* specification.

Bit. Short for *binary digit,* the smallest unit of computer data, consisting of a one or a zero. Eight bits are usually needed to make a *byte,* which represents one alphanumeric character, though sometimes a byte may contain seven or nine bits.

Boot. 1) The process a computer goes through when it starts and loads the *operating system* into *memory.* 2) What you use to kick a *crashed* computer.

Branch. One of the six primary *keys* of the *Registry.*

Browser. The software tool that you run to view or "browse" Web servers and pages. Browsers present Web documents in a *GUI.* Browsers provide some navigation controls and may offer security and performance features.

Bus. A data highway inside a computer. Electronic traffic flows on buses between all the computer's component parts.

Byte. A chunk of computerized data corresponding to one alphanumeric character; composed usually of eight *bits.*

CD-ROM (Compact Disc-Read Only Memory). An optical disc, similar in appearance to an audio CD, that stores about 650 *megabytes* of digital computer data. You can read, but not modify or erase, data on CD-ROMs, unlike CD-R (CD-Recordable) discs.

CFGBACK (Configuration Backup). One of the *Registry backup* tools that come with Windows 95, and probably the least useful one.

Client/server network. A *network* (such as IntranetWare or Windows NT Server) in which a *server* computer running a network operating system handles resource-sharing responsibilities, such as file- and printer-sharing, for *client* computers (user workstations).

CLSID (Class ID). A unique number, such as {25336920-03f9-11cf-8fd0-00aa00686f13}, that identifies an object in Windows 95, including data file types (such as a PowerPoint slide show) and program modules (such as the code that displays and processes dialog box radio buttons). Class IDs take the form of a 16-byte number enclosed in curly braces, each *byte* expressed by a two-digit *hexadecimal* number, arranged in a 4-2-2-2-6 grouping.

Command prompt. The famous MS-DOS prompt, usually C:>,which you can use to start a Windows 95 machine. You can reach the command prompt by choosing Start⇨MS-DOS Prompt or by rebooting to a command prompt-only mode (by pressing F8).

CONFIG.POL. A *policy file* residing on a *network server* that becomes a mandatory part of every network user's *Registry.*

CONFIG.SYS. A PC startup file, essential on *DOS* PCs. The *Registry* mostly replaces the functions — loading memory managers and device drivers — of CONFIG.SYS.**Context menu.** A menu that you see when you right-click an object, such as a desktop icon or a file in Explorer.

Control Panel. A special Windows 95 program that enables you to change various system settings. Start⇨Settings⇨Control Panel displays all the available control panels in a single window. Control panels typically modify the *Registry* and are safer and more user-friendly than the *Registry Editor.*

Crash. 1) The event that causes a computer system or *application* to stop working suddenly, immediately, and irreversibly. 2) What you can do to your boat if you sail at night near the shore in the fog.

Data field. The part of a *Registry value* that contains an actual setting, as opposed to the *name field,* which contains the setting's name or identifier.

Data file. A computer file that contains information you create. A word processing document and a *REG* file are data files. See also *application program.*

Database. A collection of related information stored in a computer, such as a sales history or customer list, that you can search, edit, add to, delete from, and print. The *Registry* is a database.

DDE (Dynamic Data Exchange). A technique that Windows programs may use to exchange data and/or commands between two running programs.

Decimal notation. A way of expressing a number in base 10, with digits ranging from 0 to 9.

Defragment. To disassemble, move, and reassemble files on a disk so that all the files' data are physically adjacent rather than scattered around your hard disk. Defragmenting improves performance of disk files, including *Registry* files.

Deinstall. To remove a program from a computer. (Yeah, we think *remove* is a better term, too, but *deinstall* is what the industry uses.) Synonymous with *uninstall.*

Device driver. Software that enables a computer to communicate with a particular input or output device, such as a mouse. Device drivers interpret computer data and provide the commands or signals needed by the device.

Dial-Up Networking (DUN). Microsoft's remote access software for *Windows 95, Windows NT Workstation,* and *Windows NT Server,* which enables remote PCs to connect to a *network* over phone lines.

Directory. An organizational structure that permits the grouping of individual files in a single area, much like a manila folder permits the grouping of individual paper documents. Windows 95 typically includes most of its files under the C:\WINDOWS directory.

Diskless workstation. A computer without diskette drives or *hard drives.* Reduces security risks both outbound (confidential data) and inbound (*virus*-infected files).

DLL (Dynamic Link Library). A file containing program code (and sometimes icons). Much of the Windows 95 *operating system* consists of DLLs, which Windows 95 and *applications* can load into memory to use as needed.

DOS (Disk Operating System). The most popular *operating system* for IBM-compatible PCs until *Windows 95* became popular (earlier versions of Windows still use DOS extensively, while Windows 95 contains relatively little DOS code).

Download. To copy a file from another computer to your computer, over a network connection, modem link, or direct cable connection. See also *upload.*

DWORD (double-word) value. A *Registry* value whose *data field* consists of a sequence of four two-digit *hexadecimal* numbers, not separated by spaces, introduced by "0x" and followed by the equivalent *decimal* number in parentheses. For example, 0x0000027d.

Edit flag. A *Registry* value that specifies restrictions. For example, an edit flag may cause certain buttons to appear grayed-out and inactive in a dialog box. Edit flags are *binary values* having four *bytes.*

ERD (Emergency Recovery Disk). The *Registry restore* program that comes with Windows 95 as the counterpart to *ERU.*

ERU (Emergency Recovery Utility). One of the better *Registry backup* utilities that comes with Windows 95.

Explorer. 1) The Windows 95 file management utility. 2) The Windows 95 desktop (or *shell*). The terminology is confusing, we know — this is the sort of thing that happens when hundreds of programmers work on the same project!

Export. To create a full or partial *Registry backup* by using the *Registry Editor's* Registry⇨Export Registry File command. The result is a *REG* file. See also *import*.

FAQ (Frequently Asked Questions). A document featuring a list of common questions and their answers.

File association. In *ActiveX* (what we used to call *OLE*), a connection between a file suffix (such as .TXT) and an *application* (such as Notepad), so that double-clicking the file runs the associated application. The *Registry* maintains all file association information in Windows 95.

File attribute. Information stored with a computer file that determines under what conditions the file can be viewed, modified, copied, or deleted. For example, the attribute of "Read-only" means that you cannot modify or delete the file. Windows 95 file attributes also include System, Hidden, and Archive.

File server. A *network server* that shares files among users, as opposed to (for example) print servers (which share printers) and application servers (which share programs).

File type. A category of all files having a particular *file association.*

FILEMON. A free utility that tracks file accesses and changes as they occur.

Folder. See *directory.*

Full backup. A *backup* of all the files on your computer's *hard drive* or drives.

Gigabyte (abbreviated GB). A measure of data storage capacity equaling 1,024 *megabytes,* or roughly a billion *bytes,* a byte being equivalent to one letter or number.

Group. A collection of *network* users who have the same rights and restrictions to shared resources. With the *Registry,* you can assign access restrictions by group, using the *System Policy Editor.*

GUI (Graphical User Interface, pronounced "gooey"). A software interface, such as that of Microsoft Windows, that presents a graphical "face" to the user — as opposed to a text-mode interface like the *DOS* command line or a simple text mainframe terminal.

Happy. What you'll be if you back up the Registry religiously before making any changes to it.

Hard drive (also called "hard disk"). A computer storage device in which a stack of magnetic disks spin at high speed in a sealed enclosure. Hard drives retain information even when no power is supplied to them, unlike *RAM.* Hard drives can be written to, erased, and rewritten a large number of times. Capacity is measured in *megabytes* or *gigabytes.*

Hardware configuration. A feature of Windows 95 that lets you define multiple hardware setups; for example, a docked *notebook* and an un-docked *notebook.* The Registry stores hardware configurations in *HKey_Local_Machine\Config,* and it stores the current hardware configuration in *HKey_Current_Config.*

Hardware tree. The tree-structured representation of your PC's hardware setup, used by *Plug and Play* and viewable from the System *control panel's* Device Manager tab. The *Registry* stores hardware tree information in the *HKDD branch.*

Headache. What you get from working with the Registry too long.

Hexadecimal (hex) notation. A way of expressing a number in base 16, with digits ranging from 0 to F, where A corresponds to decimal number 10, B to 11, and so on. The *Registry* uses hexadecimal notation to express *binary values* and *DWORD values*. Hex numbers appear in the Registry grouped by two-digit *bytes*, for example, c8 06 00 00.

HKCC (HKey_Current_Config). The *Registry branch* containing information about the current *hardware configuration*. *HKCC is an **alias** to one of the keys below HKLM\Config.*

HKCR (HKey_Classes_Root). The *Registry branch* containing information about *file associations* and drag-and-drop behavior. *HKCR is an **alias** to HKLM\SOFTWARE\Classes.*

HKCU (HKey_Current_User). The *Registry branch* containing information about the current user logged on to Windows 95, including individual preferences and settings. *HKCU is an **alias** to a subkey of **HKU**.*

HKDD (HKey_Dyn_Data). The *Registry branch* containing information about the *hardware tree* and *Plug and Play.* This branch resides completely in *RAM,* and Windows 95 rebuilds it at each restart.

HKLM (HKey_Local_Machine). The *Registry branch* containing information about the computer that does vary from user to user or reflects individual user preferences. This branch includes the contents of *HKCC* and *HKCR.*

HKU (HKey_Users). The *Registry branch* containing information about all persons who can use the computer. This branch includes the contents of *HKCU.*

Import. To *merge* a full or partial *Registry backup* in the form of a *REG* file into the current *Registry* by using the *Registry Editor's* Registry⇨Import Registry File command. See also *export.*

INF file. A *text file* having a specific predefined format that can be *installed* onto the computer. *Application* software vendors and hardware vendors typically provide an INF file to modify the *Registry* as necessary and to copy required files into the proper *directories* on your *hard drive.*

INI file. A configuration *text file,* such as *WIN.INI* or *SYSTEM.INI,* that contains *operating system* settings. Windows 3.*x* makes heavy use of INI files, but Windows 95 depends on them to a much lesser extent, having moved most (but not all) of their responsibilities to the *Registry.*

Internet. The world's largest computer *network,* hosting all manner of private, public, and commercial uses. Physically, the Internet is a collection of millions of computers, each with its own unique network address to identify itself to other computers. Each computer on the Internet speaks the same basic communications language — *TCP/IP.*

Interrupt. A signal to the computer's main processor from a device that needs attention, usually to service an input or output demand (such as a keystroke or a file save request).

Key. A location for storing data in the *Registry.* Keys look like folders in the *Registry Editor* window's left-hand pane.

Key pane. The left-hand pane of the *Registry Editor* window, where *keys* appear.

Kilobit. 1,024 bits, where a *bit* is a zero or one.

Kilobyte (abbreviated K). 1,024 bytes, where a *byte* is a character equivalent to one letter or number.

Logical structure. The way the *Registry* looks when viewed by the *Registry Editor,* that is, as a single *database* with a tree-like organization consisting of *branches, keys, subkeys,* and *values.* See also *physical structure.*

Megabit (abbreviated Mb). About one million *bits,* a bit being a one or a zero.

Megabyte (abbreviated MB). A measure of data storage capacity equaling 1,024 *kilobytes,* or roughly a million *bytes,* a byte being equivalent to one letter or number.

Merge. To combine the contents of a *REG* file with the current *Registry* contents. Merging can overwrite existing Registry entries and create new ones, but cannot delete existing entries.

MIME (Multipurpose Internet Mail Extensions). A set of extensions to the original *Internet* e-mail standards that enable you to send and receive data types other than text.

MRU (Most Recently Used) list. A list of documents, programs, or *Internet* locations, maintained in the *Registry* or on disk for your convenience.

MS-DOS Mode. A special mode of Windows 95 in which Windows 95 effectively removes itself from memory and makes the PC look like a *DOS* machine; when you type EXIT at the *command prompt,* Windows 95 reloads into memory. An option on the Start⇨Shut Down dialog box. Also called *Single MS-DOS Mode.*

Name field. The part of a *Registry value* that contains a setting's identifying name, as opposed to the *data field,* which contains the actual setting.

Network. Two or more computer systems connected to enable communication or resource sharing.

Notebook. A portable computer, the size of a large and unusually heavy paper notebook.

Object. Anything that a user or programmer can manipulate in Windows 95. For example, objects include data files (such as a PowerPoint slide show) that users can click, programs (such as PowerPoint) that users can run, and program modules (such as the code that displays and processes dialog box radio buttons) that software developers can call upon in their programs. See also *ActiveX, CLSID,* and *OLE.*

OLE (Object Linking and Embedding, pronounced "oh-LAY"). A Windows technology that enables you to create compound documents with data coming from more than one program. OLE also allows in-place editing, or the ability to edit cut-and-pasted data without having to leave the application program that you pasted the data into. A big part of OLE is *file associations.*

Operating system. The basic software that enables a computer to interact with users, manage files and devices, and communicate over a *network.* *Windows 95,* UNIX, MacOS, and OS/2 Warp are all operating systems. Operating systems designed for network *servers,* such as NetWare and *Windows NT Server,* are called NOSs (Network Operating Systems).

OSR2 (OEM Service Release 2). A version of Windows 95 sold only on new PCs. An OSR2 machine displays the version number 4.00.950B on the System *Control Panel.* OSR2 contains a slightly different version of the *Registry Editor.*

PC Card. See *PCMCIA.*

PCMCIA (Personal Computer Memory Card Industry Association). A group that standardized PCMCIA devices, now called "PC Cards," which plug into *notebook* computers. The *Plug and Play* specification views PCMCIA as a separate *bus.*

Physical structure. The way the *Registry* looks as viewed by a file management program such as Windows *Explorer,* that is, as a collection of files, consisting of *SYSTEM.DAT, USER.DAT,* and an optional *policy* file. See also *logical structure.*

Plug and Play (often abbreviated PnP). A set of standards developed by Microsoft, Intel, Compaq, and Phoenix (among others) to ease the configuration of hardware devices by automatically detecting and setting device characteristics. A full implementation of PnP requires compatibility at all levels, from the *BIOS* to the *operating system* to the *device driver.* The *Registry* contains Plug and Play information in the *HKLM* and *HKDD* *branches.*

POL file. See *policy file.*

POLEDIT. See *System Policy Editor.*

Policy file. An optional *Registry* component with the suffix .POL that applies restrictions and customizations to the information in *USER.DAT* and *SYSTEM.DAT.* For example, you can create a policy that prevents users from running the Registry Editor. You create policy files with the *System Policy Editor.*

Property sheet. A window (usually, a dialog box) that displays information about a file or *control panel*. The window usually permits you to change some or all the information it contains in predefined ways, for example via text fields, radio buttons, and check boxes. You typically get to a property sheet by right-clicking an icon and choosing Properties from the *context menu.*

Protected mode. The usual mode of running Windows 95, in which programs and data use *RAM* above the 1-*megabyte* boundary and enjoy some protection from each other to help ensure reliability. If Windows 95 can't start in protected mode, for example due to a severely damaged *Registry,* you may have to troubleshoot the problem in *real mode.*

RAM (Random Access Memory). Chip-based memory in a computer, which is both faster and more expensive than disk-based memory (*hard drives*). A computer's RAM contains the currently active programs and data files, and its contents start empty every time the computer restarts.

Real mode. A mode of running Windows 95 in which only the DOS components of the *operating system* are activated, usually accomplished by restarting the computer and booting to a *command prompt*. The *Registry Editor* can run in a limited way in real mode for troubleshooting purposes. See also *protected mode.*

REG file. A *text file* having a specific predefined format that can be *imported,* or *merged,* into the *Registry. Exporting* a file from the *Registry Editor* creates a REG file, and *application* software vendors sometimes provide a REG file to modify the Registry as necessary to accommodate their particular needs.

REGCLEAN. A software utility, provided by Microsoft at its Web site, that automatically removes certain inaccurate or obsolete *values* from the *Registry.*

REGEDIT. See *Registry Editor.*

Registry. The central store of information that Windows 95 and Windows 95 programs use to track all the software and hardware on the machine, including details about how that software and hardware are configured.

Registry Editor. The tool (REGEDIT.EXE) that comes with Windows 95 and enables you to view, edit, print, *export,* and *import* the *Registry.* The Symantec Norton Registry Editor is a better version of REGEDIT.

REGMON. A free utility that tracks *Registry* accesses and changes as they occur.

Remote Registry Service. Software that comes with Windows 95 that enables a user on one computer to view and edit the *Registry* on another computer on the same network. This service only works in a *client/server network.*

Rescue disk. A diskette (or, more likely, a set of diskettes) created by a utility such as Norton Utilities that enables you to start your computer from the diskette drive and *restore* critical system files. Most rescue disk programs can't handle *Registry* files that don't fit on a single diskette; the Norton Utilities 3.0 Rescue Disk program can, if you use the ZIP disk option, but you have to add the Registry files to the list manually.

Restore. To copy files to your computer's *hard disk* that you previously *backed up.* You can restore the *Registry* by using a variety of techniques and utilities, including *CFGBACK* and *ERD.*

Root directory. The top-level *directory* on a disk, under which all other directories reside.

Sad. What you will be if you don't back up the Registry religiously before making changes to it.

Safe mode. A Windows 95 startup option that you activate by pressing F8 at startup and choosing either "Safe Mode" (which loads the *GUI*) or "Safe Mode, Command Prompt Only" (which takes you to a *command prompt*). You may need to restart in safe mode to perform certain *Registry* troubleshooting and *restore* operations.

Server. 1) A computer that provides *network* services, such as file and printer sharing. 2) The combination of server hardware and programs.

Shell. The part of an *operating system* that presents computer resources to you and enables you to work with the machine, as opposed to the part of the operating system that talks to devices or software. In Windows 95, the usual shell is *Explorer.*

Shortcut. A file (with the suffix .LNK) that points to a local or *network* file, *directory,* program, *control panel, disk drive,* or printer in order to increase user convenience by making resources more easily accessible (for example, via a desktop icon).

Startup disk. A diskette you create with the Control Panel's Add/Remove Programs option to enable you to start your computer from the diskette drive. Windows 95 does not copy the *Registry* to the startup disk, making it useful for starting a computer that won't boot at all, but not useful for restoring a damaged Registry.

String value. A *Registry* value whose *data field* consists of a sequence of alphanumeric characters. String values almost always appear in the *Registry Editor* surrounded by double quotes.

Subkey. A Registry key that resides underneath another key.

Swap file. An area of *hard drive* space that your *operating system* (for example, *Windows*) uses as a low-speed supplement to your main memory, *RAM.* Windows 95 swap file settings reside in *SYSTEM.INI.*

System Policy Editor. The tool (POLEDIT.EXE) provided with Windows 95 that enables you to apply restrictions and customizations to the current *Registry,* or create a *policy file* that applies those changes every time your PC starts.

SYSTEM.1ST. The very first *SYSTEM.DAT* file created when you install Windows 95. This file resides in the *root directory.*

SYSTEM.DA0. A *backup* of *SYSTEM.DAT* that Windows 95 creates at each successful startup.

SYSTEM.DAT. A primary component of the *Registry's physical structure,* SYSTEM.DAT is a file that contains all machine-specific settings for both hardware and software. It resides in the C:\WINDOWS *directory.*

SYSTEM.INI. A Windows configuration *text file* that exists primarily in Windows 95 for compatibility with Windows 3.*x* programs, but that still contains some important information that the *Registry* does not contain.

TCP/IP (Transmission Control Protocol/Internet Protocol). A set of *network* standards for file transfer, network management, and messaging — the public *Internet* uses TCP/IP.

Text file. A data file consisting of nothing but standard alphanumeric characters that you can read with a wide variety of *application programs.*

TweakUI. A *control panel* that comes with Microsoft PowerToys, which you can *download* from Microsoft's Web site. TweakUI enables you to change the Windows 95 desktop in ways that normally require the *Registry Editor.*

Uninstall. See *deinstall.*

Upload. To copy a file from your computer to another computer, over a network connection, modem link, or direct cable connection. See also *download.*

URL (Uniform Resource Locator). The address that points you to a specific *Internet* or intranet location (a Web page or a file to *download*).

User profiles. A Windows 95 feature that permits multiple users to share a single PC and still see their own individual preferences and settings. User profiles also permit *network* users to log on to any networked PC and still see their preferences and settings, by maintaining multiple copies of *USER.DAT.* The *Registry* maintains user profile information in *HKey_Users* and the current user's profile information in *HKey_Current_User.*

USER.DA0. A *backup* of *USER.DAT* that Windows 95 creates at each successful startup.

USER.DAT. A primary component of the *Registry's physical structure,* USER.DAT is a file that contains all user-specific settings. If *user profiles* are not enabled, only one USER.DAT file exists, and it resides in the C:\WINDOWS *directory.* If user profiles are enabled, multiple and different USER.DAT files reside in the C:\WINDOWS\PROFILES directory.

USER.MAN. A mandatory *user profile* that resides on a *network server* and overrides any information in the network user's *USER.DAT* file.

Value. A chunk of information contained in a *Registry key.* Values have a *name field* and a *data field,* and have three types: *binary value, DWORD value,* and *string value.* A single Registry key can contain multiple values.

Value data. See *data field.*

Value name. See *name field*.

Value pane. The right-hand pane of the *Registry Editor* window, where *values* appear.

Verb. Some action you can perform on a Windows 95 object. For example, if you open a program, *open* is the verb and *program* is the object. *Edit* and *print* are other examples of verbs.

Windows. A family of *operating systems* from Microsoft that put a graphical face onto your computer, enabling you to run multiple programs at once and easing the copying and pasting of data among programs. Versions in current use include Windows 3.1, Windows for Workgroups 3.11, *Windows 95, Windows NT Workstation,* and *Windows NT Server.*

Windows 95. A very popular PC *operating system* from Microsoft that succeeds Windows 3.*x* and makes much heavier use of the *Registry.*

Windows NT Server. A network *operating system* from Microsoft featuring relatively easy installation and management and strong security. Windows NT Server 4.0 and higher use the same *GUI* as Windows 95.

Windows NT Workstation. A workstation *operating system* from Microsoft for PCs requiring high performance, high security, or high reliability; more expensive than *Windows 95,* both in purchase price and in hardware requirements.

WIN.INI. A Windows configuration *text file* that exists in Windows 95 primarily for compatibility with Windows 3.*x* programs. Most of the information that Windows 3.*x* placed in WIN.INI now exists in the Windows 95 *Registry.*

WWW (World Wide Web). The multimedia face of the *Internet.* Web pages can include color graphics and even sound and video. They can also include convenient and automatic links to other Web pages. Much *Registry*-related software is available on the Web.

Appendix B
References and Resources

● ●

*T*his book mentions several companies that offer Registry-related products, and in case you want to explore their products further, this appendix provides contact information. We also direct you to a few good books and magazines that can add to your knowledge of the Registry.

Companies Mentioned in This Book

This section provides Internet addresses (Web where available, e-mail otherwise), phone numbers (both the free-in-the-USA "800" and "888" variety, where available, and toll numbers for the convenience of international readers), and physical addresses for the companies we mention in this book.

Cheyenne (Division of Computer Associates International, Inc.)
www.cheyenne.com
800-243-9462; 516-465-5000
3 Expressway Plaza, Roslyn Heights, NY 11577

CyberMedia, Inc.
www.cybermedia.com
800-721-7824; 310-581-4700
3000 Ocean Park Boulevard, Suite 2001, Santa Monica, CA 90405

Exabyte Corp.
www.exabyte.com
800-EXABYTE; 303-442-4333
1685 Thirty-eighth Street, Boulder, CO 80301

Helix Software Company
www.helixsoftware.com
800-451-0551; 718-392-3100
47-09 Thirtieth Street, Long Island City, NY 11101

imagine LAN, Inc.
www.imagine-lan.com
800-372-9776; 603-889-5889
76 Northeastern Boulevard, Suite 34B, Nashua, NH 03062

Inso Corp.
www.inso.com
800-733-5799; 617-753-6500
31 St. James Avenue, Boston, MA 02116

Iomega Corp.
www.iomega.com
800-697-8833; 801-778-1000
1821 W. Iomega Way, Roy, UT 84067

ISES Incorporated
ises@ix.netcom.com
800-447-ISES; 908-766-1109
102 Sunrise Drive, Gillette, NJ 07933

McAfee Associates, Inc.
www.mcafee.com
800-332-9966; 408-988-3832
2085 Bowers Avenue, Santa Clara, CA 95051-0963

Microsoft Corp.
www.microsoft.com
800-426-9400, 206-882-8080
One Microsoft Way, Redmond, WA 98052

Netscape Communications Corp.
home.netscape.com
800-638-7483; 415-254-1900
501 E. Middlefield Road, Mountain View, CA 94043

Novell, Inc.
www.novell.com
800-453-1267; 801-222-6000
1555 North Technology Way, Orem, UT 84757

PowerQuest Corporation
www.powerquest.com
800-965-7576; 801-437-8900
1083 North State Street, Orem, UT 84057

Quarterdeck Corp.
www.quarterdeck.com
800-354-3222; 310-309-3700
13160 Mindanao Way, Marina del Rey, CA 90292-9705

Seagate Software (Information Management Group)
www.seagatesoftware.com
800-877-2340; 800-663-1244 (Canada); 604-681-3435
1095 W. Pender Street, 4th Floor, Vancouver, BC, Canada V6E 2M6

Seagate Technology, Inc.
www.seagate.com
800-SEAGATE; 408-438-6550
920 Disc Drive, Scotts Valley, CA 95066-4544

Steven J. Hoek Software Development
shoek@ix.netcom.com
6173 Sunningdale Drive, Hudsonville, MI 49426

Symantec Corp.
www.symantec.com
800-441-7234; 408-253-9600
10201 Torre Avenue, Cupertino, CA 95014-2132

SyQuest Technology, Inc.
www.syquest.com
800-245-CART; 510-226-4000
47071 Bayside Parkway, Fremont, CA 94538

Wedge Software
www.wedgesoftware.com
P.O. Box 431, Davisburg, MI 48350-1223

Books

These titles are worth a look next time you find yourself lost among the rows of computer books at your local bookstore-slash-coffee house — or wandering cyberspace bookstores such as www.amazon.com.

Bulletproofing Windows 95
Glenn E. Weadock
McGraw-Hill
350 pages, $34.95

Microsoft Windows 95 Resource Kit
Microsoft Press
1,348 pages, $49.95

The Mother of All Windows 95 Books
Woody Leonhard and Barry Simon
Addison-Wesley
922 pages, $39.95

Troubleshooting and Configuring the Windows NT/95 Registry
Clayton Johnson
Sams Publishing
612 pages, $49.99

The Windows 95 Bug Collection
Bruce Brown
Addison-Wesley
$14.95

Windows 95 For Dummies, **2nd Edition**
Andy Rathbone
IDG Books Worldwide, Inc.
386 pages, $19.99

The Windows 95 Registry: A Survival Guide for Users
John Woram
MIS:Press
350 pages, $24.95

Magazines

Here are a few magazines that cover Windows technology. A quick skim of these publications can keep you up on current trends.

Byte: The Magazine of Technology Integration
www.byte.com
603-924-9281
One Phoenix Mill Lane, Peterborough, NH 03458

Computerworld
www.computerworld.com
508-879-0700
500 Old Connecticut Path, Framingham, MA 01701

Information Week
techweb.cmp.com/iw
516-562-5051
600 Community Drive, Manhasset, NY 11030

Infoworld
www.infoworld.com
800-457-7866; 847-647-7925
P.O. Box 1172, Skokie, IL 60076

PC Computing
www.pccomputing.com
800-676-4722; 303-665-8930
P.O. Box 58229, Boulder, CO 80322-8229

PC Magazine: The Independent Guide to Personal Computing
www.pcmag.com
212-503-5255
One Park Avenue, New York, NY 10016-5802

PC Week
www.pcweek.com
617-393-3700
10 Presidents' Landing, Medford, MA 02155

Windows Magazine
www.winmag.com
516-733-8300
One Jericho Plaza, Jericho, NY 11753

Windows NT Magazine
www.winntmag.com
800-621-1544; 970-663-4700
P.O. Box 447, Loveland, CO 80539-0447

Appendix C

About the CD

● ●

*H*ere's some of what you can find on the *Windows 95 Registry For Dummies* CD-ROM:

- ✔ Norton Utilities 3.0 from Symantec, featuring the Norton Registry Editor, Norton Registry Tracker, and WinDoctor
- ✔ NovaBACKUP 5.0 from NovaStor software, a full-featured backup program
- ✔ Registry Monitor, which tracks Registry activity as it occurs

System Requirements

Make sure that your computer meets the minimum system requirements listed below. If your computer doesn't match up to most of these requirements, you may have problems using the contents of the CD.

- ✔ A PC with a 486 or faster processor (a Pentium processor is recommended)
- ✔ Microsoft Windows 95 or later
- ✔ At least 8MB of total RAM installed on your computer. For best performance, we recommend at least 16MB of RAM installed.
- ✔ At least 70MB of hard drive space available to install all the software from this CD. (You need less space if you don't install every program.)
- ✔ A CD-ROM drive — double-speed (2x) or faster.

If you need more information on the basics, check out *PCs For Dummies,* 5th Edition, by Dan Gookin or *Windows 95 For Dummies,* 2nd Edition, by Andy Rathbone (both published by IDG Books Worldwide, Inc.).

How to Use the CD by Using Microsoft Windows

To install the items from the CD to your hard drive, follow these steps.

1. **Insert the CD into your computer's CD-ROM drive.**

2. **Click the Start button and click Run.**

3. **In the dialog box that appears, type** D:\SETUP.EXE.

   Most of you probably have your CD-ROM drive listed as drive D under My Computer in Windows 95. Type in the proper drive letter if your CD-ROM drive uses a different letter.

4. **Click OK.**

   A license agreement window appears.

5. **Since we're sure you'll want to use the CD, read through the license agreement, nod your head, and then click the Accept button. After you click Accept, you'll never be bothered by the License Agreement window again.**

   From here, the CD interface appears. The CD interface is a little program that shows you what is on the CD and coordinates installing the programs and running the demos. The interface basically enables you to click a button or two to make things happen.

6. **The first screen you see is the Welcome screen. Click anywhere on this screen to enter the interface.**

   Now you're getting to the action. This next screen lists categories for the software on the CD.

7. **To view the items within a category, just click the category's name.**

   A list of programs in the category appears.

8. **For more information about a program, click the program's name.**

   Be sure to read the information that appears. Sometimes a program may require you to do a few tricks on your computer first, and this screen tells you where to go for that information, if necessary.

9. **To install the program, click the appropriate Install button. If you don't want to install the program, click the Go Back button to return to the previous screen.**

   You can always return to the previous screen by clicking the Go Back button. Doing so allows you to browse the different categories and products and decide what you want to install.

   After you click an install button, the CD interface drops to the background while the CD begins installation of the program you chose.

10. **To install other items, repeat Steps 7, 8 and 9.**

11. **When you're done installing programs, click the Quit button to close the interface.**

    You can eject the CD now. Carefully place it back in the plastic jacket of the book for safekeeping.

To run some of the programs, you may need to keep the CD inside your CD-ROM drive. This is a good thing. Otherwise, the installed program would have required you to install a large chunk of the program to your hard drive space, which would have kept you from installing other software.

What You'll Find

Here's a summary of the software on this CD.

CleanSweep Deluxe

CleanSweep Deluxe removes unnecessary files and Registry entries from your PC. It looks for Registry orphans (the "Registry Sweep" command), duplicate files on disk, and rarely-used files. CleanSweep "knows" about hundreds of application programs, and can deinstall them even when they can't deinstall themselves. CleanSweep also includes the ability to move entire applications from one directory to another. This is a trialware version of a commercial utility from Quarterdeck Corporation.

Filemon

Filemon is a freeware utility from Mark Russinovich and Bryce Cogswell that monitors file activity as it occurs. It tracks reads as well as writes, and after a monitoring session you can save a Filemon log to disk as a plain text file. You can also set filters to control which types of events Filemon logs. Filemon is especially useful if you're performing an application install or uninstall and you want to see exactly what happens at the file system level. It doesn't show you Registry activity in terms of specific keys and values, though; that's the province of Regmon (described later in this section).

GHOST

GHOST is a disk and/or partition copying program from Ghost Software. It is designed to minimize installation times for operating systems by "cloning" a drive and to create complete backups of disks. Using GHOST is a good solution if you want to clone an operating system over a network in which the clients are composed of the same hardware components.

MTUSpeed

MTUSpeed is freeware from Mike Sutherland that enables you to change the Registry's TCP/IP settings for more efficient Internet access. Normally, Windows 95 sets its maximum transmission unit size to a value that's appropriate for local area networks, but not efficient over a dial-up link. This utility helps you correct the problem by reducing the maximum packet size for your dial-up connections.

Norton Utilities

Norton Utilities 3.0 from Symantec Corp. contains the Norton Registry Editor, Norton Registry Tracker, and WinDoctor. The software on the CD-ROM is a trialware version.

- Norton Registry Editor is a better version of Windows 95's REGEDIT program, offering an "undo" feature as well as a read-only mode.

- Norton Registry Tracker lets you take before-and-after "snapshots" of the Registry and compares them, automatically highlighting additions, deletions, and changes.

- WinDoctor performs a raft of analytical tests, but its most common function is to help you locate Registry orphans — entries pointing to files that no longer exist on your system.

Important Note: This Software has a "time-out" feature so that it expires within thirty (30) days after you load the Software on your system. The "time-out" feature may install hidden files on your system which, if not deleted, might remain on your computer after the Software has been re-moved. The purpose of the "time-out" feature is to ensure that the Software is not used beyond its intended use.

NovaBACKUP

NovaBACKUP is a trial version of a full-featured commercial backup utility from NovaStor Corp. that supports full and partial backups, including the Registry. This versatile program features virus protection, automatic backup scheduling, multiplatform and multilanguage support, automatic log files, and more. NovaStor's Web site is http://www.novastor.com.

Registry Search and Replace

Registry Search and Replace is a shareware utility from Steven J. Hoek Software Development that enables you to find and replace specific text strings in the Registry. It's a handy tool that you might use, for example, when you manually relocate an application's files to a different directory. Registry Search and Replace can log your search or search-and-replace session to a file. It works with remote Registries as well as the local one.

Regmon

Regmon is a freeware utility from Mark Russinovich and Bryce Cogswell. The program monitors Registry activity as it occurs. You get a listing of every Registry access — read, write, or modify — and after a monitoring session you can save the log to a plain text file. Regmon is a useful utility if you want to see exactly what happens when you change a control panel setting, install or uninstall an application, or perform some other Windows 95 task, such as logging on to a network.

The Registry Surfer

The Registry Surfer (RegSurf) is shareware from ISES that enables you to find Registry entries in any key without actually running REGEDIT. RegSurf doesn't do search-and-replace, but it does have the ability to search every Registry key, something that Registry Search and Replace doesn't do. RegSurf also includes a handy option to print the results of your search. It works with the Windows NT Registry as well as the Windows 95 Registry, and it's pretty fast (especially if you choose the Minimize While Surfing option).

TweakDUN

TweakDUN is shareware from Patterson Software Design that enables you to change the Registry's TCP/IP settings for more efficient Internet access using Dial-Up Networking. Normally, Windows 95 sets its maximum transmission unit size to a value that's appropriate for local area networks, but not efficient over a dial-up link. As a result, your TCP/IP packets get chopped up and reassembled in transmission, reducing your actual data throughput. This utility helps you correct the problem by reducing the maximum packet size for your dial-up connections. It also modifies other, related TCP/IP settings for better performance.

WinHacker

WinHacker is a popular shareware utility that allows you to make many desktop changes that normally require Registry editing. With WinHacker, you can add or remove "persistent" desktop icons; activate or deactivate Windows 95's zooming windows; rename the Start button; hide drives in "My Computer;" change Windows 95 startup options, and dozens of other actions to customize your system.

WinZip 95

WinZip 95 is a shareware file compression and decompression utility from Nico Mak Computing, Inc. that's handy for moving files over modem links. It's also very useful for saving disk space by archiving little-used files. Some of the files on this CD are compressed using the ZIP format, and you can use WinZip 95 to decompress them. WinZip offers a step-by-step wizard mode for those who want to fiddle with the program as little as possible, or a "classic" mode for users who want access to all the program's features. The program also supports long filenames, and the creation of self-extracting EXE archives (which you could use, for example, to distribute a bunch of REG files containing Registry hacks you want to share with others).

If You've Got Problems (Of the CD Kind)

We tried our best to compile programs that work on most computers with the minimum system requirements. Alas, your computer may differ, and some programs may not work properly for some reason.

If you get messages like Not enough memory or Setup cannot continue, you can try the following fixes:

- ✔ Reboot your computer and close any programs that run automatically before trying to install the software again.
- ✔ Download a newer version of the software from the vendor's Web site.
- ✔ Have your local computer store add more RAM to your computer.

If you still have trouble with installing the items from the CD, please call the IDG Books Worldwide Customer Service Center phone number: 800-762-2974 (outside the U.S.: 317-596-5430).

Appendix D

Differences between the Windows 95 and NT Registries

*s the Windows 95 Registry different from the NT Registry?

The short answer: Yes. Windows 95 and Windows NT share a fair amount of software and can often run the same exact programs. So you may think that the two Registry structures would be identical. That would be nice, but Windows NT is quite a different animal under the skin than Windows 95, and the NT Registry differs in some substantial ways from the Windows 95 Registry. You need to know the differences if you work with both Windows 95 and Windows NT.

Files

Windows NT separates the Registry into more files than Windows 95 does. The Windows 95 Registry is contained in two files, USER.DAT and SYSTEM.DAT (a third file with access restriction information is optional). The NT Registry replaces USER.DAT with NTUSER.DAT, and replaces SYSTEM.DAT with a whole set of files called *hives,* which live in the \WINNT\SYSTEM32\CONFIG folder. (Whether these files are called hives because they store data in compartments similar to a beehive's or because they induce a breakout of hives when human beings try to understand them, is anyone's guess.)

Security

Windows 95 isn't a secure operating system; Windows NT is. Windows NT can keep an audit log of who's made changes to the NT Registry. Each of the NT Registry's hives has an associated LOG file that tracks changes and permits recovery if a Registry change creates a problem.

Some of the keys that appear in the Windows NT Registry, such as SECURITY and SAM, relate to NT's security system and therefore don't appear in the Windows 95 Registry.

Windows NT 101

For those of you who are new to Windows NT, here's a very brief overview of the key differences between Windows NT and Windows 95. First, the benefits:

✔ NT is a secure operating system: It has its own software to authenticate users and restrict access. Windows 95 must rely on another computer on the network — such as a NetWare or NT server — to provide security, and even then, it isn't rock solid.

✔ NT is more stable, in part because it uses extra layers of software to protect programs from each other and to protect the operating system from programs.

✔ NT supports multiple processors (CPUs) in the same computer, something called *symmetric multiprocessing* (SMP); Windows 95 doesn't.

✔ NT supports non-Intel processors (such as Alpha); Windows 95 doesn't.

✔ NT offers an improved file system, NTFS (NT File System), with better disaster recovery, security, and audit logging capabilities than the Windows 95 FAT (File Allocation Table) or FAT32 systems.

And now, the disadvantages:

✔ NT requires more muscle to operate. It needs more memory and a faster CPU to do its job at the same performance level as Windows 95.

✔ NT doesn't work with nearly as wide a variety of hardware as Windows 95 does. Version 5.0 narrows the gap somewhat — for example, by providing much improved support for the *PC Card* devices common in the notebook computer world — but the gap remains.

✔ NT doesn't work with real-mode device drivers (the kind you may specify in CONFIG.SYS or AUTOEXEC.BAT).

✔ NT 4.0 doesn't support Plug and Play in a serious way (NT 5.0 claims to redress this grievance, but it's too soon to tell for sure).

✔ NT is harder to install than Windows 95.

✔ NT doesn't run older Windows programs as well as Windows 95 does.

✔ No convenient upgrade utility exists for migrating from Windows 95 to NT 4.0 and preserving system settings.

✔ For many customers, NT is more expensive. (Big companies typically pay about the same for NT as they do for Windows 95.)

Structure

The Registry in Windows 95 has six primary branches, one of which *(HKEY_DYN_DATA)* contains the PC's Plug-and-Play database (the so-called *hardware tree*). The NT 4.0 Registry doesn't use this same primary branch (largely because NT 4.0 isn't really compatible with Plug-and-Play). The branch does shows up if you're using REGEDIT, but you can't open it.

Server or Workstation?

Here's an interesting note about critical settings buried deep in the Windows NT Registry structure. You may have heard or seen two different versions of Windows NT: Server and Workstation. The server product, which is more expensive, comes with a different license that permits more user connections. However, at least as of Version 4.0, these two products are *exactly the same from the physical standpoint* (except for the bundled software). Two Registry settings determine which is which:

✔ *HKLM\System\Current ControlS et\ Control\ProductOptions\ProductType*, which is either "WinNT" or "ServerNT."

✔ *HKLM\System\Setup\SystemPrefix*, a binary value that changes depending on whether the license specifies workstation or server.

We mention this not to suggest that you do anything illegal to violate your license agreement (you can't buy our next book if you're in jail). We just want to show that the Registry is just as important in Windows NT as it is in Windows 95.

The other five branches are the same in name, but the underlying structure varies in sometimes-unexpected ways. Features that are common to both Windows 95 and Windows NT don't necessarily appear precisely the same way in the Registry.

If you create REG files to modify the Windows 95 Registry, as we show you how to do in Chapter 12, the differences between the Windows 95 and Windows NT Registries mean that such files don't necessarily work with Windows NT.

Finally, the Windows NT Registry permits longer keys — up to 1MB, as opposed to the 64K limitation for a Windows 95 Registry key.

Data Types

The Windows NT Registry uses the three main data types that the Windows 95 Registry uses, but adds two new data types of its own: an expandable string that can include variables, and a multiple string that can contain several entries "strung" together.

You can't use REGEDIT to work with these new data types; you need to use the REGEDT32 tool, described in the next section.

Here's a brief look at Windows NT's Registry-editing and Registry backup tools.

Editing the NT Registry

The Registry Editor that Microsoft supplies with Windows 95 is REGEDIT.EXE. With Windows NT, you get two Registry Editors at no extra charge:

- REGEDIT.EXE works pretty much like it does under Windows 95. It can only edit the data types supported by Windows 95. REGEDIT can use .REG files for export and import purposes.

- REGEDT32.EXE is based on the NT 3.5*x* Registry Editor and does some things that REGEDIT can't. For example, you need REGEDT32 if you want to edit or add data using one of the Windows NT Registry's two new data types (see previous paragraph). REGEDT32 also looks significantly different from REGEDIT (see Figure D-1). Unlike REGEDIT, REGEDT32 has a read-only mode (hurrah!). The behavior of the key pane is a little different, too; you have to double-click the "+" folder icon instead of single-clicking it.

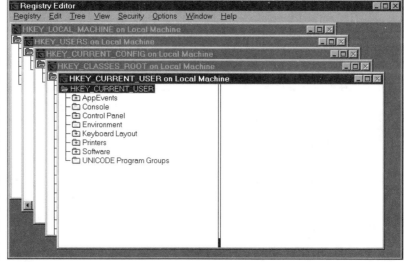

Figure D-1:
Windows NT comes with a different (and different-looking) Registry Editor called REGEDT32.

Expansion

The Windows 95 Registry grows as necessary, for example, when you install new software onto a PC. The Windows NT Registry has a software-settable maximum size value that you must increase manually for the Registry to be able to grow beyond that size.

For more details on the Windows NT Registry, see the *Windows NT Workstation Resource Kit* (Microsoft Press), especially Part V, *Windows NT Registry*. The book also comes with a CD-ROM that has a helpful "help" file, COMMON\DOCS\REGENTRY.HLP, more formally known as the *Microsoft Windows NT Registry Entry Guide*.

Index

• C •

(continued)

IDG Books Worldwide, Inc., End-User License Agreement

5. **Limited Warranty.**

   (a) IDGB warrants that the Software and Software Media are free from defects in materials and workmanship under normal use for a period of sixty (60) days from the date of purchase of this Book. If IDGB receives notification within the warranty period of defects in materials or workmanship, IDGB will replace the defective Software Media.

   (b) **IDGB AND THE AUTHORS OF THE BOOK DISCLAIM ALL OTHER WARRANTIES, EXPRESS OR IMPLIED, INCLUDING WITHOUT LIMITATION IMPLIED WARRANTIES OF MERCHANTABILITY AND FITNESS FOR A PARTICULAR PURPOSE, WITH RESPECT TO THE SOFTWARE, THE PROGRAMS, THE SOURCE CODE CONTAINED THEREIN, AND/OR THE TECHNIQUES DESCRIBED IN THIS BOOK. IDGB DOES NOT WARRANT THAT THE FUNCTIONS CONTAINED IN THE SOFTWARE WILL MEET YOUR REQUIREMENTS OR THAT THE OPERATION OF THE SOFTWARE WILL BE ERROR FREE.**

   (c) This limited warranty gives you specific legal rights, and you may have other rights that vary from jurisdiction to jurisdiction.

6. **Remedies.**

   (a) IDGB's entire liability and your exclusive remedy for defects in materials and workmanship shall be limited to replacement of the Software Media, which may be returned to IDGB with a copy of your receipt at the following address: Software Media Fulfillment Department, Attn.: *Windows 95 Registry For Dummies,* IDG Books Worldwide, Inc., 7260 Shadeland Station, Ste. 100, Indianapolis, IN 46256, or call 800-762-2974. Please allow three to four weeks for delivery. This Limited Warranty is void if failure of the Software Media has resulted from accident, abuse, or misapplication. Any replacement Software Media will be warranted for the remainder of the original warranty period or thirty (30) days, whichever is longer.

   (b) In no event shall IDGB or the authors be liable for any damages whatsoever (including without limitation damages for loss of business profits, business interruption, loss of business information, or any other pecuniary loss) arising from the use of or inability to use the Book or the Software, even if IDGB has been advised of the possibility of such damages.

   (c) Because some jurisdictions do not allow the exclusion or limitation of liability for consequential or incidental damages, the above limitation or exclusion may not apply to you.

7. **U.S. Government Restricted Rights.** Use, duplication, or disclosure of the Software by the U.S. Government is subject to restrictions stated in paragraph (c)(1)(ii) of the Rights in Technical Data and Computer Software clause of DFARS 252.227-7013, and in subparagraphs (a) through (d) of the Commercial Computer–Restricted Rights clause at FAR 52.227-19, and in similar clauses in the NASA FAR supplement, when applicable.

8. **General.** This Agreement constitutes the entire understanding of the parties and revokes and supersedes all prior agreements, oral or written, between them and may not be modified or amended except in a writing signed by both parties hereto that specifically refers to this Agreement. This Agreement shall take precedence over any other documents that may be in conflict herewith. If any one or more provisions contained in this Agreement are held by any court or tribunal to be invalid, illegal, or otherwise unenforceable, each and every other provision shall remain in full force and effect.

CD-ROM Installation Instructions

● ●

*T*o install the items from the CD to your hard drive, follow these steps:

1. **Insert the CD into your computer's CD-ROM drive and close the drive door.**

2. **Click the Start button and click Run.**

3. **In the dialog box that appears, type** D:\SETUP.EXE.

   Most of you probably have your CD-ROM drive listed as drive D under My Computer in Windows 95. Type in the proper drive letter if your CD-ROM drive uses a different letter.

4. **Click OK.**

   A license agreement window appears.

5. **We know you'll want to use the CD, so read through the license agreement and then click on the Accept button. Once you click on Accept, you'll never be bothered by the License Agreement window again.**

   From here, the CD interface appears. The CD interface lets you install the programs on the CD without typing in cryptic commands or using yet another finger-twisting hot key in Windows.

For more information on the CD (and maybe a slight case of déjà vu), check out Appendix C, "About the CD."

Discover Dummies Online!

The Dummies Web Site is your fun and friendly online resource for the latest information about ...*For Dummies*® books and your favorite topics. The Web site is the place to communicate with us, exchange ideas with other ...*For Dummies* readers, chat with authors, and have fun!

Ten Fun and Useful Things You Can Do at www.dummies.com

1. Win free ...*For Dummies* books and more!
2. Register your book and be entered in a prize drawing.
3. Meet your favorite authors through the IDG Books Author Chat Series.
4. Exchange helpful information with other ...*For Dummies* readers.
5. Discover other great ...*For Dummies* books you must have!
6. Purchase Dummieswear™ exclusively from our Web site.
7. Buy ...*For Dummies* books online.
8. Talk to us. Make comments, ask questions, get answers!
9. Download free software.
10. Find additional useful resources from authors.

Link directly to these ten fun and useful things at
http://www.dummies.com/10useful

For other technology titles from IDG Books Worldwide, go to
www.idgbooks.com

Not on the Web yet? It's easy to get started with *Dummies 101*®: *The Internet For Windows*® *95* or *The Internet For Dummies*,® 4th Edition, at local retailers everywhere.

Find other ...*For Dummies* books on these topics:
Business • Career • Databases • Food & Beverage • Games • Gardening • Graphics • Hardware
Health & Fitness • Internet and the World Wide Web • Networking • Office Suites
Operating Systems • Personal Finance • Pets • Programming • Recreation • Sports
Spreadsheets • Teacher Resources • Test Prep • Word Processing

IDG BOOKS WORLDWIDE
BOOK REGISTRATION

We want to hear from you!

Visit **http://my2cents.dummies.com** to register this book and tell us how you liked it!

✔ Get entered in our monthly prize giveaway.

✔ Give us feedback about this book — tell us what you like best, what you like least, or maybe what you'd like to ask the author and us to change!

✔ Let us know any other ...*For Dummies*® topics that interest you.

Your feedback helps us determine what books to publish, tells us what coverage to add as we revise our books, and lets us know whether we're meeting your needs as a ...*For Dummies* reader. You're our most valuable resource, and what you have to say is important to us!

Not on the Web yet? It's easy to get started with *Dummies 101*®: *The Internet For Windows*® *95* or *The Internet For Dummies*®, 4th Edition, at local retailers everywhere.

Or let us know what you think by sending us a letter at the following address:

...*For Dummies* Book Registration
Dummies Press
7260 Shadeland Station, Suite 100
Indianapolis, IN 46256-3945
Fax 317-596-5498

BUSINESS AND
GENERAL
REFERENCE
BOOK SERIES
FROM IDG

COMPUTER
BOOK SERIES
FROM IDG